World Financial Crisis

World Financial Crisis

K.R. Gupta

ATLANTIC
PUBLISHERS & DISTRIBUTORS (P) LTD

Published by

ATLANTIC

PUBLISHERS & DISTRIBUTORS (P) LTD

7/22, Ansari Road, Darya Ganj,
New Delhi-110002
Phones : 23273880, 23275880, 23280451
Fax : 91-11-23285873
Web : www.atlanticbooks.com
E-mail : info@atlanticbooks.com

Branch Office
5, Nallathambi Street, Wallajah Road,
Chennai-600002
Phones : +91-44-64611085, 32413319
E-mail : chennai@atlanticbooks.com

ISBN 978-81-269-1233-9

Printed in India at Nice Printing Press, A-33/3A, Site-IV,
Industrial Area, Sahibabad, Ghaziabad, U.P.

Preface

The world is going through a financial crisis triggered by a dramatic rise in mortgage delinquencies and foreclosures in the United States, with adverse consequences for banks and financial markets around the world.

The crisis can be attributed to a number of factors pervasive in both housing and credit markets. The causes of crisis *inter alia* include inability of homeborrowers to make their mortgage payments, due primarily to resetting of adjustable rate mortgages, high-risk lending, excessive speculation during the boom period, high personal and corporate debt levels, financial products that distributed and perhaps concealed the risk of mortgage default, international trade imbalances, and last but not least, lack of proper government regulation. There is a consensus of opinion that the two important catalysts of the subprime crisis were the influx of large funds from private sector and banks entering into the mortgage bond market, and predatory lending practices of mortgage brokers, especially the adjustable rate mortgage loans.

It is also believed that the credit rating agencies, which are now under scrutiny for having given investment-grade ratings to mortgage based securities (MBSs), were instrumental in effecting a large scale sale of such risky securities. Some people believe that these ratings were justified because of risk reducing practices, such as credit default insurance and equity investors willing to bear the first losses. However, there are clear indications that some agencies knew that the rating process was faulty. Critics have alleged that the rating agencies suffered from conflicts of interest as they were paid handsomely by investment banks and other firms that organize and sell structured securities to investors.

Sharp eyes were able to notice the crisis much before it snowballed into a global turmoil. The crisis began to affect the financial sector in February 2007 when Hong Kong & Shanghai Banking Corpn (HSBC), the world's largest bank, wrote down its holdings of subprime-related MBS by US$ 10.5 billion—the first major subprime-related loss to be reported. During 2007 over 100 mortgage companies either shut down, suspended operations or were sold. The CEOs of Merrill Lynch and Citigroup resigned in late 2007. The crisis started causing panic in financial markets in 2008 and induced investors to take their money out of risky mortgage bonds and shaky equities. As the mortgage defaults started piling up, the financial firms around the globe had to write down their holdings of subprime-related securities. According to an IMF estimate, the financial institutions all over the world will eventually have to write off $1.5 trillion. When Lehman Brothers and other important financial institutions failed in September 2008, the crisis hit its peak point.

The failure of large financial institutions in the United States rapidly evolved into global credit crisis, deflation, sharp reductions in shipping and commerce, leading to failure of several European banks, declines in various stock indexes, substantial reductions in market values of equities and commodities all over the world including centrally-controlled economies, e.g. China and Russia. In America, Section 128 of the Emergency Economic Stabilisation Act of 2008 aggravated the crisis, as it permitted the Federal Reserve Bank to pay interest on excess reserve requirement balances held with it as deposit from banks, removing the long-standing incentive for banks to extend credit instead of keeping hard cash with the Federal Reserve Bank. It led to a liquidity problem and the de-leveraging of financial institutions, particularly in the United States and Europe where the liquidity crisis intensified and decline in international trade became sharper. Inspite of coordinated efforts of the governments and finance and central bank directors to mitigate fears, the crisis went on worsening, resulting in currency crisis leading to transfer of vast capital resources by investors in stronger currencies like yen, US dollar and Swiss franc. It compelled many emerging economies to seek aid from the International Monetary Fund.

When the financial crisis erupted in a comprehensive manner on Wall Street, there was some premature triumphism among the Indian policymakers who argued that India would be relatively immune to this crisis because of the strong fundamentals of its economy and a well-regulated banking system even while the other developing countries in Asia clearly showed signs of significant negative impact through domestic credit stringency. However, the crash in the Indian stock market, triggered by a pull-out of Foreign Institutional Investors (FIIs) funds, October 2008 onwards is not only an indicator of the impact of international contagion, but also a sign of the integration of Indian economy with the world economy despite claims of decoupling.

Global response to the financial crisis has been prompt, and by and large adequate. There have been bailouts, relief plans and stimulus packages in several countries of Europe, Asia, America and Africa. Banks around the world have reduced interest rates to boost the economy. Federal Reserve Bank has reduced its lending rates and brought them to near zero level. The US Government has signalled that its financial rescue efforts may have reached their high watermark as the much anticipated 'stress tests' conducted by regulators showed that the banks can withstand an adverse economic scenario though they will be required to raise fresh capital to boost their reserves against losses. Ten of America's largest 19 banks need a combined $74.6 billion of extra funds to increase their cash reserves. Federal Reserve chairman Ben Bernanke said that the Treasury stands ready to provide whatever additional capital may be necessary to ensure that our banking system is able to navigate a challenging economic downturn. The Reserve Bank of India has cut its short term lending rates by 4.25 per cent in six steps since October 2008. The Interim Budget announced 2 per cent cuts in excise duty and service tax besides providing for expansion in infrastructure investment. The European Central Bank and Bank of England have pumped in billions of dollars in the money-market auction.

The most significant measure being taken is the sweeping overhaul of the financial regulation. In America, hedge funds, private equity firms and derivative markets will come under government supervision for the first time. These regulatory changes are necessary to restore confidence in business enterprises, institutions, markets and public at large. The G20 meeting of 2 April 2009, held in London, can be termed as landmark in many ways. The member countries—which are virtually world's main financial powers—pledged more than $1 trillion for emergency loans to reverse the recession. They not only decided to reject protectionism but also to bring tighter financial regulation. Positive results can be expected sooner than later, though much will depend on the extent to which policy interventions—at the national and global levels—are successful.

The book *World Financial Crisis* attempts to provide a holistic view of the financial turmoil afflicting the world today, which has been widely accepted as the biggest contagion after the Great Depression of 1930s, and has presented new challenges to the entire world. It analyses the factors like subprime mortgage failures, excessive leveraging of available capital and lack of financial regulation that led to this crisis. The book studies its debilitating effect on economic growth, industrial production, employment, wages and salaries, stock markets, foreign direct investment (FDI), liquidity, rate of interest, money market, fiscal position, infrastructure development, and completion of projects and undertaking of expansion programs in public as well as private sector.

To complete this monumental task I had to refer to a number of sources like, reports by established institutions, newspaper reports, articles and editorials, information portals and websites. I take this opportunity to acknowledge them all.

The book will be useful to the students, teachers and researchers of Economics, parliamentarians, policymakers, economists, and entrepreneurs in India and abroad. Common readers interested in knowing about the present global economic conditions will find it inculcating and informative.

K.R. Gupta

Contents

Introduction

Global financial markets are showing strains on a scale and scope not witnessed since the Great Depression of 1930s. Though the crisis can be attributed to several causes, the subprime mortgage failure is unarguably the major among these. Subprime lending is mainly in the form of mortgages for the purchase of residences to borrowers who do not meet the usual criteria for borrowing at the lowest prevailing market interest rate. These criteria pertain *inter alia* to the borrower's credit score and credit history. If a borrower is delinquent in making timely repayment to a loan servicer—usually a bank or financial institution—the lender can take possession of the residence acquired using the proceeds of the mortgage, in a process known as foreclosure.

The Origin of Crisis

The crisis began with the bursting of housing bubble in the United States, marked by high default rates on subprime and adjustable rate mortgages (ARM), beginning approximately in 2006. According to *New York Times*, "Government policies and competitive pressures for some years prior to the crisis encouraged high risk lending practices." An increase in loan incentives such as easy initial terms and a long-term trend to escalating housing prices encouraged borrowers to assume difficult mortgages in the belief that they would be able to quickly refinance at more favourable terms. However, once the interest rates began to rise, and housing prices started to drop—moderately in the beginning but significantly later on in many parts of US—refinancing became more difficult. Defaults and consequent foreclosure activity started rising dramatically as easy initial terms expired, the home prices did not go up as anticipated, and ARM interest rates were reset higher.

Foreclosures went up 79 per cent in 2007 from those in the preceding year.

It is also believed that the credit rating agencies, which are now under scrutiny for having given investment-grade ratings to mortgage based securities (MBSs), were instrumental in effecting a large scale sale of such risky securities. Some people believe that these ratings were justified because of risk reducing practices, such as credit default insurance and equity investors would bear the first losses. However, there are clear indications that some agencies knew that the rating process was faulty. Critics have alleged that the rating agencies suffered from conflicts of interest as they were paid handsomely by investment banks and other firms that organize and sell structured securities to investors.

Financial products called mortgage-backed securities (MBS) which derive their value from mortgage payments and housing prices, had enabled financial institutions and investors around the world to invest in the US housing market. Major banks and financial institutions who had borrowed funds and invested heavily in MBS, reported losses of approximately US$435 billion in July 2008. The liquidity and solvency concerns regarding key financial institutions drove central banks to take action to provide funds to banks to encourage lending to worthy borrowers and to restore faith in the commercial paper markets which are integral to funding business operations. The US Government bailed out key financial institutions, assuming significant additional financial commitments.

The Bear Stearns bailout, the Government takeover of Fannie Mae and Freddie Mac, the Lehman Brothers bankruptcy, the sale of Merrill Lynch & Company, and then a drop of more than 62% in AIG's share price, combined to create a financial atmosphere verging on panic. The debacle of the hyper-buoyant housing market and the freewheeling attitude of the subprime mortgage industry, leading to the collapse of Lehman Brothers, have resulted in a take down of giant financial institutions that had successfully weathered the stock market crash of 1930s.

The failure of large financial institutions in the United States rapidly evolved into global credit crisis, deflation, sharp reductions in shipping and commerce, leading to failure of several European banks, declines in various stock indexes, substantial reductions in market values of equities and commodities all over the world including in the centrally-controlled economies like China and Russia. The crisis was sharpened by Section 128 of the Emergency Economic Stabilisation Act of 2008 which permitted the Federal Reserve Bank to pay interest on excess reserve requirement balances held by it as deposits from banks, removing the long standing incentive for banks to extend credit instead of keeping hard cash with America's premier bank which plays a leadership role in monetary policy, financial supervision and the payment system. It led to a liquidity problem and the de-leveraging of financial institutions, particularly in the United States and Europe which aggravated liquidity crisis and brought about a decline in international trade. In spite of coordinated efforts of the Governments and central bank directors to mitigate fears, the crisis went on worsening, resulting in currency crisis leading to the transfer of vast capital resources by investors in stronger currencies like yen, US dollar and Swiss franc. It compelled many emerging economies to seek aid from the IMF.

The crisis which originated from widespread subprime mortgage failures quickly engulfed the entire financial system as well as industry resulting in widespread layoffs, for example, 70,000 job losses in a single day in six companies ranging from manufacturing to telecom across the United States and Europe as a cost-cutting measure to grapple with sharp slump in consumer spending. Construction machinery manufacturer Caterpillar, carmakers General Motors and Chrysler, pharma major Pfizer, telecom firm Sprint Nextel Corporation and home improvement retailer Home Depot were among the top companies adversely affected.

China's Undervaluation of its Currency, Yuan

Some experts believe that apart from subprime mortgage failures, China has also been an important culprit in bringing the current economic meltdown. China intentionally undervalued its currency yuan. Thus its goods became cheaper in the international markets. It flooded United States market and accumulated trillion-plus dollars. In such a situation in a free economy the exchange rate of the country's currency would have risen on the principle of demand for and supply of the currency. But since Chinese economy is controlled, the rate of yuan did not rise as the Government of China kept it artificially low.

China used an important part of thus accumulated dollars in financing US Government debt which encouraged American extravagance. A vicious circle was created: more US spending resulted in more Chinese exports leading to more US debt involving more US spending. In the same way oil-rich Gulf countries controlled supply of oil leading to a substantial rise in oil prices. They also got huge amounts of dollars which flowed into US securities.

Cheap capital availability led to a boom of real estate in the United States creating a subprime monster. The United States became a nation of spenders and the earlier habit of saving disappeared. Keeping the currency undervalued is an indirect way of subsidising and dumping goods and is contrary to the provisions of World Trade Organisation.

Global Impact of the Crisis

When the financial crisis erupted in a comprehensive manner on Wall Street, there was some premature triumphism among the Indian policymakers who argued that India would be relatively immune to this crisis because of the strong fundamentals of its economy and a well-regulated banking system even while the other developing countries in Asia clearly showed signs of significant negative impact through domestic credit stringency. However, the crash in the Indian stock market, triggered by a pull-out of Foreign Institutional Investors (FIIs) funds, October 2008 onwards is not only an indicator of the impact of international contagion, but also a sign of the integration of Indian economy with the world economy in the present times of globalization despite claims of decoupling.

As worldwide recession has taken over boom, Indian professionals, technicians and workers in various industries are facing layoff. Even those in sales and marketing have been hurt because they were mostly subcontracted by large companies which now look upon these staff as dispensable. Indian workers in the Gulf contribute nearly 40 per cent of the $27 billion in overseas remittances that come to India—accounting for 3 per cent of India's GDP. World Bank has said that the remittances generated by South Asian workers in the Gulf will come down by 9 per cent. If the Middle East economic crisis deepens, India will face a double whammy of dipping remittances on one hand, and jobless returnees flooding the domestic market on the other.

The Times of India had first reported in its 28 February 2009 edition that Government's estimate of 7.1 per cent GDP growth for 2008-09 may not be achieved after third quarter (October-December) figure revealed that growth had dipped to 5.3 per cent.

The IMF expects average inflation to moderate to 2 per cent in 2009-10 from about 8.8 per cent in 2008-09. Inflation has been coming down consistently after touching a peak of 12.9 per cent in August 2008. India's growth rate in 2008-09 was projected at 6.25 per cent by the IMF, as against the Government's forecast of 7.1 per cent. The IMF expects the growth rate in 2009-10, to fall to 5.25 per cent.

India is staring at deflation, or negative inflation, with the official inflation rate falling below one per cent—the lowest since 1977. Food prices, however, continued to be high, with food grains roughly 9 per cent costlier than a year ago, reinforcing a cruel paradox for consumers that they hear about zero inflation but face high prices when they buy their groceries. With the wholesale price index (WPI) falling by one point to 226.7 for the week ending 7 March 2009—the same level at which the index was on 29 March 2008—it now means the year-on-year inflation rate will become zero in the near future even if the index for the current year falls no further. In the current scenario, prices are falling not because of improved productivity but due to sharp fall in demand. If deflation sustains for a long period of time, it could lead to lower production, weak economic growth and rising unemployment.

As many as 1.5 million people could end up losing their jobs in India, as exports contracted for the third successive month plunging by 1.1 per cent in December 2008 amid the worst slowdown in the world economy in the last 80 years. "If these projections continue...it's quite likely that you can expect another five lakh losses...", Commerce Secretary said. About 1 million jobs have already been lost since August 2008.

Exports for the month of December 2008 stood at $12.69 billion, according to the latest available trade data. It had declined by 12.1 per cent and 9.9 per cent in October and November 2008 respectively. Exporters employ about 150 million people in India and the sector is India's biggest provider of jobs after agriculture. Nervous exporters, smarting under severe earnings erosions, are struggling to ink new contracts as demand shrinks amid growing bankruptcies in the US—India's largest export market. In recent months the Government has taken a slew of fiscal measures, including sharp cuts in excise duties and increased plan spending, to help the economy tide over a recession in the world's developed countries.

The global economic slowdown has adversely impacted nearly every sector of India's economy except perhaps agriculture. Businesses in industry, trade and manufacturing are declining. Flagship steel companies take Tata Steel and Arcelor Mittal have reported sharp slump in sales. As a matter of fact 110 firms out of BSE 500 have seen much lower profits, and even losses in some cases, in the last quarter of the financial year 2008-09. High interest cost, fall in domestic demand and decline in exports have led to a contraction in their profitability. The sectors that faced the maximum pressure include automobiles and auto ancillaries, financial services, infrastructure, real estate, airways and retail. Even the production of consumer durables has suffered a blow following a sharp decline in demand.

Although the banks in India have not been affected as much as the banks and financial institutions abroad, the formers' Non Performing Assets (NPAs) are rising at a worrying pace. There has been a 25 per cent rise in NPAs of 26 banks, in absolute terms. The delinquency in retail and realty segments has been more pronounced. This has made banks in general, hesitant in lending—leading to a credit crunch. A survey entitled "India's Top Banks-2009" has pointed to the fact that the amount of loans restructured has gone up by 61 per cent in 2008-09. The State Bank of India, and ICICI Bank, the country's major credit card issuers have reported losses for the second consecutive year in 2008-09. The officials feel that the market has gone extremely difficult.

Downturn and Poverty Situation

About 53 million people in developing countries will remain poor because of the world economic slowdown, the World Bank has said. The Bank says the downturn will reverse many of the gains made in reducing poverty in developing countries. It estimates that 40 per cent of the world's 107 developing countries are "highly exposed" to the global crisis. And it calls on the rich countries to devote 0.7 per cent of their bailout packages to help the poor in the developing nations. The global crisis is likely to keep 46 million more people below the absolute poverty line of $1.25 per day, and another seven million under $2 per day, compared with previous World Bank forecasts for 2009. An earlier version had incorrectly stated that 100 million more people would remain poor. "The global crisis threatens to become a human crisis in many developing countries unless they can take targeted measures to protect vulnerable people," said World Bank President Robert Zoellick. "While much of the world is focused on bank rescues and stimulus packages, we should not forget that poor people are much more exposed if their economies falter," he added.

The World Bank says the crisis will also delay progress towards reducing infant mortality, which could see 200,000-400,000 more children a year die if the crisis persists. These developments will undermine the plans agreed by the UN to reach the world poverty targets agreed in the Millennium Development Goals by 2015.

Global Response—Stimulus Measures

Global response to the financial crisis has been prompt, and by and large adequate, though it will take some time to have the desired impact. There have been relief plans, bailout packages, etc. in many countries of Europe, Asia and America. China has announced a $556 billion domestic stimulus package. Federal Reserve has reduced its fund rates six times in 2008—from 3.5 per cent to 1.5 per cent. The European Central Bank and the Bank of England have pumped in billions of dollars in the money-market auction.

Stimulus Package—I

In September 2008, the then Secretary of the United States Treasury, Henry Paulson and President George W. Bush proposed legislation for the Government to purchase up to US$700 billion of "troubled mortgage-related assets" from financial firms in hopes of improving confidence in the mortgage-backed securities markets and the financial firms participating in it. Discussions, hearings and meetings among legislative leaders were held, and the administration made clear that the proposal would undergo significant change before it could be approved by Congress. On 1 October 2008, a revised compromise version was approved by the Senate with a 74-25 vote. The bill, HR1424, was passed by the House on 3 October 2008 and signed into law. The first half of the bailout money was primarily used to buy preferred stock in banks instead of troubled mortgage assets.

Federal Reserve Response

In an effort to increase available funds for commercial banks and lower the fed funds rate, the US Federal Reserve announced on 29 September 2008, plans to double its Term Auction Facility to $300 billion. Because there appeared to be a shortage of US dollars in Europe at that time, the Federal Reserve also announced it would increase its swap facilities with foreign central banks from $290 billion to $620 billion.

As of 24 December 2008, the Federal Reserve had used its independent authority to spend $1.2 trillion on purchasing various financial assets and making emergency loans to address the financial crisis, above and beyond the $700 billion authorized by Congress from the federal budget. This included emergency loans to banks, credit card companies, and general businesses, temporary swaps of Treasury bills for mortgage-backed securities, the sale of Bear Stearns, and the bailouts of American International Group (AIG), Fannie Mae and Freddie Mac, and Citigroup.

Stimulus Package—II

Members of both houses of Congress reached a deal in February 2009 over US President Barack Obama's economic stimulus plan. Senate majority leader Harry Reid said the deal "bridged differences" between an $820 billion House version of the bill and a $838 billion Senate version. "The package...worth $789 billion (£549 billion), includes tax cuts and spending aimed at rescuing the US economy. The middle ground we have reached creates more jobs than the original Senate bill and costs less than the original House bill," said Senate majority leader Harry Reid. He said the stimulus bill should create 3.5 million jobs. He added that more than one-third the package it would be dedicated to tax cuts and incentives for middle-class Americans.

The House approved its $825 billion version of the package without any Republican support. The Senate voted 61-37 to approve a different $838 billion version with few Republicans opting to back it. The bill included help for victims of the recession in the form of unemployment benefits, food stamps, health coverage as well as billions for states that face the prospect of making deep cuts in their own public spending. Vice President Joe Biden said the passage of the bill would be an important psychological moment for the country as it grapples with the economic downturn. "It is the thing that will kick-start the confidence, the psychology that we can climb out of this," he said.

Measures in India

In October 2008, the supplementary demand for grants provided for a gross expenditure amounting to Rs. 2,37,286 crore with net cash outgo of Rs. 1,05,613 crore mainly to finance schemes/plans announced in the Union Budget for 2008-09. However, no provisions were made for the same.

On 7 December 2008, the three major *ad valorem* rates of central excise duty, viz. 14 per cent, 12 per cent and 8 per cent applicable to non-petroleum products were reduced by 4 percentage points each.

For promoting exports, pre-shipment and post-shipment export credit for labour intensive exports, i.e. textiles (including handlooms, carpets and handicrafts), leather, gems and jewellery, marine products and Small & Medium Enterprise (SME) sector was made more attractive by providing an interest subvention of 2 per cent up to March 31, 2009 subject to minimum rate of interest of 7 per cent per annum. An additional fund of Rs. 1,100 crore to ensure full refund of terminal excise duty/central sales tax (CST) was announced. Furthermore, an additional allocation of Rs. 350 crore for export incentive schemes was announced.

The Interim Budget 2009-10 presented on 16 February 2009 provided 2 per cent cut in exercise duty and service tax to boost the economy. Under the PPP mode, 54 Central Sector infrastructure projects worth Rs. 27,900 were approved for validity gap funding. The India Infrastructure Finance Company Ltd. (IIFCL) was authorized to raise Rs. 10,000 crore to ensure that the projects do not face financing difficulties arising from the current downturn.

The unprecedented economic stimulus packages announced by governments will take time to have an effect on economic growth and employment. The recent turmoil has presented a new set of challenges to most, if not all, regions of the world by rendering the achievement of a path, toward sustainable and socially equitable growth, and decent work for all, increasingly more difficult. According to the International Monetary Fund, the world economy is now entering a major downturn in the face of the most dangerous shock in mature financial markets since the 1930s, and governments have to act accordingly. The most significant measure being taken is the sweeping overhaul of the financial regulation. In America, hedge funds, private equity firms and derivative markets will come under government supervision for the first time. These regulatory changes are necessary to restore confidence in business enterprises, institutions, markets and public at large.

The G20 Summit on Financial Markets and the World Economy, in Washington DC in November 2008 also mandated a substantial action plan of measures to support international economy, strengthen financial sector supervision and reform global economic governance. The vein of international cooperation to fight global recession was visible at the London G20 meeting of April 2009 where the member countries pledged to "restore confidence, growth and jobs; repair the financial system to restore lending; strengthen financial regulation to rebuild trust; fund the reform... international financial institutions to overcome this crisis and prevent future one; promote global trade and investment and reject protectionism, to usher in prosperity; and to rebuild an inclusive, green, and sustainable recovery."

The Issue of Protectionism

There has been in the US and UK, a rise of legislation aimed at protecting industries and jobs through some anti-trade measures. The most notable examples of the same have been the insistence by the Democratic congressional leadership in the US to require that the stimulus money come with strings like "Buy America", and strikes by workers in the UK showing slogans "British jobs for British workers" on the placards.

The World Trade Organisation (WTO) Director General, Pascal Lamy, calls such measures catastrophic, and says, "If you start killing imports, you will kill exports." The political impulse to protect domestic economies during times of crisis is understandable, but "that's precisely why we have these rules, to avoid the slippery slope of protectionism," he adds.

However, there are people who believe that such a policy is necessary under the present conditions. For example, John Judis feels that the US has to do something like this to ensure that its spending does not simply disappear in a flood of imports. Complaints by other countries are immaterial. As things stand today, it seems difficult to hold back the tide of protectionist sentiment.

World leaders reiterated their rejection of protectionism, and trade barriers that threaten to deepen the global financial crisis. At the London meeting, the heads of the Group of 20 nations vowed "to do whatever is necessary to promote global trade and investment and reject protectionism." That pledge is almost identical to one made at a November 15, 2008 summit where they decided to "underscore the critical importance of rejecting protectionism and not turning inward in times of financial uncertainly." Since then, 17 of the G20 members have implemented 47 trade restrictions, a 1 March 2009 study by the World Bank showed.

Outsourcing

India Inc has expressed concern over Barack Obama's plans to clamp down on the outsourcing industry. Such a move will clearly make outsourcing unattractive to US companies, which is bad news for the Indian tech sector. Reiterating one of his election campaign agenda, in one of his more recent speeches, Obama made it clear that there would not be any tax benefits for American companies that outsource jobs to other countries. It would create/save 3.5 million jobs in the country. The domestic industry in general said such a move will only hurt US as outsourcing makes a lot of economic and logical sense to the country. Reacting to Obama's statement, Kris Gopalakrishnan, CEO Infosys said, "Outsourcing has enhanced the competitiveness of US corporations and has created more jobs within US economy. US is an open economy and a strong proponent of free trade globally. We are confident that US will not take any measures which might hurt its own global competitiveness."

The Future of Capitalism

The leaders of the former bastions of communist bloc have blamed capitalists for dragging the world into a serious economic crisis. In the opening address of the World Economic Forum at Davos, Switzerland, the Russian Prime Minister, Vladimir Putin spoke of a "perfect storm" that has decimated the old system, rendering it obsolete. He said that the fundamental stability and "the investment banks once considered the pride of Wall Street have virtually ceased to exist." But the damage has gone beyond Wall Street. Putin said, "The entire economic growth system where one regional centre prints money without respite and consumer material wealth, while another regional centre manufactures inexpensive goods and saves money printed by other Governments has suffered a major setback." The Chinese premier, Wen Jiabao also blamed the United States for economic slowdown. "Inappropriate macroeconomic policies ...unsustainable model of development characterised by prolonged low savings and high consumption...the blind pursuit of profit and the failure of financial supervision, all have contributed to the present crisis."

Marx saw the power of unbridled capitalism as a kind of myth which became more real than it actually is. In the present era of unchallenged capitalism, the only reality is money and its purchasing power. People want money in their pockets and their accounts, and the liberty to buy what they want to. That is how they understand the system. People believe in capitalism as it talks about profits, incentive and consumers' sovereignty.

Some experts feel that the present global crisis cannot be attributed to capitalism as much as to the structural changes which have taken place within global capitalism since the economic crisis of mid-1970s, and the neo-liberal policies introduced to combat it. The distribution of wealth in the leading capitalist countries like America, England, France, among others, has shifted to a large extent to the benefit of high-income individuals. Real wages have risen only marginally since then; the increase in social wealth has benefited almost entirely those already possessing a good amount of wealth. A large amount of these gains was invested in the financial markets which wooed the investors with increasingly novel speculative financial instruments like derivatives after the sweeping deregulation of markets in the 1970s.

The biggest charge being leveled against capitalism these days is that it privatises profits and socializes losses. During good times, the rich get richer while the poor keep waiting for the multiplier effect to percolate down to them, whereas during bad times, the lower-middle classes suffer more because their capacity to absorb economic shock is very low. Some economists have questioned the legitimacy of using taxpayers', money to bail out ill-functioning institutions including banks.

Keynes' Viewpoint

There is wide agreement that the world capitalist system is in the midst of its most severe crisis since the Great Depression of 1930s. Keynes' *The General Theory of Employment, Interest and Money*, which was published in 1936, recommended massive Government investment that would inject purchasing power into the economic system, which would help resuscitate the economy through the multiplier effect.

Keynes' persuasive power was formidable and among the earliest converts to his thinking—other than a close band of students and select professional colleagues—was President Franklin D. Roosevelt. Roosevelt's "New Deal" ushered in a massive public works program as per the Keynesian prescription. The Keynesian idea of having an interventionist state particularly when economic activity was sluggish remained the cornerstone of economic policymaking in the Western capitalist world in the post-World War II era. For more than three decades the capitalist countries in the West recorded uninterrupted economic growth that was without any historical precedence.

In fact, what we require is a combination of reasonable wages, monetary policy in the form of low interest rates, as well as fiscal policy in the shape of public expenditure on infrastructure, i.e. education, transportation, power supplies, buildings, communication networks, etc.

It is believed in some circles, and rightly so, that capitalism is reinventing itself. They feel that capitalism is not dead. "Recessions are not aberrations of capitalism but an intrinsic part of it. Markets create boom and bust cycles, arising from human tendencies to swing from euphoria to fear and back. A bust is an occasion for cleaning out deadwood and failed experiments, and reinventing capitalism."

Conclusion

There is no question that the global financial crisis has crippled economic growth around the world. But there is a lesson in this crisis. The rumours about the demise of capitalism may be exaggerated but the warning signs are clear and scary. In the present age of globalisation, an unregulated market—which is susceptible to manipulation by a few rogue characters—can plummet and send out strong ripples. Capitalism may have an in-built self-correcting mechanism, but how painful such mechanism is, can be realized from the present global economic conditions which have jolted the entire world.

"The financial crisis roiling the world today is the result of serious shortcomings in domestic financial governance that have exposed gaps in the global governance of institutional finance and capital." Its immediate roots lie in the excessive and not so transparent leverage of complex securities and derivatives that inflated the real economy to excessive proportions. The US regulatory regime governing its financial and banking worlds—which had far-reaching repercussions for the entire globe—can be euphemistically described as light, incomplete and fragmentary. Thus, the need for efficient, effective and transparent regulatory and surveillance instruments and institutions is quite obvious. The role of global governance institutions, now more than ever before, is to contain the contagion. Only a new regulatory regime will reassure the world at large that the balance has been restored between the risks and the benefits of integrating with an open world economy.

The comity of nations has joined hands to take short-term emergency measures to deal with the financial crisis. There is a growing recognition that the system to manage the modern world of banking, capital and finance has to be redesigned. The corporations, markets and financial flows are global, but regulatory and financial systems are national—or in a few cases like Europe—regional. The world at this juncture needs "some sort of visionary internationalism" like Bretton Woods Conference in 1944 that founded the IMF and the World Bank and restructured the international monetary system.

It is also being felt that the existing political or economic institutions like IMF and G7 have not proved equal to the task of coordinating an adequate response to global crisis. The way things are, it is hard to imagine that any major global challenge can be effectively addressed without involving all three Asian giants—China, India and Japan. But two of them, viz. India and Japan are not permanent members of the UN Security Council, and two, viz. China and India are not part of the G7. These anomalies need to be removed to give these countries more say in international affairs.

The G20 meeting of 2 April 2009, held in London, can be termed as landmark in many ways. The member countries—which are virtually world's main financial powers—pledged more than $1 trillion for emergency loans to reverse the recession.

Emerging markets and developing countries, which have been the engine of recent world growth, are also now facing challenges which are adding to the current downturn in the global economy. It is imperative for global confidence and economic recovery that capital continues to flow to them. This will require a substantial strengthening of the international financial institutions, particularly the IMF. G20 members have therefore agreed to make available an additional $850 billion of resources through the global financial institutions to support growth in emerging markets and developing countries by helping to finance counter-cyclical spending, bank recapitalisation, infrastructure, trade finance, balance of payments support, debt rollover, and social support. They not only decided to reject protectionism but also to bring tighter financial regulation. Positive results can be expected sooner than later.

INTRODUCTORY

The world is going through its worst economic slowdown since the Great Depression of 1930s, as a massive financial crisis has slashed global investment, brought sharp drops in commodity prices and severely hurt exports. The World Bank has lowered its estimates of global growth to 0.9 per cent in 2009—well below the 3 per cent rate typically considered the dividing line between growth and contraction. Releasing its annual report on global economy, World Bank's chief economist, Justin Lin said, "The financial crisis is now likely to result in the most serious recession since the 1930s."

The current economic slowdown is notable for both its length and breadth across all the regions of the world, leading to a contraction in the most-wealthy nations and a sharp downturn in emerging economies, including China, India, Russia and Brazil. The Major indicators of this slowdown are contraction of world trade volumes for the first time since 1982; nearly 50 per cent fall in investment from the 2007 levels; and an unprecedented liquidity crunch, which has affected business all over the world. The liquidity crunch has cut access to loans in advanced as well as developing countries —pulling investment out of poor nations which need them most—and an across the board reduction in consumer spending. The world is witnessing large job cuts in almost every sector, cancellation or postponement of future projects, erosion of margins and extremely low profits or even losses in businesses while the Governments across the world are taking monetary and fiscal measures to revive their respective economies. Various aspects of this slowdown are discussed below.

ORIGIN OF MELTDOWN

Though sharp eyes noticed the global financial crisis much earlier, it became prominently visible to everyone in September

2008 with the failure, merger and conservatorship of several large financial firms of the United States. The crisis was faced by leading United States and European investment banks, insurance firms and mortgage banks as a consequence of subprime mortgage crisis.

The failure of large financial institutions in the United States rapidly evolved into global credit crisis, deflation, sharp reductions in shipping and commerce, leading to failure of several European banks, declines in various stock indexes, substantial reductions in market values of equities and commodities all over the world including in the centrally-controlled economies like China and Russia. The crisis was sharpened by Section 128 of the Emergency Economic Stabilisation Act of 2008 which permitted the Federal Reserve Bank to pay interest on excess reserve requirement balances held by it as deposits from banks, removing the long standing incentive for banks to extend credit instead of keeping hard cash with America's premier bank which plays a leadership role in monetary policy, financial supervision and the payment system. It led to a liquidity problem and the de-leveraging of financial institutions, particularly in the United States and Europe which aggravated liquidity crisis and brought about a decline in international shipping and commerce. In spite of coordinated efforts of the Governments and central bank directors to mitigate fears, the crisis went on worsening, resulting in currency crisis leading to the transfer of vast capital resources by investors in stronger currencies like yen, US dollar and Swiss franc. It compelled many emerging economies to seek aid from the IMF.

The crisis which originated from widespread subprime mortgage failures quickly engulfed the entire financial system as well as industry resulting in widespread layoffs, for example, 70,000 job losses in a single day in six companies ranging from manufacturing to telecom across the United States and Europe as a measure of cost-cutting to grapple with slump in consumer spending. Construction machinery manufacturer Caterpillar, pharma major Pfizer, telecom firm Sprint Nextel Corporation and home improvement retailer Home Depot were among the top companies adversely affected.

China an Important Culprit for Recession

China intentionally undervalued the exchange rate of its currency yuan. Thus its goods became cheaper in the international markets. It flooded United States market and accumulated trillion-plus dollars. In such a situation in a free economy the exchange rate of the country's currency would have risen on the principle of demand for and supply of the currency. But since Chinese economy is controlled, the rate of yuan did not rise as the Government of China kept it artificially low.

China used an important part of thus accumulated dollars in financing US Government debt which encouraged American extravagance. A vicious circle was created: more US spending resulted in more Chinese exports leading to more US debt involving more US spending. In the same way oil-rich Gulf countries controlled supply of oil leading to a substantial rise in oil prices. They also got huge amounts of dollars.

Cheap capital availability led to a boom of real estate in the United States creating a subprime monster. The United States became a nation of spenders and the earlier habit of saving disappeared.

Keeping the currency undervalued is an indirect way of subsidising and dumping goods and is contrary to the provisions of World Trade Organisation.

GLOBAL FINANCIAL CRISIS: A CHRONOLOGY

Though the present global crisis can be attributed to several causes, the subprime mortgage crisis is unarguably the major among these. What started it all was the dramatic rise in mortgage delinquencies and foreclosures in the United States, with major adverse consequences for banks and financial markets around the globe. The crisis, which has its roots in the closing years of the 20th century, became apparent in 2007 and has exposed pervasive weaknesses in financial industry regulation and the global financial system.

Many US mortgages issued in recent years were made to subprime borrowers, defined as those with lesser ability to repay the loan based on various criteria. When US house prices began to decline in 2006-07, mortgage delinquencies soared, and securities backed with subprime mortgages, widely held by financial firms, lost most of their value. The result has been a large decline in the capital of many banks and USA Government sponsored enterprises (GSEs), tightening credit around the world.

The Bear Stearns bailout, the Government takeover of Fannie Mae and Freddie Mac, bankruptcy of Lehman Brothers, the sale of Merrill Lynch & Company, and now a drop of more than 62 per cent in AIG's share price, combined to create a financial atmosphere verging on panic.

The debacle of the hyper-buoyant housing market and the freewheeling attitude of the subprime mortgage industry, most recently illustrated by the collapse of Lehman Brothers have resulted in a takedown of giant financial institutions that had successfully weathered the stock market crash of 1929.

Lehman Brothers Holdings Inc. was a global financial-services firm that, until declaring bankruptcy in September 2008, did business in investment banking, equity and fixed-income sales, research and trading, investment management, private equity, and private banking. It was a primary dealer in the US Treasury securities market. Its primary subsidiaries included Lehman Brothers Inc., Neuberger Berman Inc., Aurora Loan Services Inc., SIB Mortgage Corporation, Lehman Brothers Bank, FSB, Eagle Energy Partners, and the Crossroads Group. The firm's headquarters were in New York City, with regional headquarters in London and Tokyo, as well as offices located throughout the world.

On September 15, 2008, the firm filed for Chapter 11 bankruptcy protection. The filing marked the largest bankruptcy ever in US history.

The subprime crisis had begun to show its signs in the early 2007 which reached a critical stage during September 2008. It was characterised by substantial decline in liquidity in the global credit markets and insolvency threats to investment banks and other financial institutions. In February 2008, the US Congress approved a $168 billion economic stimulus package and sent it to the then US President George W. Bush for his approval. In March, the US investment bank Bear Stearns got emergency funding from JPMorgan Chase with the backing of Federal Reserve Bank of New York. During this time JPMorgan Chase announced plans to buy investment bank Bear Stearns for $2 a share following the liquidity problems caused by the crisis. The US Federal Reserve System became lender to various other large investment banks. It cut the federal funds rate by 75 basis points to 2.25 per cent, which was followed by another cut of quarter percentage points to 2 per cent.

In May 2008, the United States Federal Reserve System auctioned off $24.12 billion in Treasury Securities to help relieve the subprime mortgage crisis. Further, lending standards on home mortgages, other types of consumer loans and business loans were tightened. In June, premier US banks and insurance companies like Wachovia (the fourth largest bank in the US) and the American International Group (AIG) world's largest insurance company) sacked their CEOs for the losses incurred because of the subprime mortgage crisis. During the time Ireland's Economic and Social Research Institute declared for the first time that the country was in the grip of recession. However, it predicted that the economy would regain its growth momentum towards the end of 2009 and would be back to normal growth by 2010.

In July 2008, the European Central Bank increased interest rates in the Eurozone to 4.25 per cent to tackle inflation. The US Federal Reserve tightened mortgage regulation in an attempt to stamp out the practices that had led to the subprime mortgage crisis. In response to the subprime mortgage crisis, the then US President George W. Bush signed the Housing and Economic Recovery Act in 2008. The unemployment in the United States rose to 5.7 per cent, the highest in more than four years. The New York Attorney General Andrew Cuomo reached a $7 billion settlement with Citigroup to buy back auction rate securities from about 40,000 clients throughout the United States. The UK home repossessions rose by 48 per cent. The Consumer Price Index in the United States rose by nearly one per cent in July 2008, leading to an annual inflation rate of 5.6 per cent, the highest in 17 years.

In the beginning of September 2008, reserve balances from banks in the Federal Reserve System started increasing over required levels of about $10 billion just before the stock market crash. Gradually, the signs of recession began to appear in other parts of the country as well. In September, the European Commission predicted the fall of UK, Germany and Spain into recession and further added that the outlook for the rest of the Eurozone was gloomy. The Washington Mutual, the largest savings and loan company in the United States, fired its Chief Executive due to heavy losses incurred due to the subprime mortgage crisis. It was this time that the AIG sought an emergency $40 billion loan from the United States Federal Reserve. The AIG which is not only the largest insurer but also a significant participant in the credit default swaps markets suffered a liquidity crisis following the downgrade of its credit rating. The Federal Reserve took several measures to expand emergency lending to tackle the crisis. At the request of AIG, it agreed to lend it $85 billion in exchange for a 79.9 per cent equity interest and the right to suspend dividends to previously issued common and preferred stock.

On September 7, 2008, the United States Director of the Federal Housing Finance Agency (FHFA) announced the decision to place two United States Government-sponsored enterprises—Fannie Mae (Federal National Mortgage Association) and Freddie Mac (Federal Home Loan Mortgage Corporation)—into conservationship run by FHFA. Conservation was the only form in which taxpayer's money was committed to the GSEs.

On September 16, The Reserve Primary Fund, an important money market mutual fund, lowered its share price below $1 as a consequence of exposure to Lehman debt securities. This led to demands from investors to return their funds as the intensity of the financial crisis increased. By morning September 18, money market sell orders from institutional investors totalled $0.5 trillion, out of a total market capitalisation of $4 trillion. However, $105 billion liquidity injection from the Federal Reserve averted immediate collapse. On September 19, the United States Treasury offered temporary insurance (similar to FDIC insurance bank accounts) to money market funds. Towards the end of the week, short selling of financial stocks was suspended by the Financial Services Authority in the United Kingdom and by the Securities and Exchange Commission in the United States. The authorities in other countries took similar measures.

On September 19, Troubled Assets Relief Program (TARP), a plan to combat the subprime mortgage crisis was proposed by the Secretary of the Treasury, which was later incorporated into the Emergency Economic Stabilisation Act. It permitted the United States Government to purchase illiquid assets—formally termed toxic assets—from financial institutions. Within a couple of days the Secretary of the Treasury and President Bush announced a proposal for the federal Government to buy up to $700 billion of illiquid mortgage-backed securities to increase the liquidity of the secondary mortgage markets and reduce potential losses encountered by the financial institutions. This draft proposal of the plan was received favourably by investors in the stock market. US President George W. Bush addressing the nation on prime time television to discuss the crisis warned that the United States would face a "long and painful recession" if the package was not passed.

Unemployment in the United States rose to a seven year high, and orders for durable goods fell to their lowest level in 18 months. Home sales during August 2008 fell to a 17 year low. Goldman Sachs and Morgan Stanley, the two last remaining independent investment banks on Wall Street became bank holding companies as a result of subprime mortgage crisis. The US Congressional leader and the George W. Bush administration reached an outline Emergency Economic Stabilisation Act of 2008 for the bailout of financial institutions hit hard by the subprime mortgage.

The Russian Government lent the country's three biggest banks—Sberbank, VTB Bank and Gazprombank—1.13 trillion roubles ($44 billion) to boost liquidity. Trading remained suspended for the third consecutive day in Russia's two main stock exchanges—the MICEX and the dollar-denominated RTS—amidst fears of financial collapse. Russian President Dmtry Medvedev ordered ministers to inject another 500 billion roubles (£10.8 billion, US$20 billion) of funds from the state budget to stabilize the markets.

The key risk indicators became highly volatile during September 2008, which led the US Government to pass the Emergency Economic Stabilisation Act of 2008. As mentioned earlier, Section 128 of the Emergency Economic Stabilisation Act of 2008 permitted the Federal System to pay interest from October 6 onwards, on the excess balances, causing further pressure on international credit markets. By the end of second week of January 2009, excess on the balances reached $870 billion as against the increase in reserve balances of only $65 billion after September 2001 before declining to normal levels within a month.

In the first week of October 2008, a major banking and financial crisis emerged in Iceland with a decline of 30 per cent in its currency, krona, against the Euro. An emergency meeting was held the same day and a legislation was passed granting great powers to Government to seize and regulate banks. Standard and Poor's cut Iceland's foreign-currency sovereign credit rating. It also lowered Iceland's banking industry country risk assessment from Group 5 to Group 8. Iceland's Financial Supervisory Authority took control of troubled Landsbanki Bank. Iceland's largest bank, Kaupthing Bank, was nationalised by the country's Financial Supervisory Authority. Russia agreed to provide Iceland with emergency loans of €4 billion ($5.4 billion). Significant losses were marked on stock exchanges all across the world. The Dow Jones Industrial Average slipped by as much as 800.06 points which is the biggest intra-day drop ever recorded. The Dow closed below the 10,000 mark for the first time since 26 October 2004. The US Federal Reserve announced plans to buy billions of dollars of short-term commercial paper to restore liquidity to the money market. The Chairman of the Federal Reserve proposed to cut interest rates in the wake of emerging situations. The shares plunged nearly 20 per cent in Russia amid fears of global crisis and fall in oil prices. Trading was suspended in Russia's leading stock exchanges.

Britain also took certain measures to tackle the situation. Britain's Chancellor of Exchequer released details of a rescue package to restore confidence in British banks. As part of the package, the British Government announced to provide £50 billion of investment, a further £200 billion in short-term loan and guarantee up to £250 billion of intra-bank loans. The German Parliament passed a €500 billion ($673.8 billion) bailout package for banks.

The Australian Prime Minister Kevin Rudd announced to guarantee all deposits in all Australian banks for a period of three years to combat the situation emerging from subprime mortgage crisis. The Reserve Bank of Australia pumped $1.5 billion into the banking system to mitigate the severity of crisis. The amount was nearly three times as much as the market's estimated requirements. New Zealand and United Arab Emirates also announced to guarantee all bank deposits in their banks. Greece, as a part of measure to combat the situation, introduced a €100,000 guarantee for the €230 billion bank deposits in the country for three years—well above the EU-wide Ecofin-mandated minimum of €50,000 for one year. It also assured about the stability of its banking system. The US Federal Reserve Board cut interest rates by half a percentage point to 1.5 per cent as part of a coordinated activity with the European Central Bank and other central banks. It approved the merger of Wells Fargo and Wachovia after Citigroup withdrew the legal case to put on hold a proposed merger. The head of the International Monetary Fund expressed concern over the US financial crises and warned of a global meltdown. It also offered to lend countries, if required.

In *World Economic Outlook* the IMF presented a gloomy projection for the global financial system. The Finance

Ministers of G7 who met with the IMF Chief and World Bank President in Washington announced a plan to combat the crisis with the help of "all available tools" to support key institutions. The then US President George W. Bush committed to a collaborative action with G7 Finance Ministers. He announced new measures to attack the current economic crisis including plans for the US Government to buy stakes in major banks. The heads of 45 countries from Asia and Europe met in Beijing to discuss the situation emerging from the financial meltdown. The Reserve Bank of India added almost $1.32 billion, through a refinance operation, to cope with the situation.

On 7 October 2008, the Federal Reserve announced the formation of a Commercial Paper Funding Facility, intended to serve as a funding backstop to facilitate the issuance of term commercial paper by eligible users. Several countries announced new deposit guarantees, some increased them. Taiwan outlined plans to double the guarantee to NT $3 million ($92,000). European Union agreed to increase guarantees across the EU to at least €50,000 per saver. Several EU states such as Netherlands, Spain, Belgium and Greece announced increases on top of this minimum. They announced to guarantee up to €100,000. On October 8, the British Government announced £25 billion, available as "Tier 1 capital" preference share capital or PIBS (Permanent Interest Bearing Securities), to various financial institutions such as Abbey, Barclays, HBOS, HSBC Bank, Royal Bank of Scotland, and Standard Chartered as part of a bank rescue package. An additional £25 billion was scheduled for other financial institutions, including British subsidiaries of foreign banks. Besides, the plan included increased ability to borrow from the Government, assistance in raising equity and a support for international efforts. The European Central Bank, Bank of England, Federal Reserve, Bank of Canada, Swedish Riksbank, and Swiss National Bank announced simultaneous cuts of 0.5 per cent to their base rates. Following them, the Central Bank of People's Republic of China also cut its interest rates. Stock markets all across the world witnessed a sharp fall which led to suspension of trade in Russia and Indonesia. The Japanese benchmark index Nikkei fell over 9 per cent.

On October 9, the cost of short-term credit rose, while there were heavy losses in the United States stock market. The Dow plunged to 8600, lowest in the last five years, though the losses were moderate in Europe. The following day, there were heavy losses in Asian and European markets. Russia's stock markets remained closed on October 10 due to falling stock prices. The Russian parliament passed a plan authorizing lending of $36 billion—gained from global oil sales—to banks that met creditor-worthiness requirements. In the United States, the Government authorized by the Emergency Economic Stabilisation Act, announced plans to infuse funds into banks by purchasing equity interests in them—in effect partial nationalisation like Britain. Stock markets crashed across Europe and Asia. London, Paris and Frankfurt dropped 10 per cent within an hour of trading. The Wall Street also opened weak for trading and kept on falling further. Global markets experienced their worst week since 1987.

The Dow Jones Industrial Average dropped 697 points within the five minutes of trading session on Wall Street. It fell below 7900 to its lowest level since March 17, 2003, though it improved in the afternoon and experienced a loss of just 128 points or 1.49 per cent at the end of the day. The New York Stock Exchange, with the Dow at 8,451, was trading at 40 per cent down from its record high on October 9, 2007. The day was marked by extreme volatility in US markets. On October 11, the US Government announced a shift in emphasis in its rescue efforts from buying illiquid assets to recapitalising banks, including strong banks, in exchange for preferred equity.

On October 12, European leaders, meeting in Paris, announced recapitalisation plans for Europe's banks. Plans were also announced to guarantee bank deposits for five years. Mechanisms were also outlined to increase the availability of short-term credit. It was decided that the European countries would finance their own rescue plans and tailor them to local conditions. A total €1 trillion rescue plan was announced.

Bank guarantee plans were also announced by Australia and New Zealand. Norway, which is not in the Eurozone, announced in a hastily called press conference, a US$57.4 billion (350 billion Norwegian kroner) plan of offering Norwegian banks new Government bonds.

In their meeting in Washington, the G7 nations pledged to support the important financial institutions to prevent their failure. This decision came in the wake of the bankruptcy of Lehman Brothers which led to the loss of funds by other financial institutions. It was thought that the losses may have triggered a tightening of the credit crunch as banks ceased to lend to one another. However, no enforceable mechanism was created to support the pledge.

On October 13, stock markets worldwide rose. The International Monetary Fund offered possible technical and financial aid to Hungary which suffered during the crisis due to the flight of investors to euro, Swiss franc, and dollar-denominated investments. As in the rest of the world, stock prices rose on the Hungarian exchange and pressure on forint, the national currency, eased, which had dropped to 30 per cent against the dollar since July 2008. The Prime Minister of Spain, Jose Luis Rodriguez announced to provide up to €100 billion of guarantees for new debt issued by commercial banks in 2008. The UK Government initiated the process of nationalisation by injecting £37 billion in the three largest banks. The banks, in return for the bailout, agreed to cancel dividend payments until the loans are repaid, have board members appointed by the Treasury and limit the executive pay. The European Central Bank attempted to revive credit market by weekly injecting of unlimited euro funds at an interest rate of 3.75 per cent. Following its European partners, Italy pledged to intervene to prevent any bank failures in its country. Its Finance Minister Giulio Tremonti, announced to guarantee new bank bonds of up to 5 years until the end of 2009 and the Bank of Italy would provide €40 billion in Treasury bills to banks to refinance inferior assets that cannot be currently used as collateral. Coordinating with the Eurozone countries, the Dutch Government announced to guarantee interbank lending up to €200 billion. It was followed by setting up of a €20 billion Dutch fund in order to help recapitalise banks and insurance companies.

On 14 October, the US announced a plan to take an equity interest of $250 billion in US banks with 25 billion for each of the four largest banks of the country. The plan also included an option allowing the Government to purchase common stock according to a formula which could return substantial profit to the taxpayers, should the stock price of the companies substantially appreciate. It was thought that the additional capitalisation and the guarantees will help banks resume a normal lending pattern with each other and borrowers as well. Japan also took many such measures to help its market and to prevent the worse of the credit crisis. It lifted restrictions on companies buying back their shares, strengthened disclosure on short selling and temporarily suspended the sale of Government-owned stocks. The Australian Government also released a $10.4 billion stimulus package to support its economy. The Economic Security Strategy was designed to help pensioners, low income families and for the first time, the home buyers to withstand the impact of global meltdown. It was followed by Australian Government's announcement to guarantee all bank deposits for three years, all term wholesaling funding by Australian banks in international markets and double its planned purchase of residential mortgage backed securities.

On 15 October, the London Stock Exchange FTSE 100 fell substantially. It slipped down by 7.16 per cent. The losses sparked off more losses in the US, as the Dow Jones Industrial Average suffered the biggest fall in terms of percentage since 1987, dropping over 733 points, while the NASDAQ dipped almost eight and a half per cent and Standard and Poor's plunged over nine per cent.

As a result of various measures taken, there was some improvement in the availability of credit, though stock markets and currencies like British pound and euro continued to decline worldwide during the last days of the October. Asian markets particularly suffered heavy losses while the losses in the

European markets were substantial. The Dow Industrial Index experienced the highest volatility during the week. The dollar and the yen showed particular strength which had a baleful effect on global economies, including the US and Japan. On 22 October, Pakistan along with Hungary, Siberia, Ukraine, etc. approached the IMF for aid in dealing with severe balance of payments difficulties. A great number of countries like Turkey, South Africa, Argentina, Romania, Bulgaria, etc. were facing financial difficulties. Although they had not held securities based on subprime mortgages, they were unable to borrow money and hence, were experiencing a severe credit crisis.

On October 24, stock markets plunged all across the world amidst fears of imminent global recession. This was aggravated by the remarks of Alan Greenspan that the crisis was "a once-in-a-century credit tsunami". It was further fuelled by the comments of Gordon Brown, the UK Prime Minister, who in his speech admitted that Great Britain was already in the grip of recession. Following the trends, the US stock markets also fell sharply on opening and closed with the Dow Industrial Index down 312 points. On October 24 and 25, the 7th Asia-Europe Meeting was held in Beijing with the European Union meeting Asian states to draw out a common approach ahead of the Emergency International Meeting scheduled to be held on November 15 in Washington.

On October 26, Hungary and Ukraine made tentative arrangements with the International Monetary Fund for emergency aid packages. In Poland, the value of stocks dropped 50 per cent for the year, the Polish currency zloty, fell against both the dollar and the euro. South Africa was badly affected by the crisis, due to dramatic decline in the price of platinum which is widely used in automobile industry. Various countries of the world were engaged in emergency discussions with the IMF. The Gulf Cooperation Council met in Riyadh in the wake of falling prices of oil and a 40 per cent drop in equity prices to formulate a coordinated response to the crisis.

On October 27, Hong Kong stocks crashed, losing more than 12 per cent of their value while Nikkei 225 index in Japan fell by 6.4 per cent to its lowest level since 1982. There were mixed results in European stock markets. After initial drop, the Dow Jones Industrial Average showed a slightly positive trend but eventually closed down 203 points. Oil futures continued to decline and the yen continued to rise against all other currencies.

In the second round of recapitalisation, the US Treasury funded 20 banks with 38 billion dollars. Criteria for funding was based on the strength of the bank. The stronger the banks with higher CAMELS ratings, the greater the chance of being offered aid.

On October 28, stocks rose dramatically worldwide in anticipation of rate cuts by central banks. In the US, the Dow Industrial Average rose 10.8 per cent and closed above 9000. On October 29, the US markets closed slightly down despite the announcement of a reduction in the federal funds by the Federal Open Market Committee. The US markets were up on 30 and 31 October, cutting losses to the Dow Industrial Average during October to 17 per cent down 30 per cent for the year thus far. In Russia, stock markets had crashed down 70 per cent. Despite significant foreign reserves, Russia was faced with sharply reduced commodity prices.

In Asia, Japan announced its second economic stimulus plan of $51 billion on 30 October. Hong Kong and Taiwan cut interest rates while Japan announced an interest cut to 0.3 per cent. The Federal Reserve established a $30 billion currency swap line with South Korea, Singapore, Brazil and Mexico.

JPMorgan Chase, the largest bank in the United States announced to work with those home owners who were ready to pay their mortgages by reducing interest payment or principal. Counseling centers were planned for the affected areas. Bank of America and Countrywide Financial also announced similar programs.

The United States Government announced a second bailout of AIG. The total value of the new plan, roughly amounting to $150 billion, is the largest Government support package extended to a private company in US history. Employment data released by the Labour Department on November 7, showed that about 500,000 jobs were lost in the United States during September and October 2008 with unemployment rising to 6.5 per cent in October. There is an anticipation that unemployment will rise to 8 per cent by the middle of 2009. On November 6, amidst predictions of deep recession in the UK and the Eurozone, the Bank of England, in anticipation of the danger of inflation, lowered its base rates by 1.5 percentage points, from 4.5 to 3 per cent. It was accompanied by a 50 basis point drop in the base rate to 3.25 per cent by the European Central Bank. The IMF predicted for 2009, a worldwide –0.3 per cent decrease of the BIP for the developed economies (–0.7 per cent for the USA and –0.8 per cent for Germany).

On November 9, the People's Republic of China announced a domestic stimulus package of $586 billion to finance programs in 10 major domestic areas in the next two years. Economic growth declined in China with sharp drops in property and stock values. Some Chinese factories engaged in low-end export manufacturing, were badly affected by the emerging situation. On November 12, the US Treasury Secretary Henry Paulson scrapped the original Troubled Asset Relief Program and announced a shift in focus to consumer lending. The remaining portion of the TARP budget was to be used to help relieve pressure on consumer credits like car loans, student loans, credit cards, etc. On November 13, the Dow Jones Industrial Average marked another dramatic session, opening at 8,282.66, with sharp fluctuations, eventually closing at 8,835.25 with a net gain of more than 550 points (third largest ever). On November 15, the leaders of the G20, at the invitation of the then US President George W. Bush, held the initial session of the Summit on Financial Markets and the World Economy. They agreed to cooperate with respect to global financial crisis and issued a statement regarding immediate and medium term goals and actions, required to be taken to reform the international economy.

The Eurozone entered the first recession during November as the combined Gross Domestic Product of the 15 members dropped 0.2 per cent in the second and third quarters of 2008.

In the third quarter, the GDP of Japan fell 0.4 per cent, following a 3.7 per cent drop in the second quarter. The Japanese economy posted consecutive second quarter contraction for the first time since 2001, officially putting the country in a recession. On November 19, proposed bailouts of US automakers, were rejected. Automobile sales declined sharply in Europe and bailouts were under consideration. On November 19, the Dow Jones Industrial Average fell sharply by 427.47 points or 5.07 per cent closing below 8,000 points for the first time since March 2003. The US financial stocks led the way with Citigroup and showed a 23 per cent drop. The UK FTSE 100 fell by about the same percentage, closing just above 4000. The BBC Global 30, combining Europe, Asia and North America, in a single index, fell by 5.1 per cent.

On November 20, the Dow Jones Industrial Average dropped 445 points, closing at 7,552, the lowest point in six years. Shares of Citigroup plummeted another 26 per cent and shares of other major US financial institutions dropped by more than 10 per cent. On November 21, the Dow Jones Industrial Average recovered slightly closing above 8,000. However, stocks of Citibank, Bank of America and JPMorgan Chase continued to decline. As of the week of November 16, stock losses in United States markets during 2008, as measured by S&P 500, were equivalent to those suffered in 1931, i.e. over 50 per cent. Total losses during the Great Depression exceeded 80 per cent but that was over a period of three years.

November 21 and November 22 marked the largest two session gain in Dow Jones Industrial Average since October 1987. The Dow gained 891.10 points, 11.8 per cent and closed at 8,443.39 points. On November 23, the United States Government agreed to a rescue plan for Citigroup. It was announced in a joint statement by the Treasury Department, the Federal Reserve and the Federal Deposit Insurance Corp that in exchange for preferred stock valued at $27 billion paying 8 per cent interest, a further $20 billion would be invested into the company and that the Government would be invested into the company and that the Government would limit loss on $306 billion in risky loans and securities to

$29 billion plus 10 per cent of any remaining losses. Citigroup received US$32 billion under the United States Emergency Economic Stabilisation Act. The company announced to cut 75,000 jobs by early 2009. The US Federal Reserve announced a new stimulus package of US$800 billion to buy debt and mortgage-backed securities and make loans to holders of consumer debts. During the month, the IMF approved a US$2.1 billion reserve package for Iceland to combat the financial crisis. The European Union proposed a €200 billion stimulus package which included already spent money.

On 1 December, the National Bureau of Economic Research officially declared that the US economy had entered recession in December 2007. The Labour Department reported that the US lost 533,000 jobs in November 2008, the biggest monthly loss since 1974. The unemployment rate rose from 6.5 per cent to 6.7 per cent. After experiencing a positive trend in the last week of November 2008, the S&P fell 80 points to 816, down 9 per cent. Financial stocks in the S&P 500 declined 17 per cent. The Dow Jones Industrial Average dropped 679 points and closed at 8149 with a fall of 7.7 per cent. Oil prices fell below $50 a barrel in New York trading.

On December 9, the Bank of Canada lowered its key interest rate by 0.75 to 1.5 per cent, the lowest since 1958. The bank officially announced that the economy of Canada was in recession. Canada lost 70,600 jobs in the month of November, the highest since 1982. The US Government announced a proposal for a US$17.4 billion bailout package for three major US automakers—Chrysler, General Motors, and Ford—to avoid bankruptcy. The money was proposed to be taken from the $700 billion bailout package originally intended to rescue the US banks. President George W. Bush said that it would not be a "responsible course of action" to allow the companies to collapse. In the third week of December, the US industry leader asked the Federal Reserve for assistance unfreezing the commercial real estate market, which had not securitized any loans in the last six months of 2008. The US consumer price index had fallen in November by 1.91 per cent on a non-seasonally adjusted basis, the biggest decline since the Great

Depression of 1930s. Bernard Madoff, former chairman of the NASDAQ exchange market, was arrested on a single securities fraud charge for operating a $50 billion Ponzi scheme which was found affecting banks, individuals and charities in the US and Europe.

The Central Bank of America spent US$30 billion in currency market interventions in November 2008. Canada announced a US$3.3 billion bailout for its troubled automotive industry. In December, Toyota Motor Corporation, the world's largest automaker, forecast its first operating loss in 70 years caused by the automotive crisis.

In the second week of January 2009, Sony announced $1.1 billion operating loss. On 18 January, the Danish Parliament agreed to a financial package worth 100,000,000,000 Danish krone (US$ 17,596,339,961). On January 20, Philippines expressed fears of 60,000 IT job losses due to Intel shutdown. On January 19, the Royal Bank of Scotland lost around 70 per cent of its share price after the news of a GB£28 billion loss for 2008 and the UK Government's increased stake of 70 per cent in the company. The Royal Bank of Scotland's shares fell by more than 10 per cent both in London and New York stock exchanges.

American International Group (AIG) reported a record $61.7 billion quarterly loss and received a new dollop of US taxpayer aid as part of a plan to break the company into smaller, easier-to-manage units. The struggling insurance company has received $30 billion in new federal assistance, indicating that the policymakers still believe that AIG is too big to fail. Chief Executive Edward Liddy said the company has become "too complicated, too unwieldy and opaque" to be run as a single business.

The Government said the purpose of the aid was to stabilize and reduce the size of the company, which it believes poses a risk to the financial system. It was for that reason that the United States acquired 79.9 per cent of AIG in an $85 billion September 2008 bailout. In November 2008 the company was allowed to increase its borrowings to $150 billion.

The decision came as AIG announced that it lost $61.7 billion during its fourth quarter, surpassing the $54.2 billion record set by Time Warner in the first quarter of 2002. Edward Liddy said his company was in a much dire condition than expected. He also stated that the deal with the Government keeps a difficult economic situation from deteriorating further by making sure the company survives, but he couldn't guarantee AIG wouldn't need more federal aid.

Despite the loss, the company's credit rating remains intact, at least for now. Fitch Ratings said the Government's support overrides the quarter's loss for most of the parameters for company's ratings. AIG's stock rose 16.7 per cent, or 7 cents, to 49 cents in morning trading. Ironically, the report sent the rest of the stock market tumbling, finally pushing the Dow Jones Industrial Average below 7,000 points. It was alarming to note that AIG has lost almost all of its market value over the past year, falling an extraordinary 99 per cent. In the last three months of 2008, the New York-based firm lost $22.95 per share. It lost $5.3 billion, or $2.08 per share, in the previous year's corresponding period. Sales fell to negative $23.8 billion, as the company had to reverse gains it had recorded from investments in past quarters.

The dramatic reshaping of AIG is similar to drastic steps being taken at Citigroup to shore up its operations. In early 2009, Citi announced plans to hive off a mountain of bad loans, shed noncritical businesses like US mortgage lending, and refocus on its traditional commercial, retail, and private banking operations globally. It even decided to change its name back to Citicorp.

The US Government agreed to convert $25 billion of its preferred equity stake in Citigroup to common shares, giving it a 36 per cent stake in Citi and helping the bank restructure its capital base in the face of mounting losses from bad loans and other assets. Citi has also taken $45.0 billion in new capital from the Government's Troubled Asset Relief Program and got federal guarantees on $300 billion of assets.

False Belief

For most of the last decade America was a nation of borrowers and spenders, not savers. The personal savings rate dropped from 9 per cent in the 1980s to 5 per cent in the 1990s, to just 0.6 per cent from 2005 to 2007, and household debt grew much faster than personal income. According to Paul Krugman, it should not have expected its net worth to go up.

Yet until very recently Americans believed they were getting richer, because they received statements saying that their houses and stock portfolios were appreciating in value faster than their debts were increasing. The belief of many Americans that they could count on capital gains forever sounds naive, but it is worth remembering that many influential voices promoted that belief, and even ridiculed those who worried about low savings and high levels of debt. When the reality struck, it turned out that those who worried had been right all along. The surge in asset values had been an illusion—but the surge in debt had been all too real.

And as the great American economist Irving Fisher pointed out in the 1930s, the things people and companies do when they realise they have too much debt tend to be self-defeating when everyone tries to do them at the same time. Attempts to sell assets and pay off debt deepen the plunge in asset prices, further reducing net worth. Attempts to save more often translate into a collapse of consumer demand, deepening the economic slump.

As the current economic slowdown is a global phenomenon, let us have a look how it has impacted various other economies.

IMPACT ON VARIOUS ECONOMIES

The Chinese Economy

International financial crisis has inflicted rather big impact on Chinese real economy. During 2007-08 its growth rate was nine per cent, but economy grew at 6.8 per cent in the fourth quarter of 2008-09. "Under these circumstances we have set the target of the growth rate of eight per cent for 2009,"

Chinese Premier Wen Jiabao said at the World Economic Forum meeting held in January 2009 in Davos. Calling the achievement of eight per cent growth rate a tall order, Wen said this is a necessary and attainable target through hard work. "I still hold the conviction that with hard work we will be able to attain this goal," he said. The Chinese Premier said his country's economy is facing severe challenges, including notably shrinking external demand, overcapacity in some sectors, difficult business conditions for enterprises, rising unemployment in urban areas and greater downward pressure on economic growth.

Without taking the name of any country, Wen blamed the current financial crisis to inappropriate macroeconomic policies of "some economies" and their unsustainable model of development characterised by prolonged low savings and high consumption and excessive expansion of financial institutions in blind pursuit of profit. It will be interesting to note and pertinent to mentioned here that China's own economy started growing of a high rate of above 8 per cent of GDP annually, ever since if adopted the open policies of the West.

Guangdong province, which has been at the heart of China's economic miracle, is at present in serious trouble. The local Government has admitted that 2,452 manufacturing companies have shut down. But industry sources said the situation was grimmer. It is said that more than 20,000 companies in the province have cut back their operations to just 30-40 per cent as the export market has dried up. Over 450,000 migrant workers employed in these factories have lost their jobs. "This will be the toughest year for Guangdong since economic reforms as the global financial crisis has still to bottom out and the world economy is slowing down. We anticipate a growing downward pressure on the country's economy," Huang Huahua, the governor of the province said.

China observers have pointed out that the official figures do not cover companies that have either closed down since January 1 as the crisis deepened or those that are on the verge of closure. The next two to three months are expected to see a lot more companies closing down. Guangdong's high growth in 2007—a dizzying 14.7 per cent—is faltering. During 2008, the figure fell to 10.1 per cent. The governor said that in 2009 it would be a challenge to achieve 8.5 per cent, the lowest in 30 years. "The economy of our province is closely linked to the outside world, and the task of maintaining stable and fast economic growth is extremely difficult," he said. "The province will have to transform and upgrade itself from low-end manufacturing to high-end industries in order to survive the crisis," he added.

Liang Yaowen, head of the Guangdong provincial department of foreign trade and economic cooperation, said that 96 per cent of the companies that have downed shutters are small or medium-sized firms. Guangdong has more than 70,000 registered factories and its exports exceeded $417 billion in 2008. The province accounts for one-third of China's international trade. Companies in the province employed 61 million people in 2008. As a desperate attempt to salvage companies, the local Government has offered to reduce the contributions that companies make towards social insurance premiums by $2.2 billion in the year 2009.

China's Exports See Sharp Decline

China's exports fell more than expected in January 2009, down 17.5 per cent from a year earlier, marking the biggest drop in more than 10 years. Imports were down 43.1 per cent in the month compared with a year ago, as China's economy continued to be hit by the global economic slowdown. Analysts say the slowdown could prompt more factory closures and job losses. China's global trade surplus widened to $39.1 billion in January 2009 after recording a surplus of $39 billion in December 2008. Some analysts argue that this worsening trend will continue, as the world economy contracts.

In January 2009, China's crude oil imports fell to their lowest level for 15 months—down 8 per cent year-on-year. The country shipped in 12.82 million tonnes of crude oil, nearly 11 per cent lower than in December, 2008.

World Bank Cuts China's 2009 Growth Forecast to 6.5 Per cent

The World Bank cut its forecast of China's 2009 growth from 7.5 per cent to 6.5 per cent due to plunging exports but expressed confidence in Beijing's ability to keep the world's third-largest economy expanding amid global turmoil. The drop in trade will hurt investment and job creation, the bank said in a quarterly report released in the March 2009. But it said China still should grow faster than other major countries due to its huge stimulus package and strong banks, which were unhurt by the global crisis.

"China is hit very hard by an external shock," Louis Kuijs, the bank's senior China economist and the report's main author, said at a news conference. Kuijs said that could also push down prices, which can force companies to cut wages and investment. Premier Wen Jiabao said that China should meet its official 8 per cent growth target despite a 25.7 per cent drop in exports in February 2009. He said Beijing was ready to expand its 4 trillion yuan ($586 billion) stimulus if the impact downturn worsens, though he gave no details.

Beijing still has "plenty of space to implement forceful stimulus measures," with more spending and interest rate cuts, the World Bank report said. "We see China as a relative bright spot in a rather gloomy global economic picture," said David Dollar, the bank's country director for China. The stimulus is intended to reduce reliance on trade by pumping up domestic consumption through spending on building highways and other public works. But retail sales growth is weakening, suggesting Beijing has yet to spur a rebound in private sector spending. Kuijs said Government outlays alone cannot fill the gap left by falling exports.

The World Bank says it estimates that each percentage point less growth in China's non-agricultural GDP growth means 5.4 million fewer jobs. There are no comprehensive data on China's employment or job losses but the Government says the crisis has thrown some 20 million migrant laborers out of work. It was the second time in four months that the Washington-based World Bank had cut its China growth forecast for 2009, following a reduction in November 2008 from 9.2 per cent to 7.5 per cent. Growth at 6.5 per cent would be the weakest since 1990's 3.8 per cent and below 7.6 per cent reported in 1999. "We don't foresee any significant recovery in China's growth until the world economy recovers," Kuijs said. Dollar said the global economy is expected to shrink by 1.5 per cent, with no recovery until late in 2009 or in 2010.

The Japanese Economy

Strangled by the collapse in global export demand, Japan's economy shrank at its fastest rate in 35 years in the fourth quarter and shows no signs of reversing course anytime soon. Japan's GDP contracted 3.2 per cent from the previous quarter, or an annual pace of 12.1 per cent, in the October-December period, the Government said.

World stock markets fell after Japan's figures came out. Drops in Europe followed losses in Asia, but trading volumes were subdued as US markets remained closed for President's Day. Britain's FTSE 100 closed down 1.3 per cent at 4,134.75, Germany's DAX sank 1.1 per cent to 4,366.64, and France's CAC 40 dropped 1.2 per cent.

The GDP drop was worse than expected and the steepest slide for Japan since the oil shock in 1974. It is more than triple the 3.8 per cent annualized contraction in the US in the same quarter. "There is no question that this is the worst economic crisis since the end of World War II," said economy minister Kaoru Yosano. "The outcome clearly shows that Japan's export-dependent economy has been severely hit." Chief Cabinet Secretary Takeo Kawamura went further, calling the economic downturn a "once-in-a-century calamity". Rattled officials hinted that they may soon call for more Government steps to stem the widening damage.

Japan's exports plunged 45.7 per cent in January 2009 compared with a year ago to hit the lowest figure in 10 years, official figures have shown. Japan's trade deficit hit 952.6 billion yen ($9.9 billion; £6.8 billion) in January 2009, the largest since records began in 1980. Demand for Japanese cars in particular dropped by 69 per cent. Trade in electronics and other goods has also slumped as global economies and consumer spending contract, pushing Japan deeper into recession.

Japanese exports to the US, which are at the centre of the slide, fell nearly 53 per cent in January 2009 while shipments to the European Union decreased by 47 per cent, Japan's finance ministry said. "Exports to Asia, particularly to China, are tumbling at about the same pace as shipments to the United States, signalling that even China's economy may be shrinking," said Takeshi Minami, chief economist at Norinchukin Research Institute. Exports to Asia dropped 47 per cent, while those to China fell 45 per cent.

Japan's export-led economy had previously been thought to be immune to the worst effects of the global recession, the AFP news agency reported. The Government said that Japan's economy was in its most serious crisis since World War II, after it contracted at an annualised rate of 12.1 per cent in the last quarter of 2008. This was its worst performance in almost 35 years, officials said. In response, the Government is pushing bills through parliament to implement a stimulus plan, including a cash handout of at least $130 for each Japanese taxpayer. US President Barack Obama and Japanese Prime Minister Taro Aso have agreed to work together to stimulate economic demand and fight protectionism. The US and Japanese economies are respectively world's largest and the second-largest.

Actually Japan's economy shrank less than the earlier estimates of 13 per cent in the fourth quarter of 2008. Its economy appears to have been hit hard by the global downturn, choked demand for cars, high-tech goods and other exports. "The figures are not good," said Taro Aso, adding, "The economy is worsening." The latest snapshot was slightly less bleak than an initial estimate, but it was still the worst quarter since early 1974. The revision "is hardly something to cheer about," said Rabobank International strategist Jan Lambregts, noting that the improvement was due to higher inventories, which is not positive for the economy. Japan was once seen as relatively immune to the financial crisis, but its economy is now shrinking much faster than many other economies, including that of the US. The Government says the crisis is the deepest since World War II.

"Exports fell off a cliff in the fourth quarter of 2008" said David Cohen, director of Asian Economic Forecasting at Action Economics in Singapore, who sees more trouble ahead. In 2009 the economy is likely to shrink by 5.7 per cent.

Japan Economy: Japan Joins US in Recession

It's official: Japan is now in a recession. The world's second-largest economy reported a 0.1 per cent drop in its third quarter, after a 0.3 per cent fall in its second quarter. Japan's GDP has dropped by almost half a per cent in 2008.

The world is bracing with the two largest economies in recession. The US officially fell into a recession after its financial markets collapsed. The US lost 240,000 jobs in October and unemployment reached 6.5 per cent, the highest in 14 years. Europe is in a similar state with the 15-nation EU reporting a GDP decline of 0.2 per cent for the second consecutive quarter. Germany and Italy, the two largest economies that use the euro are in recession, although France is not.

The yen has been strong which has had serious negative effects on the country's stock markets, which spread to European and US exchanges. The yen has strengthened as investors shied away from higher-yielding currencies such as the pound and the euro. The result was the yen and dollar increasing in value as they are considered safer and more secure.

But with this appreciation in the yen exports have been hurt as well, as it has become more expensive to purchase Japanese goods. This was reflected in the fact that Nissan Motor Co. announced it would slash production by a further 72,000 vehicles from now until March 2009. Last month it announced it would cut production of 65,000.

Takahiko Murai, Nozomi Securities general manager, expressed concern that Japan relied so heavily on exports, "We have no factors to expect the GDP figures will be revised up later as a deterioration in US consumer spending is happening really fast, and a resulting firmer yen could further damage Japan's economic outlook."

Hong Kong and Singapore are also in recession. They too, like Japan, are heavily export-reliant nations that are thus vulnerable to any global slowdown. One consolation these slowing Asian economies have is China as a neighbor, which is projected to still grow by 7 per cent or more.

Europe Hit by Economic Slowdown

European economies contracted in the fourth quarter of 2008 with some countries registering the worst figures in decades, official data showed. The Eurozone economy shrank by 1.5 per cent in the previous quarter and 1.2 per cent on the year, Eurostat said. Germany's economy shrank by 2.1 per cent compared with the previous quarter, which is its worst quarterly performance since 1990. Germany is being punished for its heavy dependence on exports. France shrank by 1.2 per cent, initial data showed, while Italy registered a drop of 1.8 per cent, the steepest drop since 1980.

The percentage change in growth rates of GDP of major European economies and the Eurozone in the fourth quarter of 2008 as compared with third quarter is shown in Fig. 1 below.

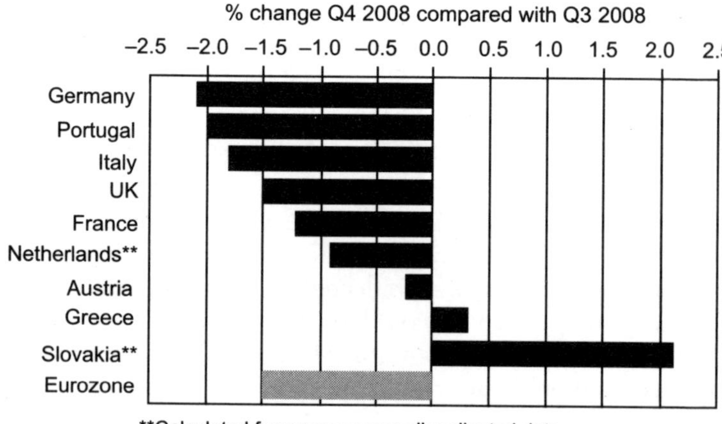

Fig. 1: Growth Rates of GDP in Volume—Seasonally Adjusted Data

Source: Eurostat

The data put pressure on the European Central Bank to cut interest rates. In the whole of 2008, the economy in the 15 countries using the euro grew by 0.7 per cent against the previous year, Eurostat said. Slovakia joined the Eurozone on 1 January 2009, making it a 16-country club. The Dutch economy shrank 0.9 per cent during the quarter while the Austrian economy contracted by 0.2 per cent, the first drop in nearly eight years. In the same quarter, Portugal's economy contracted by 2 per cent on the previous quarter and 2.1 per cent on the previous year.

"These are huge contractions in Europe, the largest in living memory in most cases," said Ken Wattret, economist at BNP Paribas. Companies have cut investment and exports have dropped as the global recession has taken hold. European companies hit by the slowdown include Air-France KLM, which reported a third-quarter operating loss, and Michelin, whose final-year profits fell as the crisis in the global car industry took its toll on the tyre maker. The decline in demand for cars was further highlighted by the data released. The number of new cars sold in Europe in January 2009 was down 27 per cent compared with January 2008, the European carmakers' association, Acea, said.

German Gloom

The slowdown has been the most dramatic in Germany, which registered the biggest fall since German reunification in 1990. The 2.1 per cent contraction was the third consecutive quarterly drop in Europe's biggest economy, according to the initial data from the Federal Statistics Office, worse than the 1.8 per cent anticipated by analysts.

Year-on-year, the German economy shrank by 1.6 per cent, after growing by 1.4 per cent in the third quarter. Many are now gloomy about the prospects for 2009. "This shows things went downhill sharply at the end of the year," said Juergen Michels, an economist at Citigroup. "We'll likely head down again the first and second quarter," he added. "This number makes it plain that we are in a very serious recession—the most serious since World War II. It is no surprise that exports and investment have tumbled," said Dirk Schumacher at Goldman Sachs, adding that the rise in inventories did not bode well for the first quarter. The situation "can hardly get worse," said Carsten Brzeski at ING Financial Markets. "The German industrial production has run out of steam with companies working only off their backlogs. Foreign demand has plummeted over the last months," he added. The German Government has forecast that the economy would shrink by 2.25 per cent in 2009.

France Slowdown

The slowdown in the French economy was slightly worse than the analysts' expectations of a 1.1 per cent drop. The French economy expanded slightly in the third quarter of 2008, by 0.1 per cent, which means that France has not officially entered a recession—which is defined as two consecutive quarters of contraction.

With consumer spending up by 0.5 per cent, some analysts found cause for hope. "Consumer spending has held up quite well so you can say there is still money out there to be spent and French households are spending it," Alexander Law, chief economist at Xerfi said. Companies also reduced their inventories in the fourth quarter of 2008, shaving 0.9 per cent off Gross Domestic Product, a fact that could augur well for industrial production in the subsequent quarters of 2009. With warehouses emptier, companies may increase production. Many say that tough times lie ahead. "The first quarter will be difficult," Christine Lagarde, France's economy minister, said.

The data increased pressure on the European Central Bank to cut rates. The bank cut the benchmark rate to 2 per cent in January 2009, the lowest in the bank's 10-year history.

Britain's National Debt to Cross £2 Trillion

The national debt of Britain could pass £2 trillion or £33,000 per capita, according to the independent Office of National Statistics (ONS). The national debt figure took a quantum leap when the ONS decided to add the debts of Lloyds Banking Group and Royal Bank of Scotland estimated at between £1 trillion and £1.5 trillion, to the public balance sheet. ONS confirmed that it considered both Lloyds and RBS to be public sector companies. At £2.2 trillion, the national debt would be about 150 per cent of the Gross Domestic Product—the worst debt total since the 1950s, when Britain was paying back its war debts.

Taxpayers are jittery as well as angry with the Labour Party's economic management. However, the Government says that the eventual cost to the taxpayer—even in the case of a further severe financial slide—would be only a fraction of this total. According to the *Telegraph*, Goldman Sachs, has estimated that the taxpayers would have to foot about £120 billion on account of the banks' bailout.

Noted economist Megnad Desai told *Hindustan Times* that the impact of the figure was more psychological than causing long-term danger to the economy. He however agreed that its immediate effect could be to make recession "slightly deeper." "But the Government would be making a mistake if it does not nationalise these banks quickly to be able to turn them around," he warned. "It took six months to nationalise Northern Rock, which added to the losses," he said.

Australian Growth Shrinks 0.5 Per cent

Australia's ability to escape the recession that has enveloped most developed economies was called into question after the country reported an unexpected contraction in the fourth quarter of 2008, its first in eight years. The Government said the economy shrank by 0.5 per cent from the third quarter, surprising economists who were predicting that the economy would remain flat or even show slight growth. Year-on-year, the economy grew by 0.3 per cent, the slowest pace since 1991 when the country was last in recession. A 10.4 per cent rise in the farming sector for the fourth quarter offset a dramatic 0.8 per cent shrinkage in the non-farm sector. "If it weren't for a slight improvement in farm production because of the vagaries of the weather, we would officially be declaring ourselves in recession," said Shane Oliver, chief economist with Australian Mutual Provident (AMP), noting that non-farm growth had fallen for two consecutive quarters. Wayne Swan, treasurer, said the economy had fared better than those of G7 members. He pointed to the "sharpest synchronised global downturn" in their lifetime and called the national accounts a "sobering but unsurprising outcome".

Stephen Walters, JPMorgan chief economist, predicted the economy would contract further over the next two quarters. "At that point we are looking at an economy that is stagnant or has been going backwards for at least a year," he said. The figures dispelled Government optimism. "The Government didn't predict recession," Mr Walters said. "They predicted the economy would weaken. This has been a big surprise to them." Economists say the weak third quarter was a direct result of the central bank's policy of increasing interest rates from late 2007 to March 2008, well past the point when other leading economies were cutting rates to try to stave off recession.

The central bank has cut cash rates by 400 basis points since September 2007 and the weak data for the third quarter of 2008 revived the prospect of more interest rate cuts. The Gross Domestic Product figures came a day after the central bank decided to hold the official cash rate steady at 3.25 per cent on the basis that Australia had not experienced the same large contractions in growth as other countries. Ministers expressed hope of improvement as the impact of the rate cuts and the Government's A$42 billion (US$27 billion, €21 billion, £19 billion) stimulus package flowed through the economy. Kevin Rudd, the Australian Prime Minister, defended his handling of the economy. He admitted some consumers would have saved their handout rather than spending it. "I have consistently said that Government can't mandate how individual consumers use their money," the Prime Minister said. Mr Walters warned that since unemployment was soaring, households would increase savings and the burden of managing the downturn would fall on the central bank.

Recession Jolts Gulf

It is not quite the end of the petro-dollar dream yet, but hundreds of Indians employed in the Gulf were forced to return home in the fourth quarter of 2008 as the global recession hit the region. If the steady trickle of Gulf returnees turns into a tide, India could face a major crisis. Authorities say the situation at the moment is not alarming, though reports of wage cuts and spiked jobs have been pouring in from the region hit hard by sinking oil prices and tottering construction, real estate and tourism sectors.

There are no hard numbers on the extent of the crisis. The Indian embassy in UAE confirmed that 20,000 Indians have returned from that country alone from October 2008 to January 2009. But these include those who were anyway planning to return as well as others coming on leave. "Some of them have been sent back for the time being and may return soon," ambassador to UAE, Talmiz Ahmed, said. Sources in airlines say, across carriers, there has been a dramatic increase in bookings to India from the Gulf. Of the 5 million overseas Indian workers, 90 per cent have jobs in the Gulf and South-East Asia. Till early 2008, the Gulf was in the midst of a construction and realty boom and had been attracting thousands of Indian workers. Migrations from India had increased from 4.66 lakh in 2003 to 8.09 lakh in 2007. But things have changed since then as the global economic slowdown has hit the Gulf Countries.

There are reports of construction projects coming to a halt across the Middle East. A case in point is the prestigious Nakheel Harbour and Towers in Dubai. Earlier known as Al Burj and expected to be the world's tallest tower, work on the project was suspended in January 2009.

South Africa Sees Economy Shrink

South Africa's economy has shrunk for the first time in 10 years, official figures have shown. Gross Domestic Product (GDP) fell by 1.8 per cent in the last three months of 2008 from the previous quarter. Lonmin, the world's third-biggest platinum producer, said it was cutting up to 5,500 jobs at two South African mines. A worldwide commodities slump has seen dramatic falls in demand and prices of metals and other mined products. UK-listed Lonmin said a deal to cut 4,000 jobs at the Marikana mine in North-West province and 1,500 in Limpopo province had been agreed with unions. It has been hit by tumbling demand from the car sector which uses platinum to manufacture catalytic converters. "With the current backdrop of challenging economic conditions, these agreements are an important milestone in our objective of restructuring the company," said Lonmin chief executive Ian Farmer.

Overall, South Africa's economy grew by 3.1 per cent in 2008, official figures showed. This was well below the Government forecast of 3.7 per cent and the previous year's 5.1 per cent. Construction ahead of the 2010 Football World Cup is expected to continue giving the country an economic boost. However, Southern African economy which relies heavily on commodities such as diamonds, gold and industrial metals has been particularly badly affected. Gold production dipped 13.6 per cent to the lowest level since 1922, according to the Chamber of Mines—meaning it is now only the third-largest gold-producing nation behind China and the US. Mining giant Anglo American said it would cut 19,000 jobs during 2009 after a 29 per cent fall in profits. It blamed the fall in earnings on sliding demand for raw materials. Debswana, a diamond-producing firm jointly owned by Botswana's Government and De Beers, said it would close two mines for the rest of the year because of falling demand. Debswana's four diamond mines were temporarily closed on 25 February, but two of them resumed work on 14 April.

However, Debswana's Damtshaa mine and Orapa No. 2 Plants are likely to remain closed till the end of 2009, directly affecting 580 employees. These workers will be redeployed within the company or offered voluntary early retirement and other incentives. "These actions are being taken to mitigate the effects of the global downturn by reducing production during 2009 to align with demand, conserving cash for the company, protecting employment and maintaining readiness for an eventual upturn in the market," said De Beers.

Diamond giant De Beers, the world's largest diamond producer by value, said in a statement that it produced 48.1 million carat in 2008, while Debswana produced 32.3 million carat, down 4 per cent from 33.6 million carat in 2007. The ongoing global financial and economic crisis forced even wealthy consumers to cut their spending on luxury goods, including jewellery. Luxury-jewellery retailer Tiffany said in

January its same-store sales for the holiday season fell by 24 per cent.

Forecast on Recession in US

US Federal Reserve chief Ben Bernanke has warned Congress that without the right policies from the Government, the US recession could last into 2010. But he said if the Obama administration and the central bank can restore some measure of financial stability, 2010 could be a year of recovery. Mr Bernanke made the comments to the Senate Banking Committee. He also warned that the global nature of the downturn was a threat because exports would be hit.

In its attempts to revive the economy, the Federal Reserve has cut its key interest rate to nearly zero, while the Obama administration has recently signed a $787 billion (£546 billion) economic stimulus package. Mr Bernanke said that the potential economic turnaround would hinge on the success of such measures in getting credit and financial markets to operate more normally again. "Only if that is the case, in my view there is a reasonable prospect that the current recession will end in 2009 and that 2010 will be a year of recovery," he said.

Mr Bernanke reassured legislators that he was, "committed to using all available tools to stimulate economic activity and to improve financial market functioning". But he also outlined long-run predictions for the economy, which he said reflected "the view of policymakers that a full recovery of the economy from the current recession is likely to take more than two or three years".

The Indian Scenario

As the recession spreads, also facing the axe are Indian professionals, technicians and low-skilled workers. Even those in sales and marketing have been hurt because they were mostly subcontracted by large companies which now look upon these staff as dispensable. Indian workers in the Gulf contribute nearly 40 per cent of the $27 billion in overseas remittances that come to India—accounting for 3 per cent of India's GDP. World Bank has said that the remittances generated by South Asian workers in the Gulf will come down by 9 per cent. If the Middle East economic crisis deepens, India will face a double whammy of dipping remittances on one hand, and jobless returnees flooding the domestic market on the other.

Kerala is likely to bear the brunt if things go from bad to worse. Remittances earned by Malayalees have fuelled construction, tourism and education in the state. In the past decade, however, many Malayalee emigrants had left the Gulf as labour laws there got harsher and the wage-expenditure mismatch widened. But that doesn't seem to have dimmed expectations back home. Many people believe that the situation is not all that dire. Going by the findings of the Indian embassy in UAE, which accounts for 1.5 million out of the 4.8 million Indian workers in the Gulf, there is no reason to panic, at least not yet. "As of now, we have found no evidence to suggest large-scale departure of Indian workers," ambassador Ahmed said. He added that reports on layoffs in the construction business were highly exaggerated. "I can say that out of 10 projects, at least five are going ahead. Of the remaining, some are merely on hold. In fact, the overall sentiment is one of optimism as the financial base of the country is sound. That's true for other Gulf countries as well," he said. Several people share Ahmed's view and feel that the impact of global meltdown has not been as harsh in the Middle East as in Europe, America and South-East Asia.

It is also being argued that Kerala is no longer as dependent on remittances as in the past. Researchers Irudaya Rajan and Zachariah call the migration situation in Kerala in the last four years "immobility in mobility". "The number of emigrants was 18.4 lakh in 2003; it was 18.5 lakh in 2007. The number of return emigrants had been 8.9 lakh in 2003; it was 8.9 lakh in 2007 also," states a study conducted by the duo.

The IMF advised India to initiate more monetary steps to battle the country's slowing economic growth, which the international multilateral agency expects to moderate to

6.25 per cent in 2008-09 and fall further by one percentage point in 2009-10.

The Times of India had first reported in its February 28 edition that Government's estimate of 7.1 per cent GDP growth for 2008-09 may not be achieved after third quarter (October-December) figure revealed that growth had dipped to 5.3 per cent.

With inflation softening to a six-year low of 2.43 per cent, there is scope for further easing of monetary policy, the IMF said in its review of the economy following Article IV consultations with the Indian authorities. "A number of (IMF) directors saw scope for further monetary easing, in light of the projected decline in inflationary pressures and the need to reinforce confidence and sustain bank credit," the review said.

The IMF expects average inflation to moderate to 2 per cent in 2009-10 from about 8.8 per cent in 2008-09 financial year. Inflation has been coming down consistently after touching a peak of 12.9 per cent in August 2008. The GDP growth rate in 2008-09 has been projected at 6.25 per cent by the IMF, as against the Government's forecast of 7.1 per cent. The IMF expects the growth rate in 2009-10, to fall to 5.25 per cent.

As part of the annual exercise to review the economies of the member countries, the IMFs executive board had held consultations with the Indian authorities on 6 February 2009. While suggesting that India focus on monetary measures, the IMF cautioned that additional expenditure and more tax reliefs for fighting economic slowdown could raise public debt to unsustainable levels. Noting that the key short-run policy objective should be to sustain liquidity and credit flows, the review said "monetary and structural policies will have to continue to carry most of the burden of adjustment".

The "sizeable fiscal stimulus" of 2008-09 would support economic growth in India, the review said, adding, "given the high ratio of public debt to GDP, significant further expansion of the deficit could raise concerns about fiscal sustainability".

Indian Economy Staring at Deflation

India is staring at deflation, or negative inflation, with the official inflation rate falling below one per cent—the lowest since 1977. Food prices, however, continued to be high, with food grains roughly 9 per cent costlier than a year ago, reinforcing a cruel paradox for consumers that they hear about zero inflation but face high prices when they buy their groceries. With the wholesale price index (WPI) falling by one point to 226.7 for the week ending 7 March 2009—the same level at which the index was on 29 March 2008—it now means the year-on-year inflation rate will become zero in the first quarter of 2009-10 even if the index for the current year falls no further.

If deflation lasts for some time, as seems possible, it would be a new experience for India. Japan went through a decade-long deflation in the 1990s, termed as the "lost decade" for that country. At present, most major economies are witnessing disinflation—a lowering of the inflation rate—and some have also seen deflation kicking in. Japan and China have already reported negative inflation rates in the latest data and there are signs that the US, too, could be heading the same way.

While a fall in prices may sound like good news to most laymen, economists see this as an ominous sign of a collapse in demand in the economy. A recent Citibank report echoed this concern in the Indian context saying that the present trend of decline in inflation was not because of any improved efficiency in the economy but because of falling demand. The report warned that this trend would weaken economic activity and discourage investments, which would affect the economy in the longer term.

In the current scenario, prices are falling not because of improved productivity but because of fall in demand. If deflation sustains for longer period of time, it will have a more adverse impact on demand. "Deflation results in less demand, lower production and weak economic growth," said Citibank in a report "India Macroscope".

A negative inflation discourages investments in the economy. The real interest rate difference between nominal interest rate and inflation becomes very high, making funds costlier. As demand goes down, capacity utilization of manufacturing units declines. This discourages investment in capacity expansion.

The fear about investments not materializing is aggravated by the fact that nominal interest rates are at relatively high levels. When prices are falling, this means the real interest rates—the difference between the nominal rate and the rate of inflation—are becoming very high for producers, making it unviable for them to raise funds.

Demands for the RBI to intervene to induce a further round of cuts in interest rates are bound to mount in the face of the latest data. However, planning commission deputy chairman Montek Singh Ahluwalia said that the inflation rate would rebound from its present level. While not ruling out the possibility that inflation could go into negative territory, he maintained that it would last for only a few weeks. Hence, he said, it should not be termed as deflation, a term that implies sustained negative inflation.

From the common man's point of view, what makes the situation worse is that prices of essential commodities like foodgrains stubbornly refuse to come down. According to the latest data, the index for foodgrains rose by 9.3 per cent in the week ending March 7 as against 10.06 per cent in the previous week. Under the "food articles" head, inflation fell to 7.4 per cent after having been stable at 8.3 per cent in the previous two first of March 2009.

The foregoing establishes that the world economy is under severe meltdown. The crisis has hit every region—America, Europe, Asia, Australia and Africa. The figures of quarter ended December 2008 of various economies have been worse than expected.

IMPACT ACROSS SECTORS

In order to get a comprehensive view of world financial crisis it is necessary to have a look at how it has impacted the major sectors of economy like industry, transport, trade, manufacturing, airways, automobile, banking, etc. The performance of these sectors in general and some major Indian as well as foreign companies in particular is discussed below.

Industry, Trade and Manufacturing

Tata Steel Sees Big Profit Fall

Tata Steel has seen profits at its Indian operations slump 56 per cent after it was hit by both the falling price of steel and higher raw material costs. India's biggest steel producer said its domestic net profit declined to 4.7 billion rupees ($95 million; £66 million) for the last three months of 2008. This compares with 10.7 billion rupees for the same quarter a year earlier. Tata Steel owns Corus in Europe, but Corus data was not included in these figures.

Tata Steel's latest quarterly profit for its Indian operations was less than half the market expectations of more than 11 billion rupees. Sales during the quarter were down 4 per cent to 47.4 billion rupees. Like other steelmakers, Tata Steel has been hit by the drop in global steel prices as the worldwide economic downturn gathered pace.

Arcelor Mittal in First Ever Quarterly Loss

Arcelor Mittal SA, the world's largest steel maker, reported its first ever quarterly loss—at $2.6 billion—during the fourth quarter of 2008 as it wrote down the value of assets amid collapsing demand. The loss compares with a $2.44 billion profit a year earlier. Sales during the three months to December 31, 2008 fell 21 per cent to 122.1 billion from a year ago, the company said. It blamed the loss on pre-tax charges of $4.4 billion to write down stockpiled steel and raw material contracts as well as payouts to workers being laid off.

Whirlpool Quarterly Profit Falls 76 Per cent

Whirlpool, the world's biggest appliance maker, reported lower quarterly profit as sales fell worldwide and it posted an operating loss in North America, its biggest market. The company's fourth quarter profit fell 76 per cent to $44 million, or 60 cents a share, from $187 million, or $2.38 a share, a year earlier. Quarterly sales fell 19 per cent to $4.3 billion. Whirlpool's debt ratings have been downgraded recently. The company said it was in full compliance with bank covenants, but had begun talks with banks to "seek additional flexibility within its capital structure."

110 Firms in BSE 500 See Lower Profit

High interest cost, fall in domestic demand and decline in exports have led to a contraction in the corporate profitability of the 110 companies in the list of BSE 500 companies that had declared their third quarter results for 2008-09 till the third week of January 2009. While margins contracted and profits dipped by 10 per cent over the same quarter previous year, revenues witnessed a growth of 18 per cent, indicating the bad state of the economy and bleeding corporate profitability. The aggregate profits of the 110 companies in the list came down from Rs. 18,017 crore to Rs. 16,377 crore. "I expect the pressure on profits not only in this quarter but also in the next quarter," said Pankaj Pandey, head of research, ICICI Direct.

Except for banks that managed to show good revenue and profit growth because of high Treasury income, companies from across sectors and sizes remained under pressure. "Banks have benefited from the fall in bond yields that have come down by 400 basis points, leading to a gain in their Treasury incomes," said Pandey. "However, they are witnessing pressure from the non performing assets," he added.

The sectors that faced the maximum pressure were automobiles and auto ancillaries, financial services and firms in the oil refinery business. The big losers were Ranbaxy (net loss: Rs. 680 crore), Mangalore Refinery (net loss: Rs. 285 crore) and Jet Airways (net loss: Rs. 214 crore).

Industrial production fell 2 per cent year-on-year in December 2008, the Government said. The contraction in December slowed industrial growth between April and December—the first nine months of the fiscal year 2008-09 to 3.2 per cent from 9 per cent from a year earlier. Consumer durables, consumer non-durables, intermediate goods—all showed a decline in production with the durables falling the most.

"In December we were expecting that the situation will be unsatisfactory, that is why the Government has taken big stimulus steps. In January we expect it to be better," Industry Secretary Ajay Shankar said. The Government has offered both tax breaks and increased spending. The fall in industrial output was also because of a "base effect"—a statistical phenomenon that shows slowing down of growth because of a very high growth rate in the corresponding period the previous year. Industrial output grew by 8 per cent in December 2007. "Industrial activity will likely improve slightly over the course of the current quarter as a combination of improving local liquidity conditions, lower interest rates, and the Government's fiscal measures," said Rajeev Malik of Macquarie Securities.

The country's macroeconomics managers would have to thrash out ways and means for raising extra borrowing for next year as most expect the new Government to unveil a fresh set of measures to stimulate a decelerating economy. "It is important to take considered steps in the emerging situation," Aran Ramanathan, Finance Secretary said. "The Government's fiscal stimulus package was the key." The Government in 2009-10 will raise Rs. 3,08,647 crore, which is 17 per cent higher than in 2008-09, of which Rs. 45,000 crore will come from sources other than market borrowings and private placement. "We will neither raise it through market borrowing nor private placement or bonds. We will decide on the modalities later," Ramanathan added.

India's exports contracted for the third successive month plunging by 1.1 per cent in December 2008 as policymakers grope for options to sustain growth amid the worst slowdown in the world economy in the last 80 years.

The Government's immediate job is to ensure that the "economic growth comes back to its high growth path. Public spending therefore is crucial to revive general demand." All eyes are on the Reserve Bank of India (RBI) to use the monetary lever. P. Chidambaram, who steered the economy to sizzling heights, said, "The Indian economy has weathered the global crisis reasonably well and is expected to post a growth rate of 7.1 per cent in 2008-09." But with the downturn more serious than ever, the GDP growth rate for 2008-09 remanded below 7 per cent.

The International Monetary Fund has recently revised downward, India's annual GDP growth below 5 per cent for the year 2009 and barely above 5 per cent for the year 2010. However, the Government is hopeful that despite the financial crisis the country's economy is likely to register a reasonable good growth of around of 6 per cent. The Government fully aware of the seriousness of the current global economy slowdown and is ready to take all the measures required to put the economy back on track, through it may take some time to show signs of removal.

Durables Worst Hit as People Hold Spending

Following the slump in December 2008, growth in industrial output for the first nine months of the financial year 2008-09 is a mere 3.2 per cent, against 9 per cent in the corresponding period of the previous year. Consumer durables production was the worst hit in December 2008, falling by 12.8 per cent. Industry Secretary Ajay Shankar said people were postponing spending because of the uncertain environment. He said the Government had expected a difficult situation in December, which is why it had announced stimulus packages. In January 2009, he asserted, the situation would be better. Output of the manufacturing sector, which constitutes 80 per cent of the total industrial production, fell by 2.5 per cent compared to December 2007. The other two segments—mining and electricity generation—also grew by just 1 per cent and 1.6 per cent respectively in December 2008, against 5 per cent and 3.8 per cent respectively a year ago. Growth in the production of capital goods was at 4.2 per cent in December 2008 and that in basic goods was pegged at 1.7 per cent. Decline in industrial production, manufacturing, growth, mining and electricity has been shown in Fig. 2. It also depicts the comparative percentage figures of basic goods, capital goods and consumer durables for 2007-08 and 2008-09 upto December 2008.

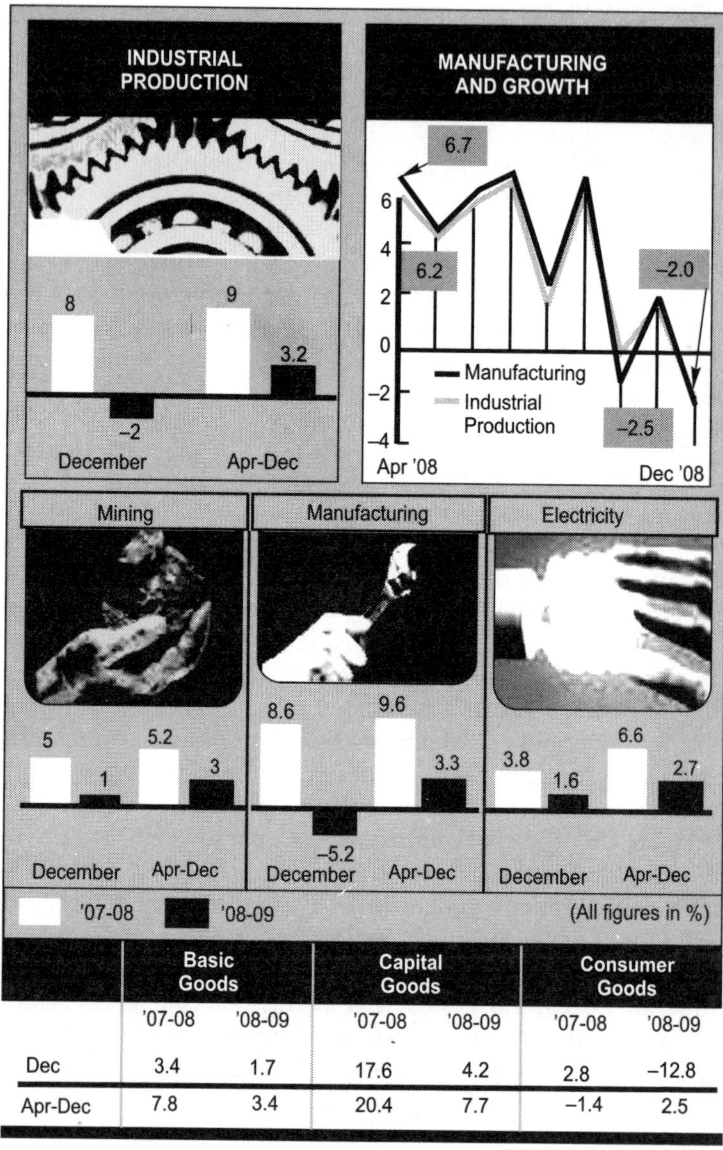

	Basic Goods		Capital Goods		Consumer Goods	
	'07-08	'08-09	'07-08	'08-09	'07-08	'08-09
Dec	3.4	1.7	17.6	4.2	2.8	–12.8
Apr-Dec	7.8	3.4	20.4	7.7	–1.4	2.5

Fig. 2: Decline in Industrial Production, Manufacturing, Growth Mining and Electricity in India—December 2008

Decline in Growth of World Trade

The financial crisis triggered a fall in world trade growth to 4 per cent in 2008, with November posting the most pronounced slowdown, estimates from the World Trade Organization showed. "Growth began to decline in the third quarter of 2008, and this became more accentuated as the year drew to a close. For the full year, the WTO secretariat estimate is 4 per cent real trade growth," said the report, which examined the impact of the economic crisis on trade.

Global trade grew by 8.5 per cent in 2006 but slipped to 5.5 per cent in 2007. The WTO has estimated that trade growth could ease to 4.5 per cent in 2008 as a sharp economic slowdown in developed countries will only be partly offset by strong gains in emerging economies. The fluctuations were most pronounced when trade was denominated in dollar terms.

Growth in dollar terms exceeded 20 per cent in the first half of 2008, but slowed sharply in the second half "and turned negative in November." Trade values were boosted by rise in commodity prices in the first half, before dropping in the second half as oil prices plummeted. "Currency developments inflated growth in value terms in the first half of the year and accentuated the decline in the second half," said the report.

Recession Talk Looms in Manufacturing

India's overall economy is growing slow but better than most of the world. However, the manufacturing sector, which has been backbone of urban growth for long, is now under the adverse effect of global slowdown.

Industrial output contracted for the second consecutive month by 0.5 per cent in January 2009, raising concerns that the manufacturing sector could slip into a "recession—which in pure technical terms—is defined to happen when any sector registers negative growth for two consecutive quarters in a year."

Within the industrial sector, the manufacturing sector contracted by 0.8 per cent. It had contracted by 0.2 per cent during the third quarter of the financial year 2008-09 and by

0.6 per cent in December 2008. Analysts do not see an early turnaround and expect the slump right through to the April-June first quarter of 2009-10. "Depressed global demand and continued inventory de-stocking suggests that a meaningful recovery is not likely until the second half of the next fiscal year," said Sonal Varma of Nomura Financial Advisory and Securities.

If the current trend continues, the manufacturing sector, of which around 40 per cent is export driven, could technically be termed as being in "recession." The current manufacturing slump is significantly driven by the decline in exports hit by shrinking world demand which has hit handicrafts, gems and jewellery, leather and textile exports, among others. This is reflected in sharp contraction in many of the country's export-driven sectors such as leather and jute products whose output growth fell by 9.8 and 8.6 per cent respectively. "The negative industrial output growth highlights the subdued pace of economic activity. Fall in global and domestic demand have taken a toll on industrial production during the last few months," said Yashika Singh of economic information firm Dun and Bradstreet.

The sequential momentum of industrial output has remained weak. It contracted by 0.6 per cent in December 2008. Industrial growth between April and January—the first 10 months of the financial year 2008-09—slowed to 3 per cent from 8.7 per cent from the corresponding period of the previous year.

UK Manufacturing Declines Sharply

Manufacturing output declined at its fastest rate since 1981 in December 2008 underscoring the fragile state of the UK economy, official figures showed. The Office for National Statistics (ONS) said it fell 10.2 per cent from a year earlier as recession hit the sector. For the final three months of 2008 output fell 5.1 per cent, the biggest quarterly fall since 1974.

According to ONS, the data meant that the contraction in UK GDP could be 1.6 per cent in the fourth quarter, compared with the preliminary estimate of 1.5 per cent. "December's UK industrial production figures maintain the picture of unrelenting gloom in the manufacturing sector," said Jonathan Loynes, economist at Capital Economics. "Various surveys suggest that things are set to get even worse over the coming months, with no signs at all that the drop in the exchange rate is yet boosting manufacturers' export order books," he added. On a monthly basis, the fall in manufacturing was 2.2 per cent—much more than the 1.4 per cent forecast.

Broader industrial output—which also includes mining, oil and gas extraction and power supply—shrank by 1.7 per cent in December 2008 and by 9.4 per cent from December 2007. Data released at the same time showed that producer output prices rose at an annual rate of 3.5 per cent in January 2009 down from 4.6 per cent in December 2008.

Huge Rise in Companies Going Bust in UK

There has been a huge rise in the number of firms going bust in England and Wales because of the recession. The Insolvency Service said that in the last three months of 2008 there were 2,428 corporate insolvencies such as administrations and receiverships. That was a 220 per cent rise in the same period the year before. In the same period, 29,444 people were made bankrupt or entered individual voluntary arrangement (IVA), 19 per cent more than a year ago. Of these, 19,100 were bankruptcies 10,344 were IVAs. Corporate liquidations, the end stage of the insolvency process, also rose strongly, with 4,607 firms being wound up in England and Wales in the last three months of 2008, which were 52 per cent more than a year before.

The figures from the Insolvency Service highlight the toll that has been taken on companies by the rapid lurch into recession. "For corporate insolvencies, this is almost a direct consequence of the economic downturn," said Pat Boyden, an insolvency expert at accountants PwC. Over the whole of 2008, the number of firms that were liquidated rose by 24 per cent to 15,535. That amounted to one in every 150 trading companies. "Liquidations in the fourth quarter of 2008 were dramatically up on liquidations in the same quarter of the previous year," said Alan Tomlinson of Tomlinsons—a licensed insolvency practitioner. "It is the small and medium-sized business, which forms the backbone of the UK economy, that has suffered the most and I expect this situation to deteriorate even further in 2009," he added.

Personal Insolvency

Global slowdown has adversely affected people who are directly or indirectly dependent on trade and industry such as dealers, accountants, brokers, contractors, etc. Personal insolvency is therefore a pertinent issue.

The number of people who were declared insolvent stood at 106,544 in England and Wales, and it was roughly the same as in 2007. But within that, the number of bankruptcies reached a record level—both for the year and the quarter. "We are now seeing victims of the recession—professionals, traders, contractors and people who have been laid off—not just people who have overspent on a credit card," said Mr Boyden. "I think bankruptcies will go much higher in 2009," he added. He explained that it was now more difficult to arrange an Individual Voluntary Arrangement (IVA), as the recession meant that people in financial trouble were less likely to be able to offer their creditors some repayments. As a result, more people on the verge of insolvency are likely to go directly into bankruptcy. "What...figures mean is that in 2008 we saw a staggering 350 people becoming insolvent in the UK every day," said Nick O'Reilly, President of the insolvency professionals' trade body, R3. "The outlook is bleak for the next two years, when insolvency practitioners expect to see in excess of 158,000 personal insolvencies annually," he said. In the UK there are following three forms of insolvency:

Bankruptcy: The traditional way of escaping overwhelming debt. It ends after one year, but you are likely to lose all your assets including your house to pay something to the creditors.

Individual Voluntary Arrangement: A deal between you and your creditors, overseen by an insolvency practitioner. There is less stigma, less chance of losing your home, but involves repaying some of your debts in one go or over a number of years.

Debt Relief Orders: Introduced in April 2009, these orders allow consumers with debts of less than £15,000 and minimal assets or surplus income to write off debts without a full-blown bankruptcy. The rising curves of individual insolvencies, bankruptcy orders and voluntary arrangements are shown in Fig. 3 below.

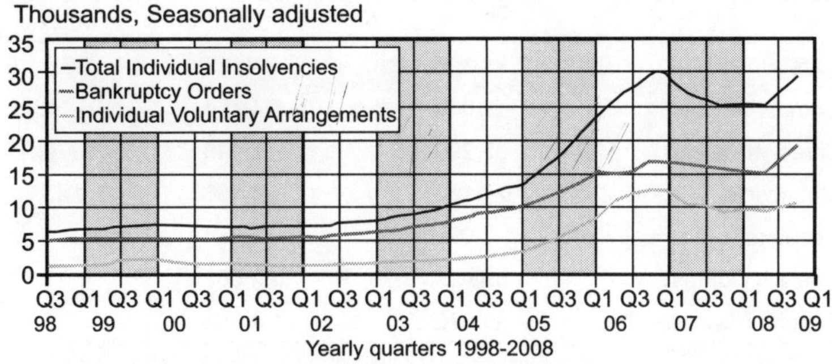

Fig. 3: Individual Insolvencies and Bankruptcy Orders 1998-2008

Source: Insolvency Service

Automobile Sector

Revenue of the auto industry slipped 7 per cent to Rs. 1 lakh crore in the April 2008-January 2009 period, from Rs. 1.1 lakh crore in the same period last fiscal, which reflects the effect of slowdown in sales (in units). Though the fall in revenue is almost across the entire spectrum of the automotive industry, commercial vehicle segment has been the worst-hit.

The commercial vehicle industry, which even saw temporary production closures by companies like Tata Motors and Ashok Leyland due to shrinkage in demand, registered a turnover of Rs. 24,724 crore in the first ten months of the financial year 2008-09, showing a 22 per cent fall against Rs. 31,843 crore in the same period last year. This comes on the back of a 20 per cent fall in sales to 3.11 lakh units in April-January, from 3.88 lakh units in the same period of the previous year.

Turnover of cars was down 0.6 per cent at Rs. 34,113 crore against Rs. 34,326 crore in the ten months of the 2007-08. The change in turnover in various segments of commercial vehicle industry in Apr '08-Jan '09 from the corresponding period of the previous year and percentage change are shown in Table 1 below.

Table 1: Change in Turnover in Various Segments of Commercial Vehicle Industry

Segment	Apr '07-Jan '08	Apr '08-Jan '09	Change (%)
Cars	34,326	34,113	–0.6
Comm. Vehicle	31843	24,724	–22
Three-wheelers	2,299	2,149	–6
Motorcycle	24,182	24,108	–0.3
Scooters	3,093	3,354	8
Overall (Domestic)	1,09,915	1,02,002	–7
Exports (Overall)	11,072	1,41,54	28

Tata Motors

Tata Motors reported a loss of Rs. 263 crore in the quarter October-December 2008 period due to foreign exchange loss and a massive decline in sales. The company had a profit of Rs. 499 crore in the same quarter of the previous financial year. This is the first quarterly loss in seven years for the company after October-December 2001. Net sales revenue for the company in the third quarter fell 35 per cent to Rs. 4,714 crore, from Rs. 7,206 crore in the same quarter of the previous year. Demand slowdown in the automobile sector has hit Tata Motors' sales of trucks, Indica cars, and Safari sport-utility vehicles very badly in India and overseas, with volumes dipping 32 per cent to 98,760 vehicles.

Tata Motors said the third-quarter result includes a foreign exchange loss of Rs. 226.5 crore due to revaluation of foreign currency borrowings. In the third quarter of the previous year the company had a foreign exchange gain of Rs. 27.5 crore. The company said the automotive sector suffered "severe contraction" in demand in the quarter due to major financial and other market upheavals. "Lack of liquidity and unavailability of consumer finance, along with contraction in freight movement in many segments of the industry, led to a massive drop of 61 per cent in the medium & heavy commercial vehicle segment," a statement said. "High interest rates and peak commodity prices also affected the auto industry and its supply chain," it added.

Tata Motors' net sales revenue in the nine months ending December 31, 2008, also declined to Rs. 18,629.9 crore against Rs. 19,823 crore in the same period last fiscal. Net profit in the period stood at Rs. 409.8 crore, that includes an exchange loss of Rs. 632.5 crore on revaluation of foreign currency borrowings, deposits and loans. Against this, it had a net profit of Rs. 1492.6 crore in the nine months of the previous fiscal that included a notional exchange gain of Rs. 264.2 crore.

The company said it has "a pipeline of new products" that it intends to launch in the next few months. "The company's actions on various cost reduction initiatives and working capital management efforts have been significantly accelerated," it said.

Toyota Reports Third Quarter Losses

Toyota reported abysmal third quarter results and warned that it was heading towards its first annual loss since 1950. For the last 57 years, this company has been profitable and growing. In 2007-08 the company made $18.8 billion in profit. But since then, Toyotas business has plunged. The company has lost $1.8 billion in the third quarter. It lost around $3.8 billion during the year 2008-09 and will build 1.42 million fewer vehicles during the year.

The fall off in sales in the US and Europe is huge, but the exceptionally strong yen combined with Japan's slowing auto market are also squeezing the world's largest automaker. Things are so slow in Japan that Toyota has idled all but one assembly line in that country. People are putting off buying a new car or truck for a whole host of reasons. There are many steps the Big 3, viz. Toyota, General Motors and Peugeot, could and should have taken in recent years that could have better prepared them to ride out an economic storm, but that's history now.

The question is which auto companies will survive the global car contraction? Will the Big 3 make it? Will only two get through? Toyota has the finances and flexibility to ride this out, but even the strongest of the Japanese automakers is finding out just how rough the worldwide recession has become.

Toyota Motor has offered buyouts to some 18,000 US workers and said it would cut pay for executives and blue-collar workers in its North American manufacturing operations in response to plunging auto sales. The Japanese automaker said it would shut down production for additional days in the coming months at plants in the United States, Canada and Mexico. It said it would also cut pay and eliminate bonuses for executives. The unprecedented cost-cutting steps for Toyota underscored how the world's top automaker and a perennial blue chip in a notoriously volatile sector is struggling amid the worst auto slump in decades. Toyota said the moves were intended to keep as many of its North American workers on the payroll as possible. "We hope the new measures will help us adjust while protecting jobs," Toyota Motor Engineering and Manufacturing Vice President Jim Wiseman said.

Toyota is on track to post an operating loss of some $4.95 billion for the fiscal year that ends in March 2009. The loss will be the first group-wide operating loss in Toyota's 70-year history. The automaker has cut North American production of top-selling cars such as the Camry and Corolla after sales dropped 15 per cent in 2008 in the United States, Toyota's largest single market. It has also suspended work on a new plant in Mississippi, slated to produce its Prius hybrid car beginning in 2010. Rivals Honda Motors and Nissan Motors have also been forced to cut output. Toyota said the buyout program would not be offered at two plants where its workers are unionized. Those are the joint venture manufacturing operations it has in California with General Motors and a truck assembly plant in Tijuana, Mexico, the company said.

Toyota spokesman Mike Goss said the automaker expected that most of its cost savings would come from the executive pay cuts, lower bonuses, frozen wages and the savings from paying factory workers for a 10 per cent cut in work hours. "In this economy we don't expect many people to take the exit program," he said.

Toyota, whose sales fell 34 per cent in January 2009, is also planning to implement a program at some plants that would reduce work hours to 72 from 80 over a two-week period. As a result, workers would be paid 10 per cent less. The automaker has not yet decided which plants would adopt the new program, Goss said.

Like its rivals, Toyota has been stung by the collapse in US demand for cars and trucks, a downturn that accelerated in October and November 2008 amid tightening credit and deepening consumer uncertainty. US auto sales in January 2009 plunged to an annualized rate of 9.5 million, the lowest in 27 years. Toyota has about 30,000 workers in its North American manufacturing operation. That includes about 25,000 hourly workers. Toyota's two Canadian plants employ just over 6,000 workers. Another 1,000 work at its Tijuana plant.

As a cost-cutting measure the company has decided to cut pay for executives in the US and further reduce production at some factories in the US, Canada and Mexico. Toyota is introducing a range of measures—including pay cuts, voluntary redundancies, bonus cuts and shorter hours—to reduce costs. The firm has already said it would post the first group-wide annual operating loss in its 70-year history.

Car companies are cutting back salaries, allowances and perks as a global slowdown reduces demand. "We hope the new measures will help us adjust while protecting jobs," said Jim Wiseman. Executives could see their take-home pay fall by 30 per cent, including a 5 per cent pay reduction and the elimination bonuses. The company will offer buyouts—voluntary redundancy for part-time workers—to 18,000 individuals, but expects few workers to take the offer up given the worsening job situation in the US. The offer consists of

10 weeks' pay, plus two weeks of pay for every year of service, plus $20,000 (£13,900). The buyouts would not be offered to workers at two unionised plants, one in California and another in Mexico. The car company has already cut production after sales fell 15 per cent in 2008 in the US, its biggest market.

Chrysler to Idle Four Plants, Seeks to Curb Production

Chrysler said it will idle four plants as it seeks to curb production in the face of weak demand for vehicles. The struggling US automaker, which received a $4 billion emergency loan from the US Government in January 2009, is idling its plants in Sterling Heights, Michigan, Belvidere, Illinois, Conner Avenue in Detroit and Brampton, Ontario. "We are responding to market conditions, the number of orders we are getting," Chrysler spokesman Max Gates said. "We are looking at these schedules every week," he added.

Chrysler, which saw its US sales decline 30 per cent in 2008 and 55 per cent in January, 2009, had shut down all of its 30 manufacturing facilities for a month from mid-December 2008. The shutdowns at the Belvidere plant that builds the slow-selling Dodge Caliber, Jeep Patriot and Jeep Compass SUVs, and its Sterling Heights factory that builds the Sebring and Avenger Sedans had been extended for an additional week. The two factories had resumed operations on 26 January 2008. Chrysler's Brampton plant builds the 300, Charger and Challenger Sedans while its Conner Avenue plant in Detroit builds the Dodge Viper.

The Conner Avenue plant has been idled since December 2008 as the company seeks a buyer for the Viper sports car line. Chrysler said that it is considering bids from three parties interested in the brand. By idling plants, Chrysler and other automakers can cut costs on inventory, components and related charges such as utilities for operating large production facilities. The moves also keep finished vehicle inventories from piling up on dealer lots and increasing the pressure for even greater discounting to consumers. Privately held Chrysler is 80 per cent-owned by private equity firm Cerberus Capital Management.

Chrysler to File for Bankruptcy

Chrysler will file for bankruptcy as talks with a small group of creditors crumbled just a day before a Government deadline for the automaker to come up with a restructuring plan, the US President, Mr Barack Obama said.

The Obama administration said it had long hoped to stave off bankruptcy for the nation's third largest automaker, but it became clear that a holdout group wouldn't budge on proposals to reduce Chrysler's $6.9 billion in secured debt. Clearing those debts was a needed step for Chrysler to restructure by the deadline.

Chrysler will file for Chapter 11 bankruptcy protection in New York, giving Chrysler time to galvanise a partnership with the Italian car maker Fiat Group SpA. The Government, which has already poured $4 billion in loans into Chrysler, would provide up to $8 billion more to carry the company through bankruptcy, said senior administration officials. The Government will also help appoint a new board of directors.

The deals give Chrysler "a new lease on life", Mr. Obama said. "I have every confidence that Chrysler will emerge from this process stronger and more competitive." Under bankruptcy, it would still sell cars and the Government would back its auto warranties. The filing for bankruptcy protection will lead to the forming of a new corporate entity.

Details of the new Chrysler include:

- Fiat will take a 20 per cent stake, with the possibility of it rising to 35 per cent if performance targets are met. It could reach 51 per cent by 2016 if Chrysler's Government loans are fully repaid.
- The Treasury will have an 8 per cent stake, a union-run trust fund VEBA will take a 55 per cent stake, and the Governments of Canada and Ontario will gain a combined 2 per cent stake.
- Current owner Cerberus will forfeit its 80.1 per cent stake.
- Daimler will give up its remaining 19.9 per cent stake in Chrysler.

- Chrysler bondholders will receive $2 billion (£1.35 billion) in cash in exchange for forgiving their $6.9 billion debt.
- The new company will be run by a nine-person board, with six picked by the Government and three by Fiat. The board will pick a new chief executive.

Some Chrysler dealerships will close over time but no jobs will be lost in the short term, President Obama confirmed.

Chrysler will receive a further $8 billion in Government aid, up from the $6 billion the Treasury had promised it if it had successfully restructured the business by midnight.

The White House described the move as a "surgical short bankruptcy" which should last between 30 and 60 days.

The nation's third-largest automaker filed for Chapter 11 bankruptcy protection with an ambitious plan to emerge in as little as 30 days as a leaner, more nimble company. After months on Government life support, Chrysler is pinning its future on a top-to-bottom reorganization and plans to build cleaner cars through an alliance with Italian automaker Fiat. In return, the federal Government agreed to give Chrysler up to $8 billion in additional aid and to back its warranties. In the meantime, Chrysler said that it will close all of its plants and that they will remain closed until the company comes out of bankruptcy.

At least three Detroit-area factories sent workers home after suppliers stopped shipping parts over fears they would not be paid. "A lot of us are scared," said Steve Grabowski, 33, who has worked at a Warren, Mich., parts stamping plant for seven years and was sent home. "We knew something like this was going to happen, but we didn't think it would be so soon."

Chrysler CEO Robert Nardelli announced he would step down when the bankruptcy is complete and take a post as an adviser with Cerberus Capital Management LP, which will give up its 80 per cent ownership of Chrysler under the automaker's plan. Vice Chairman Tom LaSorda, who once ran the company when it was owned by the German automaker Daimler, said he would retire.

Chrysler's bankruptcy filing is the latest step in a drastic reordering of the American auto industry, which has been crushed by higher fuel prices, the recession and customer tastes that are moving away from the gas-guzzling SUVs that were once big money makers. The administration has sunk about $25 billion in aid into Chrysler and rival General Motors Corp.

General Motors on the Edge of Bankruptcy

Struggling US carmaker General Motors announced a $9.6 billion (£6.7 billion) loss in the fourth quarter, pushing its net 2008 losses to $30.9 billion. It said it used up $6.2 billion in cash as it fought to stay afloat in the worst US auto sales environment for 26 years. The US's biggest domestic carmaker has been badly affected by a global slump in demand as cash-strapped consumers shun big-ticket spending. It has already received $13.4 billion-worth of federal loans since December 31. Revenue at the 100-year-old company also took a tumble, plunging more than a third to $30.8 billion from $46.8 billion in 2007.

Some of the firm's executives went to Washington to discuss GM's request for an aid up to $30 billion, in a bid to prevent it from going bankrupt. It has been kept going with the aid of Government funds since the start of 2009. Consumers' fears about job losses, rising costs and banks clamping down on lending have all converged to dampen demand for autos and batter the industry.

GM conceded in its recent report of January 2009 that it was on the edge of bankruptcy and won't be able to avoid it unless it got more Government money and successfully executed a huge restructuring plan. It was also expected that auditors would question GM's viability. The Detroit-based behemoth lost $30.9 billion in 2008, is living on $13.4 billion in Government loans, and is seeking up to $30 billion as it tries to survive the worst auto sales climate in 27 years. "The auditors' comments are serious because the threshold for raising such concerns is tilted heavily in favor of companies, and often they can negotiate them away," said John Pottow, a University of Michigan Law School professor who specializes in bankruptcy. "If you get a qualified going concern audit letter like this, that suggests you are in extreme financial distress and very likely may file for bankruptcy," he added. US Senator Charles Grassley, the top Republican on the Senate Finance Committee, said the auditors' concerns mean the Government will likely have to provide more help to GM. The senator from Iowa called for a "restructured bankruptcy" involving the Government. "It would be a process of bankruptcy but be worked out outside of the court in mutual agreement to bondholders, stockholders, management—in this case, the federal Government—because we've got a lot invested there, and also the unions," Grassley said in a conference call with reporters from his home state. Ray Young, GM's chief financial officer, said in an interview that GM can accomplish its restructuring goals without bankruptcy. The company is making progress in negotiations to swap debt for stock and to gain concessions from the United Auto Workers union, he said. "One thing for certain is there's going to be recovery," Young said. "We just need to take advantage of this situation to streamline, downsize, get ourselves leaner, so that when the recovery occurs we will emerge as a far stronger company." In its annual report filed with the Securities and Exchange Commission, GM also disclosed that Chief Executive Rick Wagoner received a pay package worth $14.9 million in 2008, although $11.9 million of his compensation was in stock and options whose value plummeted to $682,000 as GM's share price sank. GM shares, which lost 87 per cent of their value in 2008, have further fallen in 2009.

The European Commission has called for a crisis meeting among EU states hosting General Motors plants. EU Industry Commissioner Guenter Verheugen said that the way GM was "dealing with the issue of Europe is not acceptable". Earlier, the troubled carmaker's auditors said there was "substantial doubt" about the ability of General Motors to stay afloat.

General Motors and Chrysler are to get more loans from the US Treasury as the troubled carmakers work on plans to try and make themselves viable. The two carmakers are seeking to stave off bankruptcy. GM will receive a further 60-day, $5 billion loan while Chrysler is to get $500 million. The firms have already received a combined $17.4 billion in aid since December 2008. Both face collapse as the economic downturn has prompted a slump in sales of vehicles worldwide. The US Government has demanded that both firms submit viable restructuring plans before it will consider further aid. Both companies' restructuring plans were rejected at the end of March 2009. This latest funding will bridge the gap till such time they present new reorganization plans.

General Motors which has been loaned $13.4 billion before the latest tranche of cash was stated to complete its restructuring by 1 June 2009 or face seeking bankruptcy protection. The funding for the carmakers has come from the Troubled Asset Relief Program, which has about $700 billion aimed at stabilising the US financial system.

Opel 'Should Consider Insolvency'

German carmaker Opel should consider entering insolvency, the country's interior minister has said. Modern insolvency law was "not set up for the destruction but for the preservation of economic assets", said Wolfgang Schaeuble. The comments came as executives from Opel and its parent General Motors met Government officials and promised more details on a restructuring plan.

Opel has been calling for a cash injection from Germany to help its survival. But Mr Schaeuble said that insolvency was a better option for Opel than relying on a state handout, and that such a move would not mean that it would have to go bust. "The public perception is that insolvency is associated with going bust or bankruptcy," he said. "But that is wrong. We must grasp that to survive such a crisis, modern insolvency rules are a better solution than the state taking a stake." Like most global carmakers, Opel is suffering from a slump in sales. The company announced last week that it needed the money to avert plant closures and job losses among its 26,000 employees in Germany.

Airways

The economic slowdown has adversely impacted airlines all over the world. The passenger travel in Indian airlines like Spicejet, Kingfisher, Indigo and international airlines like British Airways, Japan Airlines, among others has fallen to several years' low.

The Indian Government forced airlines to drop fares in January 2009 as jet fuel prices fell dramatically. But even low fares failed to win back passengers in January 2009 in this economic slowdown. In December 2008, when fares were at their peak, 33.73 lakh people flew within the country. In January 2009, when fares were almost halved, this figure was just 33.76 lakh, showing a 14.2 per cent fall from January 2008 figure of 39.34 lakh.

Airlines now fear that the low travel season with high fares could worsen the passenger load factors. "We had lowered fares in January 2009 in the hope of getting people to fly again and attaining breakeven revenue with volumes. But in the current economic turmoil, both personal and corporate travel is down due to uncertainty over jobs and focus on cost-cutting. Obviously we can't have low fares and low load factors," said an airline CEO.

Airlines could lose more passengers in coming months after the announcement of fall in train fares in 'on account' budget for 2009-10. Now, fares of even low-cost carriers are higher than Rajdhani AC II tier level. Airlines have now launched attractive advance booking schemes so that people can plan early and get low fares. "What we need desperately is infusion of funds. That can be done by allowing FDI from foreign airlines into Indian carriers. India is one of the few countries that are still growing, when other global economies are in recession. So we remain attractive investment for foreign biggies as they can get an assured traffic here," said a senior airline official.

Air ticket prices have gone up once again. Air India has gone ahead with the hike but says it would remain 10 per cent cheaper than the other two full service carriers—Jet and Kingfisher. "Our basic fare will be lower than other full service carriers. We have also introduced a new feature—passengers who book online will get an additional 10 per cent discount on basic fares. This has been done to try and keep full service flying affordable," said Air India spokesperson Jitendra Bhargava.

The aviation ministry has allowed Delhi airport to charge Rs. 200 as fee from each outgoing domestic passenger from 1 March, which has led to a similar demand from Mumbai airport developers. The new Bangalore and Hyderabad airports levy a cess of Rs. 260 and Rs. 375 on each departing passenger. This has escalated the cost of flying and left little scope for the airlines to increase fares.

Industry insiders say they had lowered fares for a while as there was tremendous pressure from the Government to pass on benefits of cheap oil prices to passengers. There was also a threat, they say, of not getting further benefits if fares weren't reduced. However, the official version given out was that fares were lowered to stimulate demand.

"But the economic slowdown has meant that travel has not picked up despite lower fares. Having low passenger loads flying on low fares is recipe for disaster," said an airline official. A Jet spokesperson said that they "adjust fares on regular basis" which is even otherwise necessary because of the fluctuating fuel prices as well as seasonal high/low demand for air travel.

Virgin Atlantic Eyes 600 Job Cuts

Virgin Atlantic has said it is consulting with staff over the possibility of making up to 600 redundancies across the business. The airline said it was reshaping its business to ensure that it remained strong during the economic downturn. "No airline is immune from the recession," said Virgin Atlantic chief executive Steve Ridgway. The airline said it was talking to staff and unions in order to find ways to avoid compulsory redundancies.

Mr Ridgway added that airlines had to reduce their costs because of the current fall in demand for travel. "We need to stay healthy so we are ready to grow again when economic conditions allow," he said. Virgin Atlantic employs about 8,500 people worldwide. Earlier, budget airline Ryanair announced cuts in its summer schedule at Dublin airport, saying it would result in the loss of 200 jobs.

Weak Economy Hits British Airways

British Airways has announced that it made a loss of £70 million in the nine months to 31 December 2008 bruised by further economic weakness and the weak pound. In the same period a year earlier, British Airways had made a profit before tax of £816 million. The airline has many costs in dollars and the decline in sterling makes things like aircraft leasing more expensive. BA said it would try to sell more tickets in markets with stronger currencies to enable it to benefit from exchange rates. The weak pound has also meant that air traffic control and airport charges have become more costly for the airline.

Passenger traffic has declined as the economic downturn means people are travelling less. British Airways has also been offering special deals to encourage people to fly. "The industry continues to face very difficult trading conditions on the back of a weak economic environment," the airline said. However, BA's latest passenger numbers offered a glimmer of hope. While overall passenger numbers were down 4 per cent from January 2009, there had been a 1.4 per cent rise in "non-premium" traffic in January, BA said. Fuel costs climbed 48 per cent to £2.2 billion but BA said it would begin to benefit from falling fuel prices in the financial year 2009-10. Revenue rose 6.2 per cent to £7.1 billion. The airline had already warned that it expects to make an operating loss of about £150 million in the financial year 2008-09.

Japan Airlines Facing Annual Loss

Japan Airlines (JAL) is predicting an annual loss of 34 billion yen ($372 million; £253 million) as the global crisis has hit demand. International travel, business travel and cargo traffic were hit particularly hard, as JAL made a 38.5 billion yen third quarter loss. The prediction is a reversal from its November projection of 13 billion yen profit. JAL made 16.9 billion yen profit in 2007-08. The airline said it would continue with a program of job cuts, fuel-efficient planes, and focus on business customers. "With business confidence falling and demand expected to drop far more than originally expected, the pressure to increase profitability, focus on cost reduction and increased productivity levels will intensify," the airline said in a statement. JAL said it had been hit by rising fuel costs in the first half of the year 2008-09. The airline said it was expecting a significant sales decline in the fourth quarter. "The deterioration in the economy, stemming from the subprime mortgage crisis, resulted in sharp falls in our international passengers," said JAL Senior Vice President Yoshimasa Kanayama.

United Airlines Shuts Down Call Centre in India

Airlines confirmed that it was closing its call centre in India and transferring 165 jobs to the United States, which is reeling from layoffs amid recession. The move came about a month after UAL Corp, parent of the third biggest North American carrier, said it was cutting 1,000 more jobs, pushing the total to 9,000 by the end of 2009 to help stem losses. The jobs in India will be transferred to call centers in Chicago and Honolulu, Hawaii, and filled by workers who now handle reservations, the Chicago-based airline said. Beginning in April 2009, it said the workers have also started to take customer-relations duties, which involve issues or complaints after travel, said Robin Urbanski, airline spokeswoman. "More sophisticated conversations with our guests are much better-suited for us to handle instead of a third-party partner," Urbanski said. United Airlines shipped the call center positions to India about three years ago as part of a trend by US companies to move such functions overseas to save costs.

Banks

Global economic slowdown has hit banks across the globe. Actually it was crisis in two large global financial services firms that triggered the meltdown. It has been widely accepted that the collapse of Lehman Brothers was symbol of the global financial crisis. The announcement on 14 September 2008 that Lehman Brothers would file for bankruptcy after the Federal Reserve Bank declined to participate in a financial support facility for the global financial services firm played a pivotal role in the unfolding of subsequent events.

Immediately following the bankruptcy, JPMorgan Chase provided the broker deal unit of Lehman Brothers with $138 billion to settle securities transactions with latter's customers and clearance parties. The same day, the sale of Merrill Lynch, another global financial services firm to Bank of America, was announced. These two developments heralded a severe global economic slowdown. The banks and financial companies in US and Europe disclosed sharp downturn in their balance sheets as defaults in subprime mortgage loans started eroding their capital and bringing them into losses with the accumulation of toxic assets.

By and large, the banks in India are on a sound footing because they do not believe in excessive leveraging. At the time of lending to various types of industries they insist on tangible securities and guarantees. Normally, they do not become over-enthusiastic about lending in the greed to earn big profits. They also keep margins so that the value of security does not fall short of the money lent by the bank. However, some foreign banks operating in India have been affected by the current slowdown. The weakened position of some Indian foreign banks in terms of their poor earnings, rising NPAs, as well as the failure of a few banks is studied below.

ICICI Bank Writes off Rs. 1,600 Crore Bad Loans

Individuals availed of loans and used credit cards for personal consumption during the retail credit boom till 2007, but are now not in a position to repay or are intentionally defaulting. As a sufferer of this trend, ICICI Bank has had to write off a large amount of overdue retail loans where borrowers have not repaid for a long period of at least over a year.

ICICI Bank, the country's second largest bank, in the third quarter ended 31 December 2008 wrote off bad retail loans of about Rs. 1,600 crore, which were overdue for a long time. The bank still has on its books total bad loans of nearly Rs. 9,000 crore and if it had not written off the long overdue loans, then its bad loan amount would have swelled to around Rs. 10,600 crore.

In the calandar year ended December 31, 2008, ICICI Bank's bad loans have increased by a whopping Rs. 4,114 crore. In the last few quarters, the bank has been adding bad loans of about Rs. 1,200 crore every quarter, most of it because of defaults by individuals. "Outlook on NPLs (non-performing loans) remains the same...over the next couple of quarters, the current trend would continue and thereafter, we should see some easing in terms of addition to NPLs," said Rakesh Jha, Deputy Chief Financial Officer of ICICI Bank.

State Bank of India (SBI) too has been witnessing a rise in its NPLs. For the country's largest bank, small and medium enterprises (SMEs), including gems and jewellery exporters, are among the defaulters as they face difficult economic conditions in India and in their overseas markets. SBI's bad loans were Rs. 13,314 crore as on 31 December 2008, up Rs. 2,132 crore from a year earlier.

ICICI Bank lost more than Rs. 11 crore due to over 8,000 cases of credit card frauds from April to December 2008. There were 8,280 cases reported by the ICICI Bank to the Reserve Bank of India, in which it lost Rs. 11.47 crore during the said period, Minister of State for Home, Shakeel Ahmad said in reply to a question in the Lok Sabha.

A total of 703 and 2,484 cases were received by American Express Bank and HSBC Bank related to credit card frauds from April to December 2008, in which they lost Rs. 6.04 crore and Rs. 4.90 crore, respectively. According to the data, a total of 12,959 such cases were received during the said period in which various banks lost Rs. 36.54 crore. Other banks, which lost significant amount to such practices, were Citibank, which bore a loss of Rs. 4.73 crore, Standard Chartered Bank Rs. 2.39 crore and Deutsche Bank with a loss of Rs. 2.09 crore.

State Regulators Close Three Banks

FirstBank Financial Services of Georgia and Alliance Bank and County Bank of California have become latest victims of banking crisis. Deposits at FirstBank Financial Services based in McDonough, Georgia will be taken over by Regions Bank based in Birmingham, Alaska, according to the Federal Deposit Insurance Corporation. FirstBank held assets worth about $337 million, and held deposits worth about $279 million at the end of December 2008, the Federal Deposit Insurance Corporation said. Regions Bank agreed to purchase about $17 million of FirstBank's assets.

Meanwhile, deposits at Alliance Bank out of Culver City, California will be assumed by California Bank & Trust from San Diego. Alliance Bank held assets totaling $1.14 billion, and deposits of $951 million, the FDIC said. California Bank & Trust agreed to purchase $1.12 billion of Alliance's assets at a discount of $9.9 million. California Bank & Trust also agreed to share some of the asset losses with the FDIC, the agency said. Alliance Bank's five offices will reopen as branches of California Bank & Trust.

County Bank of Merced, California was closed. The FDIC said that Westamerica Bank of San Rafael, California will assume all of the deposits of County Bank. County Bank had total assets of approximately $1.7 billion and total deposits of $1.3 billion. Westamerica Bank (WABC), in addition to assuming the deposits, agreed to purchase all of County Bank's assets.

The FDIC said County Bank's 39 offices would reopen as branches of Westamerica. Customers who banked with FirstBank, Alliance Bank or County Bank will automatically become customers of the new deposit holders, and will retain their account protection under the FDIC, which insures single accounts up to $250,000, and joint accounts up to $500,000.

Those customers will be able to use cheques, ATMs and debit cards as normal. Customers who have taken out loans from a failed bank should continue to make regular payments, the FDIC said.

Altogether, the three bank failures will cost the FDIC about $452 million. The unfolding financial crisis continues to take a toll on banks. If banks continue to fail at a rate of at least one per week, on average, then 2009 could see twice as many failures as in the previous year. During 2008, 25 banks were closed nationwide, which was the highest annual total since 1993, when 42 banks went under. Economists expect the number of failed banks to continue rising in 2009 year as the financial crisis continues and the economic outlook remains bleak.

Closures in Nebraska, Florida, Illinois and Oregon have further increased the number of banks that failed in 2009 as the financial crisis continues to roll. Deposits at Sherman County Bank, based in Loup City, Neb., the first bank in the state to fail since 1990, will be taken over by Heritage Bank, based in Wood River, Nebsaska, according to the Federal Deposit Insurance Corporation. Meanwhile, accounts held by Riverside Bank of the Gulf Coast based in Cape Coral, Florida, will be assumed by TIB Bank based in Naples, Florida, the FDIC said. It is the second bank to fail in the state in 2009 and the fourth to go under in that state since the economic crisis unfurled.

Corn Belt Bank and Trust Company, based in Pittsfield, Illinois, the third bank to fail in the state since January 2008, was also shuttered by state regulators, and its deposits were turned over to The Carlinville National Bank out of Carlinville, Illinois. Pinnacle Bank, Beaverton, Oregon, was closed by the Oregon Division of Finance and Corporate Securities. The FDIC entered into an agreement with Washington Trust Bank, Spokane, Washington, to assume all of the deposits of Pinnacle Bank.

Customers who banked with Sherman County Bank, Riverside, Corn Belt Bank, or Pinnacle Bank automatically became customers of the new owners, and retained their account protection under the FDIC, which insured single accounts up to $250,000, and joint accounts up to $500,000, the Government agency said. Those customers were able to use cheques, ATMs and debit cards as normal. Customers who had taken out loans from a failed bank were asked to continue to make regular payments, the FDIC said. Sherman County Bank held assets worth about $129.8 million, and held deposits worth about $85.1 million, as of 12 February 2009 the FDIC said. Heritage Bank agreed to purchase about $21.8 million of Sherman County Bank's assets.

Riverside Bank held assets worth about $539 million, and held deposits worth about $424 million, as of December, 2008, the FDIC said. TIB Bank was not to assume $142.6 million worth of brokered deposits held by Riverside Bank, but agreed to buy $125 million of Riverside's assets. Corn Belt Bank carried assets worth about $271.8 million, with deposits of $234.4 million, according to the agency. Carlinville National did not take on $92 million of Corn Belt's brokered deposits, but bought $60.7 million of Corn Belt's assets, the FDIC said.

Pinnacle Bank had total assets of approximately $73 million and total deposits of $64 million. In addition to assuming all of the deposits of the failed bank, including those from brokers, Washington Trust Bank agreed to purchase approximately $72 million in assets at a discount of $7.6 million, the FDIC announced. Altogether, the bank failures cost the FDIC about $341.6 million.

Lloyds Bank—A Hobbled Horse

Douglas Fraser called Lloyds Banking Group (LBG) a hobbled horse: "The desperate attempts to avoid majority Government ownership of LBG have had a coach and that rampant horse on its logo driven through them. As a result, a once majestic black stallion now looks hobbled." The Asset Protection Scheme put £260 billion of toxic assets under Government insurance, in addition to the £375 billion of risky investments from the Royal Bank of Scotland, agreed sometime ago. Whereas LBG had been 43 per cent owned by the Government, following the recapitalisation in October 2008, it is now looking at 65 per cent ownership as a result of the deal. Including the Government's ownership of 'B' shares, this effectively rose to 77 per cent.

Eric Daniels, Lloyds' chief executive, fought hard to sustain the hope for his shareholders that there may be a dividend payout from 2009 onwards. The block on that has been removed, by the conversion of the £4 billion worth of preference shares the Government held since the last bailout. That removes a £480 million annual bill in payouts (at a 12 per cent rate) that was to have been the first call on the bank until the preference shares were bought off.

The Royal Bank of Scotland similarly shed £5 billion in preference shares, but the effective resulting impact of the deal, including the Asset Protection Scheme, was to take Government ownership from 68 per cent up over 90 per cent.

Daniels stressed the more robust gearing of the bank's balance sheet, but the best he could say to shareholders was that this looks like an "appropriate deal" for them. Of the assets being insured, HBOS accounted for 83 per cent and Lloyds TSB for only 17 per cent, reinforcing the message that it was the Edinburgh-based part of the merger that had brought the problems. And while the £260 billion then insured was made up of £74 billion in dodgy mortgage loans, it was dominated by the £151 billion in corporate and commercial loans, including the real estate.

It is with this background that Standard and Poor's, the credit rating agency, lowered the rating on Lloyds Banking Group and its various subsidiaries including HBOS and Scottish Windows. That means a reckoning that the financial position is less secure, but it is clear from the S&P assessment that it is only that high because the Government is standing behind Lloyds. It means, of course, that raising funds is becoming more expensive for Lloyds, just as it is for many of its customers.

Will the £14 billion in guaranteed new lending for each of the next two years feed through to hard-pressed customers? Only if the bank is willing to expose itself to more risk. This returns to the fundamental inconsistency of requiring banks to be more responsible while requiring them to take more risks. And with Lloyds now majority owned by the Government, it reinforces the other inconsistency, that the Government wants banks to behave commercially while exerting political pressure on them over their lending, dividend and pay structures. It is intensely frustrating for bankers to have to accept these terms from ministers and civil servants. But it should be intensely alarming for the taxpayer that, many stimulus packages are being given to such low-performing banks while carrying an insurance risk on billion of dodgy assets that the Government intends to buy.

A comparison of US and UK GDPs and their rescue plans is given in Fig. 4 below.

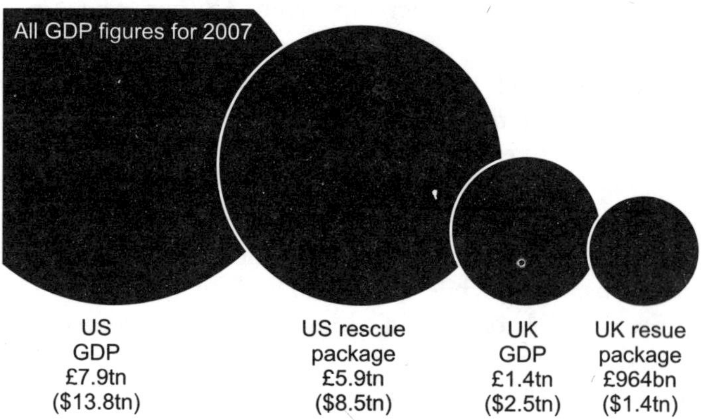

Fig. 4: US and UK GDPs and Rescue Packages

Source: US Treasury, UK Treasury, Bloomberg

The UK has spent £94 billion to prop up Royal Bank of Scotland, HBOS and Lloyds TSB as well as nationalised Northern Rock and parts of Bradford & Bingley. The Treasury and the Bank of England have pledged hundreds of billions of pounds of further support for the fragile banking system. A £250 billion credit guarantee scheme announced in October 2008 is being expanded to encourage banks to lend more, with a commitment of up to £50 billion.

The UK Government's total rescue plan and its bifurcation in different schemes is shown in Fig. 5 below.

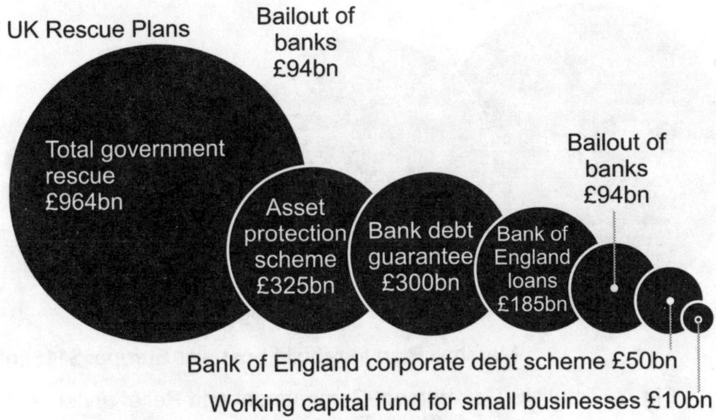

Fig. 5: UK Government Rescue Plans

Source: US Treasury, Bank of England, DBEER

The total cost to UK Government and the share of five major banks is shown in the following pie chart (Fig. 6).

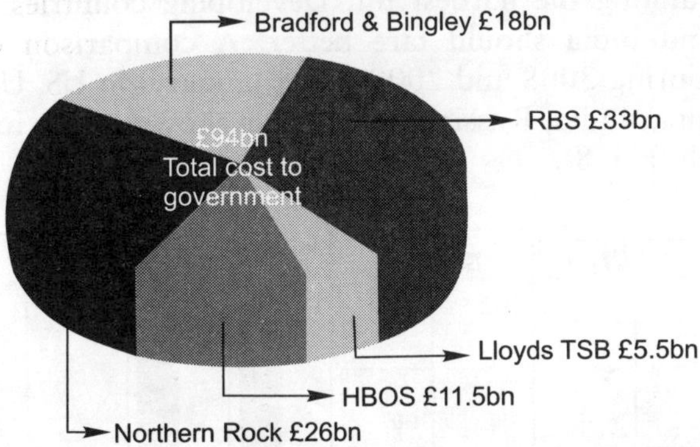

Fig. 6: Total Cost to UK Government and Share of Five Major Banks

Source: US Treasury, UK Treasury, Bloomberg

There has been an array of measures to provide support to the battered US financial system. A $700 billion scheme approved in 2008, known as the Troubled Asset Relief Program, was used to help lenders like Citigroup and Bank of America as well as the automobile industry. Major changes to the program have been announced by the new administration, including a partnership with the private sector to buy toxic assets from banks. The US Government's total commitment and relief under different programs is shown in Fig. 7 below.

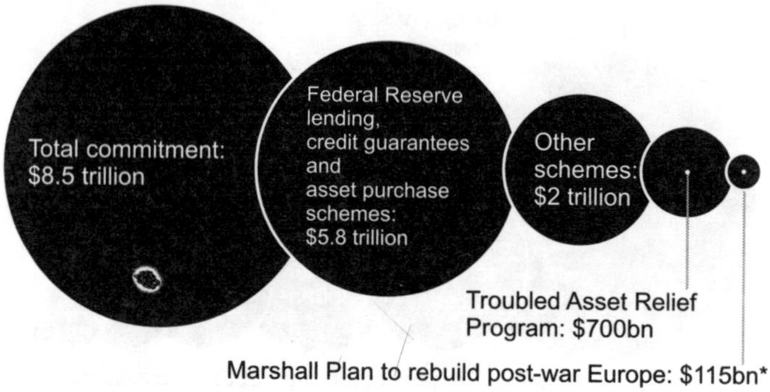

Fig. 7: Total US Government Commitment and Relief under Different Programs

* Adjusted for inflation

Source: Bloomberg, US Treasury, Federal Reserve, US National Archive

World economic growth is expected to slow sharply, with the UK among the hardest hit. Developing countries such as China and India should fare better. A comparison of GDP growth during 2008 and 2009 (upto January) in US, UK, Euro area, China, India, Russia and Brazil is shown in the following bar graph (Fig. 8).

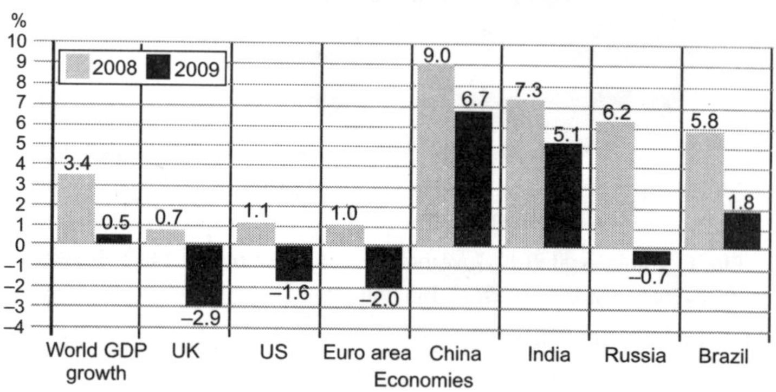

Fig. 8: Comparative GDP Growth in 2008-09

Source: IMF estimates January 2009

As countries try to spend their way out of recession, debt levels are forecast to rise. Figure 9 below shows financial liabilities as a percentage of GDP during 2008-10 (projected) in the US, UK, Germany and France.

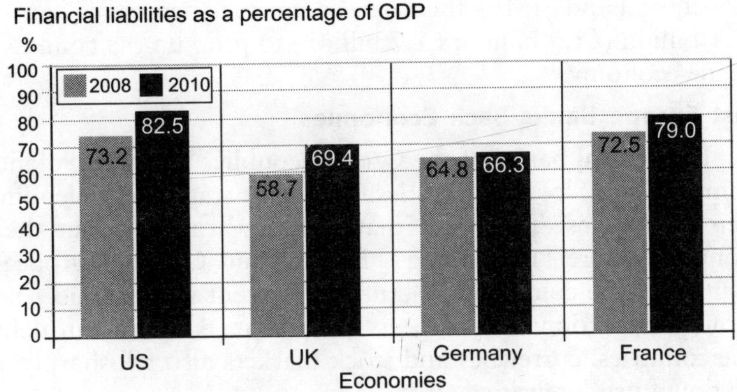

Fig. 9: Financial Liabilities during 2008-2010

Source: OECD Forecasts, December 2008

Icelandic Bank Loses Independence

The last major Icelandic bank left standing after the country's financial collapse in October 2008 was also closed down by the financial authorities. Straumur Burdaras was taken over by the Icelandic Financial Supervisory Authority (IFSA), which said it was now in the process of closing the business. The Icelandic Government took control of the country's three biggest banks in October 2008. The authority said that all deposits at Straumur were fully secure. "In spite of its strong capital position and the support of funding banks, Straumur Burdaras Investment Bank believes that its liquidity position is no longer enough to sustain its activities," a bank statement said. The IFSA suspended the bank's board and appointed a resolution committee to decide on how best to resolve the bank's problems. The bank's chief executive, William Fall also resigned.

Iceland's financial sector collapsed in October 2008 due to billions of dollars of bad debt. As a direct result, the country's three biggest banks were taken over by the authorities. First to lose independence was First Glitnir, closely followed by Landsbanki, which owned Icesave—an internet bank used by many UK customers. Finally, Iceland's biggest bank, Kaupthing, was nationalized. The International Monetary Fund (IMF) then agreed to an emergency loan of $2.1 billion (£1.5 billion; €1.7 billion) to prop up the country's fragile economy.

East Europe Banks Back Economies

The central banks of the Czech Republic, Bulgaria, Poland, Romania and Slovakia have issued a joint statement defending their economies. They said that recent warnings about their economies were "misleading". Eastern and Central European countries have come under scrutiny in recent weeks amid fears about their economic prospects and reliance on foreign debt. The countries' currencies and stock markets also fell sharply as the downturn intensified.

Hungary's central bank later said it supported the statement issued by its counterparts. The central banks urged investors to look at the prospects of individual countries and not assume that Eastern Europe was a "homogeneous region". Better-off countries like Czech Republic and Poland feel that they are unfairly lumped together with places such as Hungary or Latvia, which have been particularly hard hit. They expressed concern at the warnings recently made by credit ratings agencies and other bodies, saying it could undermine financial stability in the region. "The published information accompanying these initiatives is often simplified and misleading," the statement said.

In February 2009, Moody's warned that economic conditions in the region would hit local subsidiaries of major Western banks.

In early March 2009, the region received a 24.5 billion euro ($31 billion; £21.8 billion) rescue package from the European Bank for Reconstruction and Development (EBRD), the European Investment Bank (EIB) and the World Bank.

Euro Rates and Growth Outlook Cut

The European Central Bank (ECB) has cut its key interest rate to 1.5 per cent from 2.0 per cent, the lowest since it started setting euro rates in January 1999. It followed a cut in

UK rates by the Bank of England. US and Japanese rates are, in effect, already at zero. The European Central Bank key interest rates from 1995 till the first quarter of 2009 are shown in Fig. 10 below.

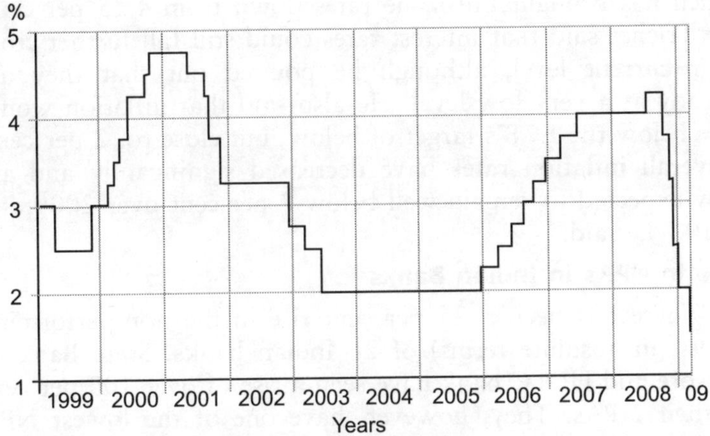

Fig. 10: European Central Bank Key Interest Rate

Source: ECB

The ECB President Jean-Claude Trichet slashed his forecasts for Eurozone growth. The ECB is now predicting the GDP in 2009 in the 16-nation bloc will shrink by between 2.2 per cent and 3.2 per cent. Its last prediction, made in December 2008 was that growth would be between no change and a fall of 1 per cent in 2009. For 2010 it was predicting growth between 0.5 per cent and 1.5 per cent. It is now forecasting growth between 0.7 per cent and minus 0.7 per cent.

The revisions reflect Mr Trichet's view that the global economy has "weakened substantially in recent months" but that it will "gradually recover" in 2010. But there were no new measures announced to help stimulate the Eurozone economy, with Mr Trichet stressing that he was already using various "non-standard measures" and saying that the ECB's rate-setters were considering various others. Slowing growth was confirmed by revised economic growth figures issued earlier. GDP for the last three months of 2008 was down 1.3 per cent from the same quarter of the previous year, worse than the initial estimate of 1.2 per cent. The figure for the previous quarter was left unchanged at a 1.5 per cent fall.

This was the ECB's fifth rate cut since October 2008, which has brought Eurozone rates down from 4.25 per cent. Mr Trichet said that interest rates could still fall further from their current level, although he pointed out that they are already at a very low level. He also said that inflation would stay below the ECB's target of below, but close to, 2 per cent. "Overall inflation rates have decreased significantly and are now expected to remain well below 2 per cent over 2009 and 2010," he said.

Rise in NPAs in Indian Banks

There has been a 25 per cent rise in the non-performing assets (in absolute terms) of 26 Indian banks. State Bank of Mysore and HDFC bank have seen a rise of over 100 per cent in their NPAs. They, however, have one of the lowest NPA levels (0.6 per cent) in the industry. NPAs are loans that fail to yield interest after a stipulated period.

Kotak Mahindra Bank and Canara Bank have witnessed a rise of 92 and 90 per cent, respectively, in their non-performing assets over the past one-year. "NPAs have been rising from the unsecured loan segment that comprises primarily of credit cards and personal loans," said the head of assets of a private sector bank. "The delinquency in the retail loans especially the unsecured loans will rise further as the GDP growth comes down," said Amitabh Chakraborth, President, Equity Religare Enterprises. "Prudent banks have already taken steps to reduce their loans to these segments," he added.

Non-performing assets for Kotak Mahindra Bank showed a 43 per cent increase in the quarter ending 31st December 2008 over the previous quarter and a 92 per cent rise on a year-on-year basis. NPAs as a percentage of total assets have gone up from 1.1 per cent in December 2007 to 2.7 per cent in December 2008. "It is because of the NPAs from other banks that we have bought for our asset reconstruction business," said Jaimin Bhatt, Chief Financial Officer, Kotak Mahindra

Bank. "It takes some time to convert these NPAs into good assets," he said.

ICICI Bank occupies the second spot with non-performing assets of 2.1 per cent. ING Vysya Bank also witnessed a year-on-year rise of 83 per cent in NPAs and a quarter-on-quater rise of 41 per cent. Most banks however arrested the quarter-on-quarter rise in NPAs in December 2008.

NPAs Rising at Worrying Pace

This is yet another proof of banks facing worsening bad loans situation. The addition to bad loans is now higher than recoveries made from defaulted loans, a reversal of the trend of previous few years when bad loan recoveries exceeded fresh slippages. In 2007-08, fresh bad loans constituted 61 per cent of total NPAs, up from 37 per cent in 2003-04, 34 per cent in 2004-05, 41 per cent in 2005-06 and 52 per cent in 2006-07, according to a report by Dun & Bradstreet titled "India's Top Banks 2009". "The movement of NPAs prior to 2006-07 was favourable as the ratio of addition to NPAs was lower than their recovery. Both these ratios were almost the same in financial year 2007," said the report.

The start of 2007-08 was marked by high interest rate regime in order to control the excess liquidity and control inflation. Furthermore, to make matters worse, the down phase in the business cycle in recent months has raised the odds of credit default. In its third edition now, the survey captures developments in the banking sector and profiles of the scheduled commercial banks in India. In the financial year 2007-08, the 77 banks surveyed, together reported 23.1 per cent growth in deposits while advances grew by 25 per cent.

"During financial year 2007-08 the total asset base of these 77 banks was equivalent to 91.8 per cent of India's GDP at current market prices," said the survey which listed Bank of India as the best performing bank in the public sector, while Axis Bank was listed as the best private sector bank. The survey also stated that there was an increase in structuring of both corporate as well as non-corporate debt. "The total amount of loans restructured went up by 61 per cent for public sector banks and more than doubled for the private sector and foreign banks," the survey said, adding that the total amount of loans restructured by foreign banks was at Rs. 1,632 million in 2007-08 compared with Rs. 578.8 million in the previous financial year.

Defaults Hit SBI Cards, Losses Ahead

SBI Cards, the nation's second largest credit card issuer, 60 per cent owned by State Bank of India (SBI), is likely to report a loss for the second consecutive year as defaults mount. ICICI Bank, the top player, has faced similar defaults as well. Both have tightened salary and other norms for the issue of credit cards. CRISIL Ltd., the Indian arm of the global rating agency Standard & Poor's, said in a recent report that SBI Cards & Payment Services Ltd. was expected to report more losses in 2008-09 on high credit costs and lower fee income. In the quarter ended December 31, 2008, ICICI bank, relatively better off but still weak, saw a pre-tax profit of Rs. 85.7 crore in retail banking on business worth Rs. 5,683 crore, as defaults and receivables in loans hit home. Sachin Khandelwal, Head of Credit Cards, ICICI Bank, said: "In 2007-08 the credit cards business grew by 20 to 25 per cent. We had done 1.5 million cards in 2007-08 which has been reduced by 60 per cent in the first 10 months of 2008-09. The credit losses have increased by more than 1 percentage point (of the spread between lending rates and cost)."

SBI Cards, which is 40 per cent owned by US-based GE Money, reported a loss of Rs. 60 crore on total income of Rs. 440 crore in the six months ended September 30, 2008. The card issuer had suffered a loss of Rs. 150 crore in 2007-08 against a net profit of Rs. 60 crore in 2006-07. A senior official of SBI Cards said, "We have consciously slowed down sourcing customers by more than 50 per cent from a peak of 1 lakh cards a month last year to 20,000 to 30,000 a month now to ensure a good portfolio. It's a difficult market. We have consolidated this year and are better placed to tackle losses." The SBI official said credit checks had increased while the minimum salary criterion for issue of cards has been revised to Rs. 2 to 2.4 lakh per year from last year's Rs. 1.44 lakh.

These measures, however, may result in decrease in customer base. In these difficult times of very low consumer spending such steps prove counter-productives to the revival of the economy.

Slowdown Doubles up Cheque-bouncing Cases

Economic slowdown has further burdened the judiciary with cheque-bouncing almost doubling in 2008 as compared to 2007. The number of cheque-bouncing cases has increased steeply in the second half of 2008, when the global meltdown actually started showing its affect. Statistics show that in 2008, the Mumbai courts received 1,14,328 cases of dishonoured cheques as compared to 58,752 cases in 2007. This means, 2008 saw more than 300 cases of cheque-bouncing registered every day in Mumbai. The payment defaults increased from August when the slowdown severely started hitting the Indian economy. In the second half of last year, Mumbai saw an average of 12,627 cases filed every month in various courts. As compared to this, the first half of 2008, on average witnessed only 7,320 cases per month.

Legal experts said that there is a huge increase in the payment defaults to banks besides that in regular business transactions. "I see an average of 15 cases of cheque-bouncing filed by banks in a single metropolitan court daily," said Advocate Pankaj Bafna, who is handling many such cases. He added that increased number of cheque-bouncing cases are coming to judiciary despite hike in court fee from September 2008. The court fee for cheque-bouncing cases was only Rs. 200 earlier which was increased to two per cent of the amount involved. However, the minimum fees is kept at Rs. 200. Statistics show that last year, 2,28,750 cases of cheque-bouncing were pending in Mumbai courts. The year 2008 witnessed disposal of only 41,599 cases. Bafna said a few months ago the Supreme Court ordered faster disposal of cheque bouncing cases. The apex court ordered that cheque-bouncing cases should be disposed of in two years.

Standing by the Private Banking System

The White House is standing by the private banking system. White House Press Secretary Robert Gibbs was asked about speculation that the Obama administration may seek to nationalize two financial bellwethers, Citigroup Inc. and Bank of America Corp. Gibbs responded that the administration continues to "strongly believe that a privately held banking system is the correct way to go." Along with that, he said, the Government must ensure that banks are sufficiently regulated.

Lord Mandelson has reiterated that the Government has no plans to nationalise the banking sector. His comments came two days after the Government increased its stake in Lloyds Banking Group to 65 per cent from 43 per cent. Speaking on the BBC's Andrew Marr show, the business Secretary said nationalisation would not be "necessary or desirable". Lord Mandelson admitted banking regulation should have been stronger, and change was now needed globally. Speaking in regard of the Government's increased stake in Lloyds, and its 68 per cent share of RBS, he said he remained "pretty confident" that taxpayers would "eventually" get something back. Ruling out full nationalisation, such as happened at Northern Rock, he said the majority ownership model at Lloyds and RBS enabled the Government to "exercise a great deal of influence...without taking that final step of removing the shareholders". Admitting that UK banking regulation "might have been wider and tougher", he said that effective reform of the regulations could only be achieved globally. He said matters to address this would be discussed in the forthcoming meeting of G20 global leaders. Turning his attention to the UK economy, he said that while we will "start to see changes taking place in the economy this year", but the Government was not "going to put a timetable on when the recovery will take place".

Fed Cuts 2009 Economic Forecast

The US Federal Reserve has cut its economic forecast for 2009 and considered setting an inflation target, the minutes from its meeting have shown. The central bank now expects a fall in output between 0.5 per cent and 1.5 per cent. In October 2008 it had anticipated output between a shrinkage of 0.2 per cent and growth of 1.1 per cent. Separately, Fed Chairman Ben Bernanke told the National Press Club in Washington that the bank sees "little risk" of high inflation. He said he expects inflation to stay low because of weak global economic activity and low commodity prices.

Fed Pumps $1.2 Trillion into US Economy

The US Federal Reserve says it will buy almost $1.2 trillion (£843 billion) worth of debt to help boost lending and promote economic recovery. It said it would start buying long-term Government debt and expand purchases of mortgage-related debt. The size of the move surprised investors, causing the Dow Jones stock index to jump almost 200 points. The Bank of England has already begun buying Government debt to expand money supply-known as quantitative easing. The Federal Reserve said it hopes the measures will boost mortgage lending and the struggling housing market by lowering interest rates on mortgages and other forms of consumer debt. "This is not only going to keep mortgage rates low for a long period of time," said Greg McBride, a senior financial analyst at Bankrate.com. "The mere announcement may produce a honeymoon effect and bring mortgage rates down to even lower levels in the coming days." The US central bank also kept interest rates unchanged at close to zero after its two-day policy meeting.

The Fed said it would employ "all available tools" to promote economic recovery. The biggest surprise was the announcement that the Fed would buy up to $300 billion worth of Government debt, known as US Treasuries, over the next six months. It also said it would buy an additional $750 billion of mortgage-backed securities to boost mortgage lending, bringing total purchases of this type to $1.25 trillion. It added that it would buy a further $100 billion in debt issued by Government-sponsored agencies like Freddie Mac, which supports the mortgage market.

The Dow Jones Industrial Average gained 90.88 points, or 1.23 per cent, to end at 7,486.58 points, reversing early losses.

The move boosted banks and financial shares, with Citigroup up 23 per cent and Bank of America vaulting 22 per cent higher. However, the announcement hurt the dollar, which hit a two-month low against the euro on fears that the measures would undermine the currency.

US Govt Eyes More Say in Banks with $2.5 Trillion Bailout

The White House plan to rescue the US financial system, announced, by Treasury Secretary Timothy E Geithner, is far bigger than anyone predicted and envisions a far greater Government role in markets and banks than at any time since the 1930s. Administration officials committed to flood the financial system with as much as $2.5 trillion—$350 billion coming from the bailout fund and the rest from private investors and the Federal Reserve, making use of its ability to print cash.

Geithner pointedly criticised the Bush administration for not acting boldly and quickly enough. "The spectacle of huge amounts of taxpayer money being provided to the same institutions that helped cause the crisis, with limited transparency and oversight, added to the public distrust," he said, in a clear swipe at the administration. But the initial assessment of the plan from the markets, lawmakers and economists was brutally negative, in large part because they expected more details.

Basic questions about how the various parts of the program would work, especially those involving the unsellable mortgages that banks are holding and preventing home foreclosures, were left for another day. President Obama welcomed the news that the Senate voted 61-37 to approve its $838 billion economic stimulus bill but dismissed the adverse market reaction to his bank rescue plan. "Wall Street, I think, is hoping for an easy out on this thing and there is no easy out," Obama said in an interview with ABC News. Many of the vital details of the program remained unsettled and were the subject of an intense behind-the-scenes debate.

"Essentially what you've got are a set of banks that have not been as transparent as we need to be in terms of what their books look like," said Obama. "And we're going to have to hold out the Band-Aid a little bit and go ahead and just be clear about some of the losses that have been made because until we do that, we're not going to be able to attract private capital into the marketplace."

Japan to Use Forex Reserves to Ease Credit Squeeze

Japan will use some of its large foreign exchange reserves to ease a squeeze in corporate financing, its Finance Minister said. Japanese firms both big and small are finding it hard to borrow as banks, hit by losses on their stock, shy away from lending, aggravating the problems the world's second biggest economy.

The Government decided to loan $5 billion in March 2009 from its foreign reserves to the Japan Bank for International Cooperation (JBIC), which has been accredited with helping ease the pressure on Japanese companies from the global credit squeeze. "We expect difficulties in corporate financing in Japan as well as overseas to reach their peak soon as economic difficulties deepen," Kaoru Yosano, Economics Minister, told a news conference after a cabinet meeting.

A financial arm of Toyota Motors has applied for about $2 billion in loans. Toyota was perhaps the first of a series of big Japanese companies turning to state-backed financial institutions prior to the closing of books for the business year at the end of March 2008.

The global economic slump has virtually frozen Japanese exports and production of cars and electronics, and its economy is seen headed for its longest recession in modern times. Corporate earnings have worsened as recession spreads around the world, eroding firms' creditworthiness and raising concerns that liquidity will remain constrained into the financial year 2009.

Banks, large holders of stocks in Japan, have been forced to raise billions of dollars in new capital as their holdings slide in value, and the Bank of Japan has already launched a scheme to buy stocks directly from them. Japan's Government is also looking at expanding stock buying and taking other steps to support the share market amid growing fears for the economy as sliding stocks erode the capital of banks. JBIC, an international arm of the state-backed Japan Finance Corporation, extends lending to Japanese companies investing abroad and is assisting them in financing amid upheavals in global financial markets.

However, Japanese stocks rallied after Citigroup Inc. said it had a profit in the first two months of this year, triggering speculation that recovery of the global financial system is in sight.

Mizuho Financial Group Inc., the Japanese bank with the biggest subprime write downs, gained 5.4 per cent, following a worldwide rebound in equities. Mitsubishi UFJ Financial Group Inc. advanced 4.1 per cent, even after a real estate company to which it lent money became Japan's third-biggest bankruptcy in 2008. Toshiba Corp. leapt 9.5 per cent on a newspaper report it may return to profit in 2009-10.

Rate of Interest in India

Bugbear of inflation appears to haunt the Governor of the Reserve Bank of India. To fight slowdown/recession a large number of countries have drastically reduced their interest rates. Table 2 given on the next page shows the current interest rates of various countries. But unfortunately the Reserve Bank of India is hesitant to further reduce the rate of interest. At the prevailing interest rate it is not profitable for industrialists to undertake investment. Similarly, the consumers cannot afford to buy homes or durables at the current high rate of interest. If the investment or consumer demand is to be stimulated, the rate of interest must be reduced quickly. Delayed decision regarding reduction in interest rate would do a lot of damage to the growth of economy. If unemployment scenario worsens a large number of people will have no money to buy goods and services. What will be the use of low prices in such case?

Table 2 on next page shows the current interest rates of 23 different countries including previous rates and the dates when they were changed by central banks.

Table 2: Current Interest Rates of Major Banks

Major Central Banks Overview			
Central Bank	Next Meeting	Last Change	Current Interest Rate
Bank of Canada	21 Apr 2009	03 Mar 2009	0.5%
Bank of Japan	28 Apr 2009	19 Dec 2008	0.1%
European Central Bank	07 May 2009	02 Apr 2009	1.25%
Federal Reserve	29 Apr 2009	16 Dec 2008	0.25%
Swiss National Bank	18 Jun 2009	12 Mar 2009	0.25%
The Reserve Bank of Australia	05 May 2009	07 Apr 2009	3%
Bank of England	n/a	05 Mar 2009	0.5%
Africa			
Country	Current Interest Rate	Previous	Last Change
Egypt	10.0%	10.5%	30 Mar 2009
South Africa	9.5%	10.5%	24 Mar 2009
Asia Pacific			
Australia	3.00%	3.25%	07 Apr 2009
China	5.31%	5.58%	22 Dec 2008
Hong Kong SAR	0.5%	1.5%	17 Dec 2008
India	5.0%	5.5%	25 Mar 2009
Japan	0.1%	0.3%	19 Dec 2008
Korea, Republic of	3.%	4.%	11 Dec 2008
New Zealand	3.0%	3.5%	11 Mar 2009
Taiwan	1.25%	1.50%	19 Feb 2009
Europe			
Czech Republic	1.75%	2.25%	05 Feb 2009
European Monetary Union	1.25%	1.50%	02 Apr 2009
Hungary	9.5%	10.0%	19 Jan 2009
Iceland	15.5%	17.0%	08 Apr 2009
Norway	2.0%	2.5%	25 Mar 2009
Poland	3.75%	4.00%	25 Mar 2009
Slovakia	2.25%	2.50%	08 Apr 2009
Sweden	1.%	2.%	11 Feb 2009
Switzerland	0.25%	0.50%	12 Mar 2009
United Kingdom	0.5%	1.0%	05 Mar 2009
Middle East			
Turkey	9.75%	10.50%	17 Apr 2009
North America			
Canada	0.5%	1.0%	03 Mar 2009
United States	0.25%	1.00%	16 Dec 2008
South America			
Brazil	11.25%	12.75%	11 Mar 2009

Source: www.whichwaytopay.com

Stress Tests

The US Government has signalled that its financial rescue efforts may have reached their high watermark as the much anticipated 'stress tests' conducted by regulators showed that the banks can withstand an adverse economic scenario though they will be required to raise fresh capital to boost their reserves against losses. Ten of America's largest 19 banks need a combined $74.6 billion of extra funds to increase their cash reserves. Federal Reserve Chairman Ben Bernanke said that the

Treasury stands ready to provide whatever additional capital may be necessary to ensure that our banking system is able to navigate a challenging economic downturn. Treasury Secretary Geithner said that the tests will help clear the clouds of uncertainty hanging over the banking system with an unprecedented level of transparency and clarity.

Obama to Test Home Loan Do-overs

Foreclosure prevention effort relies on modifying loans based on borrowers' ability to pay. Will this effort work where others have failed? Mortgage modifications have a bad rap, yet President Obama is depending on them to stop the foreclosure crisis. Modifications continue to be pushed as the best way to get struggling borrowers back on their feet. The jury is out on whether modifications work long-term. One recent study showed about half of borrowers with modified loans falling behind within six months. Still, Obama is giving modifications a central role in his $75 billion foreclosure prevention program.

The program calls for loan servicers to lower struggling borrowers' interest rates so that total payments are no more than 31 per cent of their gross income. The Government will subsidize part of the reduction, as well as kick in incentives for the servicers, borrowers and mortgage investors to participate in the modifications.

The program is getting mixed reviews. Industry experts applaud the President's emphasis on making payments affordable, a criteria made popular last year by Federal Deposit Insurance Corp. chief Sheila Bair. But, they say, the plan will fall short without a stronger push to reduce loan balances for those who owe more than their homes are worth and without a better plan for those deep in all kinds of debt.

Modification Problems

Servicers are increasingly turning to modifications as the foreclosure crisis escalates. They have modified about 1.3 million loans between July 2007 and 2009, according to statistics released by Hope Now, an alliance of the mortgage industry and housing counselors. The efforts—which usually involve adjusting interest rates, loan length or principal balance—have been largely voluntary and uncoordinated.

In recent months, modifications have come under attack as a mere short-term fix. In December 2008, the office of the Comptroller of the Currency added fuel to the fire by reporting that more than half of borrowers with loans adjusted in the first half of 2008 were behind in their payments six months later. The Hope Now survey shows that between 30 per cent and 40 per cent of modifications had defaulted again within six months. But many modification supporters said reports of redefaults don't take into account how loans were modified. Until recently, the adjustments often entailed increasing the monthly payments to make up for the arrears.

Some 34 per cent of mortgages modified in November 2008 resulted in a higher payment, while another 17 per cent had no change in payment, said Alan White, a law professor at Valparaiso University. More than nine of 10 voluntary modifications in 2008 involved no cancellation of principal, past-due interest, late fees or expenses. "The redefault problem has resulted in criticism of the very idea of modifying mortgage loans," White wrote in a January 2009 report. "On the other hand, there is considerable evidence that more aggressive modifications, especially those that reduce the principal debt, are much less subject to high rates of redefault."

In recent months, however, more servicers have focused on adjusting borrowers' payments to an affordable level, usually between 31 per cent and 38 per cent of a borrower's gross monthly income. Housing advocates as well as industry officials hope this will increase modifications' success rate. "Affordability makes sense," said Faith Schwartz, Hope Now's executive director. "It's certain a key factor in why modifications will work even better," he said.

It's too early to tell how well this new breed of modifications will perform. But a Credit Suisse study conducted in October 2008 showed that only 15 per cent of interest-rate modifications and 23 per cent of principal-reduction modifications made at the end of 2007 were delinquent eight months later, compared to 44 per cent of adjustments that resulted in higher payments. "Lots of modifications have not been done with a rigorous ability-to-pay criteria. As evidence of that, we see the high redefault rates," said Rod Dubitsky, head of asset-backed securities research at Credit Suisse. "Modifications that more carefully consider ability to pay should have a lower redefault rate," he went on to say.

Advocates also take heart in the relative success rate of servicers who have long focused on affordability. For example, Ocwen Financial Corp. boasts of a 19.4 per cent redefault rate—less than half the industry average.

The West Palm Beach, Florida-based firm says most of its borrowers remain current because of its customized approach to modifications. Ocwen looks at borrowers' income and expenses and comes up with a long-term payment plan that the homeowner can afford. The company says it has prevented more than 90,000 foreclosures since the mortgage crisis began. "If loan modifications are to have an enduring impact, the reduced mortgage payments must be sustainable by homeowners," Ocwen Chief Executive William Erbey said in a hearing before Congress. Unlike most servicers, Ocwen has embraced principal reductions. Nearly 19 per cent of its loan modifications include writing down the mortgage balance. This is an important step to achieving an affordable payment while still maximizing the payout for the mortgage investor.

Obama's plan has come under fire for not doing more to encourage servicers to reduce loan balances—a step which would help borrowers who have seen their home values plummet. The program does allow servicers to reduce principal, but makes interest rate adjustments the primary method for achieving affordable payments. One in six homeowners are "underwater," meaning they owe more on their mortgage than the house is worth, according to Zillow.com. Though experts are divided in their opinion, many say that the foreclosure crisis won't be stemmed until something is done to help these borrowers such as principal reductions to bring the loan balance in line with the home's current value. "Equity in the home is a significant driver of default," Dubitsky said. Also, many borrowers are drowning in many types of debt, experts said. So just adjusting their first mortgage, or lien, is not enough. Ocwen, for instance, takes into account all of a borrower's obligations when calculating an affordable monthly payment. Debt loads beyond the mortgage are a big factor in a borrower's ability to keep up with payments, Schwartz said. "When you have unexpected medical expenses and a lot of credit card debt, you can have an affordable first lien, but still have someone who's in trouble," she said.

Mortgage Lending at 34-Year Low

The number of mortgages lent to house buyers fell to its lowest level in 2008 since 1974, the Council of Mortgage Lenders (CML) has said. There were just 516,000 mortgages granted to house buyers, down 49 per cent from the level seen in 2007. The squeeze on mortgage funds has seen widespread rationing by lenders, which meant that first-time buyers had to put down an average deposit of 22 per cent. There is little chance of mortgage lending reviving in 2009. The CML believes that lending is likely to fall even further this year. "The shortage of mortgage funding and reduction in the number of active lenders has reshaped the mortgage landscape in the space of a year," said Michael Coogan, the CML's director general. "This low level of transactions is insufficient for the functioning of an efficient market," he added.

From a mortgage perspective, 2008 was a massacre—the entire market is barely recognisable from what it was two years ago said Andrew Montlake, Cobalt Capital mortgage brokers. The slump in lending and sales has been directly responsible for the sudden collapse of house prices seen since the credit crunch started in the summer of 2007. In 2008 the number of loans to first-time buyers fell by 46 per cent to just 194,200, which was the lowest figure since the CML's records started in 1974. And mortgages granted to people moving house dropped by more than half to 322,200.

The Government has launched a number of initiatives to stimulate bank lending, which it is widely hoped will feed through into greater lending to home buyers. But the CML expects that in 2009 new lending will fall to a level where it will be outstripped by people repaying their mortgages. "Measures are now in place to seek to restore the flow of funding to the mortgage market, but this will take time to feed through," said Mr Coogan. "Further action may still be necessary to increase transactions, stabilise prices and restore confidence," he added.

Despite the Bank of England cutting the bank rate in recent months to just 1 per cent, the dramatically lower cost of repaying a mortgage has not led to a revival in buying and selling houses. Lenders have increased the level of deposits they demand from borrowers, choking off the supply of potential buyers. About two-thirds of all new mortgage deals currently require at least a 25 per cent down payment from the borrower. And the average 22 per cent deposit currently being put down by first-time buyers is the highest since the CML's records started back in 1974. Until the end of 2007 a 10 per cent deposit was the norm. Andrew Montlake, at mortgage brokers Cobalt Capital, said business was now dire. Peter Bolton King, chief executive of the National Association of Estate Agents (NAEA), said there was now a lot of pent up demand. "NAEA figures show that there is a huge demand for property from first-time buyers, who are increasingly visiting estate agents, registering their interest and searching for property," he said. "These figures demonstrate that they are being frustrated at the final hurdle because lenders are not making mortgages available."

Banking Minister Lord Myners has said banks were "foolish" to offer 100 per cent mortgages, after Gordon Brown called for "prudent and careful" lending. Lord Myners said costly lessons had been learned worldwide "about reckless, feckless, witless lending". The Financial Services Authority is to consider controls on loans over 100 per cent. Lord Myners said it was "generally recognised in the banking community" that 100 per cent mortgages had been "a foolish thing to do". "We need to create systems through enhanced governance, more accountability and appropriate regulatory intervention to ensure that excesses do not occur," he told BBC One's Politics

Show. The minister said there needed to be a return to "safe, secure, sober lending activities". "We have learned some very, very expensive lessons globally about reckless, feckless, witless lending by a small number of banks." Writing in *The Observer*, Gordon Brown said the Financial Services Authority would be considering controls on mortgages of more than 100 per cent of a home's value, and so-called high multiple mortgages offering loans of up to six times an applicant's salary. More caution in the mortgage market, he said, would reduce chances of a future property crash. The Prime Minister added: "We do want to see the reinvention of the traditional savings and mortgage bank in Britain, for loans to be made on prudent and careful terms, not just to people with large deposits, but to those on middle and modest incomes who wish to buy their home but who have not been able to save a huge deposit."

Liberal Democrat Treasury spokesman Vince Cable said the call for an end to 100 per cent home loans was "a very belated recognition of the new reality", and questioned whether there would be regulation on the issue. He added: "...the Liberal Democrats set out a proposal for Safestart mortgages as the new models for the industry, with 85 per cent mortgages and protection against negative equity."

Gordon Brown indicated that discussions were continuing with the banks on the possibility of the Government underwriting their so-called "toxic" assets to encourage them to resume lending. "In order to get lending going, we must continue to develop agreements that remove the uncertainty arising from banks being unsure of their losses in return for improved lending conditions for families and businesses," he wrote. "We want to ensure that the new banking system that emerges over the coming years meets all these requirements—and becomes the servant of our economy and not the master." However, he ruled out legislation to create a "rigid divide" between retail High Street banks, which offer standard deposit accounts and loans, and investment banks trading globally in complex financial instruments.

Retail Malls

Retail malls are facing financial problems as a result of high rentals and decline in demand. Large retailers like the Future Group, Reliance Retail, and Aditya Birla Retail are renegotiating to bring rentals down.

A correction in the real estate industry has been long overdue, and taking advantage of the situation, modern retailers have called a war on costs to tide over the slowdown. Most of the modern retailers either purchased or rented properties at the peak of the real estate market. This has seriously dented their ability to make profits from the retail business, especially at the time of an economic slowdown. Reliance Retail spokesperson stated: "We are actively renegotiating rentals across formats and hope that, on an average, this would bring down costs by 20 per cent to 30 per cent." According to Pranay Vakil, chairman of real estate services company Knight Frank: "The headroom for reducing rentals could be anywhere between 10-35 per cent. In exceptional cases, it could even go up to 40 per cent. The exact amount would depend on the location."

Aditya Birla Retail, which was expected to more than double its turnover from Rs. 500 crore last year to Rs. 1,200 crore in 2008-09 said that if a real estate owner did not bring down the rentals of a certain store, it would not hesitate to relocate. "We hope to garner a very sizeable amount from renegotiating rentals. We are hopeful there will be softening of rentals. If this does not happen, in certain cases we will move out if the rental to sales ratio is not good enough," said Thomas Varghese, CEO, Aditya Birla Retail.

There are nearly 660 stores under Aditya Birla Retail, of which has relocated or closed down some 50-odd stores since September 2008, due to various reasons, including the fact that these stores did not fully meet good retail principles—such as right location, right catchment area—or were weighed down by high rentals.

For leading retailer, the Future Group, total rentals account for 6 per cent of sales. It plans to bring this down by another percentage point. "Given that all the players are in the midst of renegotiating rentals, to tide over the current slowdown, we are also trying to bring it down, even though we are already on the lower side," said Kishore Biyani, CEO, Future Group.

Subhiksha Eyes Stake Sale

Retail chain Subhiksha ruled out declaring bankruptcy and said it may consider selling stake to raise funds as it struggles to arrange Rs. 300 crore to meet immediate operational requirements.

The company is currently undergoing a corporate debt restructuring (CDR) exercise with lenders reviewing its books. "No, not at all, as that (declaring bankruptcy) is not a solution. We have a viable business which is cash-starved and CDR will help us revive this," Managing Director of Subhiksha Trading Services, R. Subramanian said.

He said the company, which has a total debt of around Rs. 750 crore, may have to look to the equity route to raise money to find cash for preventing the company from stopping its operations. "If there is no money, we can't run operations but if there is no debt, we have to look at options like equity," Subramanian said. "As part of CDR, the banks would need to get a current balance sheet rather than a March 31, 2008 balance sheet and they also want to ensure that events of the kind that happened...do not recur," he added.

Top Five Officials Quit Subhiksha

Subhiksha Trading Services, the city-based retail chain, said five top executives have quit the firm. The exit of Subhiksha's Senior President Atul Joshi, and Sunil Kataria, Mrinal Roy, Ashu Phakey and V. Raviganesh, Presidents in-charge of various regions, dealt another blow to the retailer after the trouble started brewing at the company in the fourth quarter of 2008.

"We had the best management team in the country in retail. Given the difficult situation some have decided to move on for better opportunities. None of these people were from retail and we recruited from outside retail and we are sure that we would get similar high quality talent when we are ready to resume," R. Subramanian told *The Times of India*. "It is a matter of great satisfaction that they continued to fight for the company for over three-four months despite the pain around them including non receipt of their own salaries," he said. Interestingly, it were these same people who had taken forward the Subhiksha growth story when the retail chain was looking at expanding across the country.

The Employees Provident Fund Office (EPFO) maintained that Subhiksha had to pay up arrears to the tune of Rs. 5 crore, even as Subramanian denied, saying that the dues were much lower. "Without going into specifics we can only say that the figures stated to you are grossly wrong and further we are co-operating with the authorities in every manner possible," he said.

Upon completion of hearing, the Subhiksha management was to be given 15 days to remit the dues, failing which properties of promoters could get attached, sources said.

Reliance Retail Goes for Revamp

Mukesh Ambani's Reliance Retail is in a consolidation mode. The company has kicked off an exercise to rationalise its existing set-up comprising 4.2 million square feet of retail space, with a focus on unlocking efficiencies.

The exercise, aimed at countering slowdown, involves relocating some stores, shutting down inefficient ones, and relaunching some others under different formats. The company operates under various formats under brands like Super, Mart, Wellness and Delite, along with exclusive formats for jewellery, footwear, vision, apparel, electronics, digital, among others. Reliance Retail has 4.2 million square feet of retail space. A spokesperson said: "We have launched a dozen different store formats. We saw...slowdown coming a little ahead of time and we had given ourselves a year to get to scale."

As part of the restructuring initiative, the firm could see up to 40-odd stores shutting down for various reasons. Given the perspective of Reliance's overall network of 940-odd stores, which include around 750 value stores, this forms a minuscule part. In fact, in 2008 alone, Reliance Retail opened some 400 stores.

Explaining the rationale behind closure of some stores, the official said, "In some cases, we are finding that some of our stores need to be larger to offer our customers a wider range of products and services. In some cases, another of our formats is a better choice for a given location, and in yet other cases, we can co-locate another format with some existing stores. All these findings do lead to relocation and resizing decisions for some of our store locations." Other reasons include the store not meeting certain criteria, or not being part of operational discipline.

New FDI Norms to Help Retail

The new guidelines on FDI will allow foreign investment in sectors like multi-brand retail where sectoral cap is zero per cent. This can be achieved through a multi-layer structure where an investing company "owned and controlled" by Indians invests in parent company. Consider the example of an investing company where 51 per cent equity is owned by Indians and the rest 49 per cent is owned by foreign entities. Under the new guidelines any investment made by this company in another company will be taken as Indian investment. Therefore, an investment by this company in a retail company will not be considered as FDI. This allows foreign companies to invest in multi-brand retail through indirect route. The new FDI guidelines say that foreign investment through an investing company "owned and controlled" by Indians would not be considered for calculation of indirect foreign investment. "This would help in attracting foreign investment in all the sectors," said Kamal Nath, Union Minister of Commerce. He also said that in case of transfer of ownership and control Government permission has now become mandatory.

Credit Crunch

Global economic slowdown has led to a severe credit crunch. As bad debts became rampant, many banks and lending institutions are in panic. A significant number of banks in the US had over-leveraged, i.e. they had borrowed beyond what was reasonable. They sought to decrease the leverage ratios by either getting rid of bad loans or raising more money. Paralysed by toxic assets, and looking to hard cash, banks have stopped lending. It no longer mattered to them the borrower was a healthy business or an individual with good credit history. Since there is already a slowdown, and interest rates have not been reduced to the extent needed to revive the economy, particularly in countries like India, there is a credit crunch. As the global credit crisis and economic slowdown takes hold, people are spending less money—aggravating the situation further.

The Mathematics of Credit Crunch

Paul Wilmott a lecturer in financial mathematics thinks that the misuse of qualitative finance has played a part in creating the current banking crisis.

In November 2007, *More or Less* asked whether the financial mathematicians known as "quants"—short for quantitative analysts—were to blame for what was then being termed "the credit squeeze". Banks and hedge funds rely on highly-paid mathematicians and economists—"quants"—to evaluate risk. So why did they not they see the credit crunch coming? Paul Wilmott says some mathematicians have a tendency to get fixated on the numbers, failing to think about the big picture.

According to him an additional cause of the credit crunch is that people simply got their sums wrong. He told *More or Less* these errors might have contributed to the mispricing of financial derivatives, and thus to the travails of the banks, the credit crunch, and the economic downturn. Many quants were paid bonuses if the banks made money. And yet, collectively, their calculations bankrupted some banks and nearly bankrupted many more. But the question is: Why did quants, paid for performance, all make the same mistake at the same time?

In October 2007, Tim Harford got a glimpse into the world of the quants. The most successful of these talented mathematicians will come up with mathematical formulae that make them and their bank or hedge fund employers millions of pounds per year. They are highly secretive about their work, not wanting others to know the details of their systems.

Companies Pledge Shares to Raise Funds

The Tata group has pledged a sizeable portion of its equity stake in Tata Steel, Tata Power and Tata Teleservices (Maharashtra) to raise funds. The value of the shares pledged from the three companies works out to Rs. 6,662 crore.

The main shareholder in each of these three companies is Tata Sons, the group's primary holding company. Over 60 per cent of Tata Sons is owned by Tata charitable trusts.

In Tata Steel, Tata Sons has pledged 9.64 crore shares, representing a 13.19 per cent stake, worth Rs. 1,924 crore. The Tatas own a 34 per cent stake in the steel company, which saw a steep decline in its profits in the third quarter of 2008-09 due to lower demand from construction, automobile and consumer durable firms.

Another group company, Tata Investment Corporation, has pledged 25 lakh shares of Tata Steel (0.34 per cent) towards security for its zero coupon convertible bonds. According to Tata Steel, the 25 lakh pledged shares cannot be invoked as no payment obligations arise from the bond issue. The total value of the pledged shares of Tata Steel stands at Rs. 1,974 crore. Tata Steel, along with Europe's second largest steelmaker Corus in its portfolio, is the largest contributor to Tata group's revenues of $62.5 billion in 2007-08.

Of the Tata group's 30 listed firms, only three have disclosed the extent of the promoters' equity being pledged for raising funds. Other Tata companies like Tata Consultancy Services and Indian Hotels Company said they are not aware if the promoters have pledged their shares, while Tata Communications, Tata Motors and Tata Chemicals said that the owners have not pledged any shares.

Tata Sons has also pledged half the 6.67 crore of Tata Power shares held by it. The 3.23 crore pledged shares of Tata Power, representing 14.59 per cent of the company's paid-up equity capital, are valued at Rs. 2,515 crore. Tatas own 33 per cent in Tata Power. The group, with interests in seven sectors from salt to software to telecom to tea, is finding it difficult to raise capital against the backdrop of an economic slowdown and financial crisis. Analysts say the group's acquisition of Jaguar Land Rover, Corus and General Chemicals, could tell on its financial health in the long run, with all the three overseas companies reporting lower sales on account of a substantial fall in consumer demand. In Tata Teleservices (Maharashtra), the promoters Tata Teleservices, Tata Power and Tata Sons—have pledged 49.7 per cent of their total 66 per cent stake in the telecom firm. The pledged lot is valued at Rs. 2,173 crore.

Real Estate Sector

The National Association of Realtors reported that home prices dropped a record 12.4 per cent in the final quarter of 2008—the biggest decline in 30 years. Home prices fell 12.4 per cent during the fourth quarter of 2008, the largest year-on-year decline since the National Association of Realtors began keeping comprehensive records in 1979. The median price for a US home sold during the fourth quarter of 2008 fell to $180,100, down from $205,700 during the last quarter of 2007. Prices fell by a record 9.5 per cent in 2008, to $197,100, compared to $217,900 in 2007. In comparison, median home prices dipped a mere 1.6 per cent between 2006 and 2007. Distressed properties, the foreclosures and short sales that have flooded the market, accounted for 45 per cent of all deals. That has driven sales volume up in Nevada, California and other states hit hard by foreclosures, but these heavily discounted homes have also pushed median prices down. "People are responding to discounted prices and are slowly absorbing the excess inventory," said NAR President Charles McMillan. "Buyers clearly see value in today's pricing." Pain is widespread. The vast majority of metropolitan areas—134 out of 153—recorded price declines compared with the last quarter of 2007. "Home markets are weak just about everywhere," said Pat Newport, an analyst with HIS Global Insight, "but in a few states, distressed sales are driving transactions." In Cape

Coral-Fort Myers, Florida, which has the third highest rate of foreclosure filings in the nation, prices fell a devastating 50.8 per cent for the year, to $110,900 from $225,300. That was the most precipitous plunge for any metro area. In Saginaw, Michigan, prices fell 41.4 per cent. In Riverside-San Bernardino, California, prices dropped 40.8 per cent and in San Jose, California, prices declined 37.7 per cent. The Beaumont-Port Arthur area of Texas bucked the national trend. Its median home price jumped 16.7 per cent to $132,600—the highest increase in the nation. Other winners included Bloomington, Illinois, up 9.6 per cent; Dover, Delaware, up 6.5 per cent; and Bismarck, Nevada, up 6 per cent. The high number of distressed sales pushed prices down for several reasons, according to Lawrence Yun, chief economist for NAR. For one thing, many sales were in low- and moderate-income housing developments where buyers during the boom years financed their purchases using subprime mortgages. In higher-end areas, fewer exotic mortgages were used. "Take Orange County, California," said Yun. "It's the lower priced areas there where homes are selling. The high priced areas along the coast are not." As a result, the median home sales price for the area skews lower. And the high number of foreclosures means banks are willing to slash prices deeply to move inventory. Many of the properties they've obtained through repossessions now sit vacant, soaking up lender money for maintenance, heating, property taxes and insurance. The banks willingly take lower prices to end those cash outlays, which brings down prices even for normal sellers. Then there's also what Yun calls a "frozen" jumbo-mortgage lending market, which has also slowed sales of higher-priced homes and reduced median prices. The good news is that bargain prices are bringing many new buyers into the market. "Many are first-time homebuyers who were priced out of the market during the boom," Yun said.

NAR hoped that a piece of the stimulus bill before Congress will build on that momentum and provide an extra incentive for buyers. "Assuming housing provisions in the economic stimulus package are quickly enacted and provide enough encouragement for homebuyers, we could see a quick lift in home sales for the critical spring home-buying season," said Yun. It appeared that the final iteration of the homebuyer's tax credit, which had very different provisions in the House and Senate versions of the stimulus package, was shaping up to be closer to the House bill, according to Yun. That means a credit of $7,500, perhaps $8,000, or 10 per cent of home price for first-time homebuyers. This windfall will not have to be repaid by homebuyers and can be taken off 2008 taxes. NAR estimates that could draw in an additional half-million buyers during 2009 year. "It could help reduce the high inventory of homes for sale and get housing markets moving again. It's hard to get the economy back to growth until that happened," said Yun.

The prices of median homes in the metro areas of USA in the fourth quarter of 2008 and their percentage decrease from the prices in the corresponding quarter of the previous year are given in Table 3 below.

Table 3: Median Home Prices 4th Quarter 2008

Metro Area	State	Median home price 4th Quarter in US$	Per cent change from 4th Quarter 2007
Akron	OH	86,100	21.1
Albany-Schenectady-Troy	NY	193,100	3.6
Albuquerque	NM	183,700	6.2
Allentown-Bethlehem-Easton	PA-NJ	238,000	3.4
Amarillo	TX	122,600	2.0
Anaheim-Santa Ana	CA	464,800	–30.8
Appleton	WI	127,600	–2.5
Atlanta-Sandy Springs-Marietta	GA	129,200	–21.4
Atlantic City	NJ	229,100	–17.8
Austin-Round Rock	TX	184,800	–0.1
Baltimore-Towson	MD	260,100	–5.5
Barnstable Town	MA	325,300	–14.9
Baton Rouge	LA	156,400	–7.8
Beaumont-Port Arthur	TX	132,600	16.7
Binghamton	NY	105,800	–3.7
Birmingham-Hoover	AL	135,400	–13.3
Bismarck	ND	164,300	6.0
Bloomington-Normal	IL	159,300	9.6
Boise City-Nampa	ID	168,800	–14.7
Boston-Cambridge-Quincy	MA-NH**	335,700	–11.8
Boulder	CO	324,400	–12.6
Bridgeport-Stamford-Norwalk	CT	379,700	–17.5
Buffalo-Niagara Falls	NY	106,200	0.8
Canton-Massillon	OH	80,400	–18.0
Cape Coral-Fort Myers	FL	110,900	–50.8

Cedar Rapids	IA	136,900	1.5
Champaign-Urbana	IL	132,000	–8.1
Charleston	WV	124,800	1.5
Charleston-North Charleston	SC	193,800	–5.2
Charlotte-Gastonia-Concord	NC-SC	186,300	–9.0
Chattanooga	TN-GA	123,800	1.8
Chicago-Naperville-Joliet	IL	217,800	–16.6
Cincinnati-Middletown	OH-KY-IN	116,000	–12.4
Cleveland-Elyria-Mentor	OH	88,300	–25.5
Colordo Springs	CO	187,000	–11.2
Columbia	MO	138,100	–4.2
Columbia	SC	139,200	–3.9
Columbus	OH	126,500	–7.8
Corpus Christi	TX	134,000	–2.8
Cumberland	MD-WV	96,900	–16.9
Dallas-Fort Worth-Arlington	TX	138,000	–4.8
Danville	IL	N/A	N/A
Davenport-Moline-Rock Island	IA-IL	98,400	–3.6
Dayton	OH	87,800	–17.6
Decatur	IL	79,300	5.9
Deltona-Daytona Beach-Ormond Beach	FL	143,600	–20.7
Denver-Aurora	CO	200,800	–12.7
Des Moines	IA	149,700	–1.9
Detroit-Warren-Livonia	MI	N/A	N/A
Dover	DE	212,500	6.5
Durham	NC	165,600	–7.0
El Paso	TX	140,700	5.3
Elmira	NY	80,900	–0.4
Erie	PA	95,200	–3.4
Eugene-Springfield	OR	212,800	–10.4
Fargo	ND-MN	140,100	–1.1
Farmington	NM	185,000	–0.8
Florence	SC	119,100	1.9
Ft. Wayne	IN	88,600	–2.5
Gainesville	FL	174,000	–11.5
Gary-Hammond	IN	115,100	–7.6
Glens Falls	NY	147,600	–9.9
Grand Rapids	MI	80,500	–35.2
Green Bay	WI	146,600	–1.5
Greensboro-High Point	NC	135,400	–10.2
Greenville	SC	146,900	–5.5
Gulfport-Biloxi	MS	129,500	–13.9
Hagerstown-Martinsburg	MD-WV	171,400	–10.8
Hartford-West Hartford-East Hartford	CT	233,700	–9.4
Honolulu	HI	610,000	–2.4
Houston-Baytown-Sugar Land	TX	142,100	–5.5
Indianapolis	IN	100,200	–12.1
Jackson	MS	126,600	4.7
Jacksonville	FL	160,700	–9.5
Kalamazoo-Portage	MI	N/A	N/A
Kankakee-Bradley	IL	125,600	1.0
Kansas City	MO-KS	131,000	–11.6
Kennewick-Richland-Pasco	WA	165,900	–3.8
Kingston	NY	224,000	–9.0
Knoxville	TN	141,700	–8.6
Lansing-E.Lansing	MI	80,000	–27.0
Las Vegas-Paradise	NV	181,700	–33.6
Lexington-Fayette	KY	138,200	–3.3
Lincoln	NE	133,100	–3.6
Little Rock-N. Little Rock	AR	125,200	–1.8

Los Angeles-Long Beach-Santa Ana	CA	354,300	–31.4
Louisville	KY-IN	124,000	–6.8
Madison	WI	227,000	–0.003
Manchester-Nashua	NH	238,600	N/A
Memphis	TN-MS-AR	100,200	–19.4
Miami-Fort Lauderdale-Miami Beach	FL	234,200	–32.3
Milwaukee-Waukesha-West Allis	WI	194,900	–11.2
Minneapolis-St. Paul-Bloomington	MN-WI	188,600	–13.2
Mobile	AL	125,000	–9.0
Montgomery	AL	126,300	–11.9
NY: Edison	NJ	343,600	–7.2
NY: Nassau-Suffolk	NY	381,300	–17.4
NY: Newark-Union	NJ-PA	373,600	–14.3
Nashville-Davidson--Murfreesboro	TN	N/A	N/A
New Haven-Milford	CT	240,400	–10.6
New Orleans-Metairie-Kenner	LA	154,900	–2.1
New York-Northern New Jersey-Long Island	NY-NJ-PA	390,400	–14.6
New York-Wayne-White Plains	NY-NJ	458,600	–11.7
Norwich-New London	CT	223,100	–11.6
Ocala	FL	121,700	–21.5
Oklahoma City	OK	124,200	–7.9
Omaha	NE-IA	129,700	–4.4
Orlando	FL	175,200	–27.1
Palm Bay-Melbourne-Titusville	FL	123,600	–18.3
Pensacola-Ferry Pass-Brent	FL	151,700	–3.0
Peoria	IL	117,200	–1.1
Philadelphia-Camden-Wilmington	PA-NJ-DE-MD	212,500	-6.3
Phoenix-Mesa-Scottsdale	AZ	155,900	-35.5
Pittsburgh	PA	109,100	–6.7
Pittsfield	MA	206,000	1.7
Portland-South Portland-Biddeford	ME	214,500	–11.4
Portland-Vancouver-Beaverton	OR-WA	264,500	–9.0
Providence-New Bedford-Fall River	RI-MA	224,500	–17.8
Raleigh-Cary	NC	230,900	–2.0
Reading	PA	155,100	1.0
Reno-Sparks	NV	231,200	–23.3
Richmond	VA	199,400	–11.7
Riverside-San Bernardino-Ontario	CA	201,300	–40.8
Rochester	NY	112,500	–6.9
Rockford	IL	111,500	–1.5
Sacramento--Arden-Arcade--Roseville	CA	187,900	–36.9
Saginaw-Saginaw Township North	MI	43,900	–41.4
Saint Louis	MO-IL	113,700	–14.8
Salem	OR	198,000	–14.4
Salt Lake City	UT	225,400	–1.6
San Antonio	TX	143,400	–5.5
San Diego-Carlsbad-San Marcos	CA	332,800	–36.4
San Francisco-Oakland-Fremont	CA	487,100	–37.4
San Jose-Sunnyvale-Santa Clara	CA	525,000	–37.7
Sarasota-Bradenton-Venice	FL	178,100	–35.0
Seattle-Tacoma-Bellevue	WA	325,900	–13.7
Shreveport-Bossier City	LA	139,200	2.8
Sioux Falls	SD	142,400	Unch
South Bend-Mishawaka	IN	80,800	–6.4
Spartanburg	SC	120,800	–0.8
Spokane	WA	185,900	–4.2
Springfield	IL	96,700	–11.0
Springfield	MA	186,400	–9.7
Springfield	MO	117,100	–3.0
Syracuse	NY	114,100	–9.7

Tallahassee	FL	150,100	–17.0
Tampa-St.Petersburg-Clearwater	FL	151,500	–24.9
Toledo	OH	75,600	–27.3
Topeka	KS	104,800	–6.7
Trenton-Ewing	NJ	247,800	–19.2
Tucson	AZ	185,900	–21.2
Tulsa	OK	N/A	N/A
Virginia Beach-Norfolk-Newport News	VA-NC	222,000	–5.9
Washington-Arlington-Alexandria	DC-VA-MD-WV	295,100	–26.2
Waterloo/Cedar Falls	IA	105,200	–8.8
Wichita	KS	118,200	3.9
Worcester	MA	217,000	–16.2
Yakima	WA	145,900	–14.4
Youngstown-Warren-Boardman	OH-PA	61,700	–0.15
US		180,100	–12.4
NE		248,800	–4.7
MW		139,500	–10.6
SO		158,300	–7.5
WE		243,200	–25.1

Source: http://news.bbc.co.uk/2/hi/business/7815994.stm

Home Loans Becoming More Difficult

Despite the fact that interest rates are coming down, people are still finding it difficult to take a home loan. The reason is that the banks now insist that borrowers need to contribute 20-30 per cent of the value of the property upfront, instead of 10-15 per cent earlier. As the finance proportion of the banks has come down from 85-90 per cent of the property value to 70-80 per cent, the borrowers are finding it difficult to go for a home loan.

The State Bank of India, which has brought down its home loan rate to 8 per cent, lends only 80 per cent of the value of house if the requirement is between Rs. 20 lakh and Rs. 75 lakh. If the loan is more than Rs. 75 lakh, the bank lends only 75 per cent of the amount. Punjab National Bank also lends 75 per cent of the loan for a property of above Rs. 20 lakh. Other PSU banks like Union Bank and UCO Bank also lend only up to 80 per cent of the value of the house. Private sector banks like ICICI Bank ask for 20-30 per cent buyer's contribution while giving a home loan.

The average price of a three-bed room apartment in metros like Mumbai, Delhi/NCR and Bangalore is around Rs. 40 lakh. In other big cities like Kolkata, Chennai and Pune, it is around Rs. 30 lakh. So, the buyer's contribution to buy a house of Rs. 40 lakh has increased to Rs. 8-10 lakh, from Rs. 4-5 lakh earlier. For a young buyer, i.e. in the age group of 30-35 years, it acts as a big deterrent.

However, bankers are not really bothered. UCO Bank Executive Director T.M. Bhasin said as real estate price is declining, banks have increased the buyer's contribution so that the market value of the property should not fall below the loan amount during the course of repayment. He said if the bank lends 85 per cent of the transaction and the market value of the house falls by 20 per cent within six months, the loan amount will become more than the value of the property taken as security. In that scenario, the borrower can decide to walk off surrendering the house to the bank, and saying recover the money by selling the property. To avoid this, the bank has increased the buyer's contribution. And this factor has played a big role in the current US crisis. The banks have lent up to 90 per cent of the value of the house. But as the market price fell below the outstanding loan amount, many borrowers decided to surrender the house to banks, which are finding it difficult to sell them to recover the money.

Banks have also made conditions related to a loan tougher. Earlier, they used to allow an EMI of up to 50 per cent of monthly income of the borrower. Now, this has been brought down to 40 per cent, making life of the borrower difficult.

Slackening Infrastructure Growth

India's infrastructure output grew by a lower 1.4 per cent in January 2009 from a year earlier, mirroring the slowdown in the broader economy. Output of the six infrastructure sectors—crude oil, refinery products, steel, cement, coal and electricity—accounts for 26.68 per cent of the country's industrial output. It grew by 3.6 per cent in January 2008, the official data released showed.

In February and March 2009, there has been a raft of weaker-than-expected economic data, including the sharp slowdown in real GDP growth in the third quarter to 5.3 per cent and contraction in export earnings for the four consecutive months. According to the RBI, the impact of the global downturn on India "has turned out to be deeper and wider than anticipated earlier."

The low growth in the infrastructure sectors was mainly due to lesser production of crude oil, which shrunk 8.1 per cent in the January 2009, against 0.2 per cent contraction in the same month of the previous year. Output of petroleum products also contracted 2.6 per cent in January 2009, as compared to 5.4 per cent increase in the year ago month. Cement production that increased 8.3 per cent as against 5.6 per cent in the same month of last year was the only silver lining.

In the April to January period of 2008-09, the core infrastructure index expanded 3.2 per cent over 5.7 per cent in the same period of the previous year. Experts expected the slowdown to continue for a few more months. "In our view, the sharp slowdown in India's economic growth will continue into the next few quarters," said Sonal Varma of Nomura Financial Advisory and Securities.

The Government had stated that the growth in infrastructure would lift the economy in these difficult times. Various projects of development kindled by high infrastructure growth would generate large employment and mitigate the effect of widespread layoffs resorted to by most companies as a cost-cutting measure in the present conditions of economic meltdown.

The declining growth in infrastructure output is a worrisome state of affairs. Various factors like lesser production of crude oil, rising prices of coal—which has decreased demand—have been attributed to this decline. But concerns have been raised that funding has not kept pace with plans for infrastructure development. Infrastructure planning underlies a fundamental premise that growth should occur where adequate facilities like buildings, transportation, power, etc. exist or are planned to exist. However, it has been felt that the public sector's ability to build infrastructure has diminished due to financial constraints, rising raw material costs and regulatory bottlenecks. The Government must therefore pay immediate attention to infrastructure development so that it may help put the economy back on track. India has a large and burgeoning private sector. It must be provided an atmosphere of actively participating in taking up large infrastructure projects.

Direct Tax Mop-up Short of Target by Rs. 1 Lakh Crore

The direct tax collections as on end of January 2009 are short by around Rs. 1 lakh crore of the target set for the current financial year, said Mr S.S.N. Moorthy, Chairman of Central Board of Direct Taxes.

The Income Tax department had targeted to collect Rs. 3,65,000 crore for the financial year 2008-09, which was revised upwards to Rs. 3,95,000 crore in September 2008, before the financial crisis broke out. The slowdown in the economy will make it tough to meet the target, said Mr P.V. Bhide, Revenue Secretary. However, the Government will mobilise all the resources at its disposal to meet the targets, Mr Moorthy said.

For the financial year 2007-08, the total direct tax collected stood at Rs. 3,14,668 crore. Of this, Mumbai contributed Rs. 1,13,991 crore, around one-third of total direct tax collections. In the financial year 2008-09, the total direct tax collections were estimated to be over Rs. 2,50,000 crore as on end of January 2009, a senior Income Tax official said.

In 2007-08 the total direct tax collections stood at Rs. 2,28,745 crore as on February 15. In 2008-09, Mumbai had contributed Rs. 87,941 crore to the direct tax kitty, upto January 2009. The Government hoped to collect around Rs. 1,50,000 crore from the financial capital by the end of the financial year.

A senior Income Tax official said that since around 30 per cent of the collections come in the month of March, the shortfall would be more or less met. The direct tax collections have been growing at around 12 per cent, said Mr Moorthy. "By the end of the year, we expect the collections to grow at around 20 per cent," he said. "The advance tax collections have seen a slowing down in the December quarter," he added.

The revenue shortfall in direct tax is close to Rs. 1 lakh crore as on end of January 2009. With an all-India target of Rs. 3.95 lakh crore, CBDT still had to collect a lakh crore. That was mainly because advance tax collections of December 2008 were lower than expected. Mr Moorthy also said that in the third quarter of 2008-09 advance tax collections were low. In Mumbai, it was lower by over Rs. 4,000 crore as compared to the corresponding figure of last year.

However, both Moorthy and Bhide ruled out the possibility of targets being revised downwards. "Some amount of shortfall is expected due to the slowdown in the economy. But we have two months to make up a lot of distance and expect to reach a reasonable target," Moorthy said. Mumbai's target is Rs. 1.5 lakh crore, of which Rs. 87,941 crore have been collected till the end of January 2009.

JOB CUTS AND RISING UNEMPLOYMENT

Global economic slowdown has led to the shrinking of businesses, trade, markets, and hence, production. Several companies across various sectors are therefore effecting job cuts in large numbers. The unemployment situation is worsening in all parts of the world. The impact of current recession on job scenario in US, UK, France, China, Japan and India is studied below.

US Jobless Rate Increases to 8.1 Per cent

The US jobless rate jumped in February 2009 to 8.1 per cent, according to official figures from the Labor Department. The number of people out of work rose by 651,000 during the month. Both figures were bigger than expected. The number of job cuts in January 2009 was revised up to 655,000 while December 2008 losses were pushed up to 681,000. December's figure was the biggest job loss in a single month since October 1949. The unemployment rate was the highest since December 1983. Rising unemployment has meant greater demand for free meals.

President Obama said that the number of jobs lost so far in the recession was "astounding". Speaking in Ohio, he added: "I don't need to tell the people of this state what statistics like this mean," saying that he had signed his economic stimulus package in order to save jobs.

The extra 161,000 job losses added to December 2008 and January 2009 figures mean that almost two million jobs have been lost in these three months. A total of 12.5 million people are now unemployed in the US. "It just continues to show the grim state of the labour market, which suggests a deepening US recession," said Joe Manimbo, currency trader at Ruesch International in Washington.

There were further signs of companies cutting back on their spending with the news that the number of people who wanted to work full-time but were forced to work part-time for economic reasons rising 787,000 to 8.6 million. The average working week stood at 33.3 hours, matching the record low set in December 2008. Jobs were cut in most sectors, with only Government, education and health services adding staff.

In the manufacturing sector 168,000 jobs were cut in January 2009 while 104,000 jobs went in construction and 375,000 were cut in the service sector. "The payroll numbers are very weak. With the revisions, we've had significant job losses in the past four months," said Gary Thayer, senior economist at Wachovia Securities in St Louis. "Companies are reducing workers and output in order to bring inventories into line with weak sales." Among the companies that announced big job cuts in February 2009 were Goodyear, Estee Lauder, Macy's and General Motors.

January 2008's job losses were worse than the forecast of a loss of 540,000 jobs by economists surveyed by briefing.com. The rise in the unemployment rate was also worse than the 7.5 per cent rate economists expected. The unemployment rate in April 2009 was at its highest level since September 1992.

As bad as the unemployment rate was, it only tells part of the story for people struggling to find jobs. It has been reported that 2.6 million people have now been out of work for more than six months, the most long-term unemployed since 1983. And that number only counts those still looking for work. The so-called underemployment rate, which includes those who have stopped looking for work and people working only part-time that want full-time positions, climbed to 13.9 per cent from 13.5 per cent in December 2008. That is the highest rate for this measure since the Labor Department first started tracking it in 1994.

Some economists are worried that the labor market is poised to get worse still. "This has just begun," said Sung Won Sohn, economics professor at California State University-Channel Islands. He projects an unemployment rate rising above 9 per cent by the end of the year 2009, while the monthly job losses could soon top 800,000. "Hiring is falling off dramatically and layoffs are accelerating," he said. "The layoffs have become an almost popular thing to do for corporations. Many businesses are scared. They want to take precautionary steps."

January 2009 was a brutal month for layoffs, as major companies ranging from Microsoft (MSFT, Fortune 500), Boeing (BA, Fortune 500) and Caterpillar (CAT, Fortune 500) to Home Depot (HD, Fortune 500) and Starbucks (SBUX, Fortune 500) all announced substantial job cuts.

Announced layoffs so far in 2008 have already topped 300,000. In addition, payroll services firm ADP estimates that small- and mid-sized businesses trimmed 430,000 jobs in January. "The breadth of job losses now surpasses the prior two recessions," said John Silvia, chief economist for Wachovia. The report showed the already battered manufacturing sector shedding 207,000 jobs, while the construction industry cut 111,000 jobs.

But it is not just the goods-producing sector that is losing jobs. The services sector, which now provides more than two-thirds of the nation's employment base, also reported widespread losses. Business and professional services, the sector that includes lawyers, accountants and tech services, lost 121,000 jobs. Retailers cut 45,000 workers, while the finance sector trimmed 42,000 workers and the leisure and hospitality sector lost 28,000. The number of temporary workers, viewed as another indicator of business and labor market strength overall, fell by 76,000. Among the only sectors posting narrow gains in jobs were education, health services, and the Government.

The White House released a statement saying the January 2009 report was proof that quick approval of the stimulus bill was needed. "These numbers, and the very real suffering of American workers they represent, reinforce the need for bold fiscal action," said Christina Romer, the chair of the President's council of economic advisers. "If we fail to act, we are likely to lose millions more jobs and the unemployment rate could reach double digits." Brian Bethune, chief US financial economist for research firm Global Insight, said how quickly the stimulus plan is passed, and how effective it is in jump-starting the economy, will determine whether the recent job losses are the peak, or if they continue to climb. He argues that stimulus needs to be for programs that get money into the economy as quickly as possible. "Business confidence is extremely weak right now," he said. "They've taken a show-me-the-money attitude. What you need to stop more job losses is a series of very effective policies. That's the only thing that will help here," he added.

Wall Street Slumps as US Cuts 100,000 Jobs in a Week

Pfizer, the leading drugmaker in terms of annual pharma sales, and Caterpillar, a heavy equipment manufacturer, each said they would cut 20,000 jobs. These are the biggest reported eliminations among US-based companies. The Chicago-based airplane manufacturer said 10,000 workers, including 4,500 previously announced reductions, would lose their jobs. The company blamed this on dwindling demand for its aircraft.

Chico's, a retailer of women's clothing said that it was cutting 180 positions. The retail industry has been hard-hit in recent months by a slowdown in consumer spending, partly because so many people have lost their jobs.

The newspaper publisher A.H. Belo has said it was cutting 500 jobs. Chief executive Robert Decherd, in a letter to colleagues, blamed the "rapid deterioration in the US economy." The US economy lost 2.6 million jobs in 2008, according to Government reports. This includes 21,137 mass layoffs, a seven-year high. In a mass layoff, 50 or more workers are laid off at a time.

Shoe Shop Chain Cuts 2,500 Jobs

The administrators of Stylo, which owns the Barratts and PriceLess chains of shoe shops, is closing 220 stores with the loss of 2,500 jobs. The remaining 160 stores and 165 concession outlets have been sold to the old management, saving 3,000 jobs. The management team of the Bradford-based firm will still be led by chairman Michael Ziff.

Barratt and PriceLess were put into administration on 26 January and the parent company followed on 17 February. "Given the difficult trading environment, we are pleased to have achieved a deal which will save 160 Stylo stores and 165 concession outlets across UK and Ireland, thereby safeguarding 3,000 jobs," said Neville Kahn, one of the administrators from Deloitte. "Due to difficult short-term financial difficulties and the long-term sector outlook, however, the store portfolio was deemed to be too large, and unable to generate sufficient profits to cover its cost base. As a result, the remaining 220 stores will be closed imminently, with the regrettable loss of 2,500 jobs," Kahn said.

Anglo American to Cut 9,000 Jobs

Mining companies are cutting jobs and production worldwide mining giant Anglo American has said it is to cut an additional 9,000 jobs as the global economic downturn hits demand for raw materials. The losses come on top of the 10,000 job cuts that Anglo's South African unit, Anglo Platinum, had already announced earlier. The job cuts follow similar moves at rivals Rio Tinto and BHP Billiton.

Anglo also announced a 3 per cent fall in 2008 pre-tax profit to $8.57 billion (£6 billion) and warned that 2009 would be tough. A spokesman said the job cuts would be across the group's operations, which are mainly in South Africa, South America and Australia. A boom in the price of metals and other commodities, sustained by China's once insatiable demand for raw materials, has to come to end.

Cynthia Carroll, Anglo's chief executive, said that the effects of the economic downturn "were difficult to overstate". "The world economy faces an unprecedented level of uncertainty," she said. "The outlook remains poor in the near term, with expectations for continuing volatility and weakness in commodity prices." She added that the board had decided to halt dividend payouts to shareholders to conserve cash. The credit crunch has made financing harder to obtain. Both prices and demand for nickel, platinum, iron ore and coking coal, used in steel production, had declined significantly, the company said.

Anglo American's downbeat assessment of the industry's prospects hurt the share prices of other mining firms. Rio Tinto shares ended 10 per cent down, while Xstrata fell 11 per cent. Anglo American shares ended 17 per cent lower at 1027 pence.

General Motors Plans to Cut 10k Jobs

General Motors is planning to slash another 10,000 salaried jobs during 2009, saying the cuts are unavoidable with a Government restructuring deadline looming and downturn in sales. GM will reduce its total number of white-collar workers by 14 per cent to 63,000. About 3,400, or 12 per cent, of GM's 29,500 salaried US jobs will be eliminated. Most of the company's remaining salaried employees will have their pay cut.

In its plan to Congress submitted towards the end of 2008, GM said it would have to reduce both salaried and hourly positions so that the company could become viable for the long term. The company said it plans to reduce its total US work force from 96,537 people in 2008 to between 65,000 and 75,000 in 2012, but it did not specify how many of the surviving jobs would be salaried or hourly.

General Motors is in talks to take back large portions of Delphi, the parts supplier spun off by the automaker a decade ago, the *Wall Street Journal* said, citing people involved in the negotiations. The discussions are part of GM's strategy to line up additional bailout funds from the US Government, which has already committed $13.4 billion to the car company, the paper said. GM is also expected to pursue the closure of more auto assembly plants beyond the nine shutdowns it has already announced, the paper said, citing people familiar with the matter.

GM has taken more than $11 billion in charges for Delphi's reorganization. GM agreed when it spun Delphi off in 1999 to assume pension and healthcare obligations for thousands of union workers should the supplier be unable to do so. Delphi has been trying to complete a revised reorganization plan since investors led by Appaloosa Management backed out of a $2.55 billion equity plan to support its re-emergence, in April 2008.

Call Centres in India

United Airlines confirmed that it was closing its call centre in India and transferring 165 jobs to the United States, which is reeling from layoffs amid recession. The move came about a month after UAL Corp, parent of the third biggest North American carrier, said it was cutting 1,000 more jobs, pushing the total to 9,000 by the end of year 2008 to help stem losses.

The jobs in India will be transferred to call centres in Chicago and Honolulu, Hawaii, and filled by workers who now handle reservations, the Chicago-based airline said.

Beginning in April 2009, it said the workers will add customer-relations duties, which involve issues or complaints after travel, said Robin Urbanski, airline spokeswoman. "More sophisticated conversations with our guests are much better-suited for us to handle instead of a third-party partner," Urbanski said. United Airlines shipped the call centre positions to India about three years ago as part of a trend by US companies to move such functions overseas to save costs.

Rise in Unemployment in UK

UK unemployment rose to 1.97 million between October and December 2008, the highest level since 1997, figures showed. The jobless number climbed 146,000 for the three-month period, data from the Office for National Statistics showed. For January 2009, the number of those getting jobseeker's allowance added 73,800 to reach 1.23 million.

The unemployment rate hit 6.3 per cent, the highest since 1998. The Bank of England had recently warned of a deep recession and rising unemployment in 2009.

Many analysts had forecast that unemployment could reach two million for the three-month period ending December 2008—which would have been the highest since 1997. But there are fears the situation will worsen further in the months ahead as the economy cools. Tony Dolphin, senior economist at the Institute for Public Policy Research said, "Unfortunately it seems inevitable that unemployment will exceed 3 million during 2009."

Peter Mooney, head of consultancy with Employment Law Advisory Services, said, "From early in December, 2008, the number of firms seeking our help in making redundancies simply exploded." As the recession bites, this strengthens still further the case for making a sharp reduction in the number of non-EU workers permitted to come to Britain. He added, "Things will certainly get worse before they get better. We would expect to see another significant increase in the number of people out of work in the figures published..., as many more firms were forced to cut staff early in the New Year." Young people between the age of 18 and 24 have been particularly hard hit, with the unemployment rate for the three-month period standing at 11.8 per cent. The number of those receiving jobseeker's allowance climbed for 12 consecutive months. At 1.23 million, it stood at the highest level since the summer of 1999.

Apprenticeships

Following the release of the data, David Kern, chief economist at the British Chambers of Commerce, commented: "Unemployment continues to rise in the face of a worsening recession. We know businesses do not want to lose key staff, but they are struggling with cash-flow." Mr Kern added that cutting business rates, freezing the national minimum wage and scrapping plans to increase National Insurance would help firms retain employees.

The companies, as well as NHS and local authority leaders, will agree to advertise all non-specialist vacancies through the Jobcentre Plus network and to start offering more apprenticeships. A local employment partnership scheme has been launched to get people back into work. Councillor Margaret Eaton, chairman of the Local Government Association, said: "The LGA has committed to working with local authorities to increase the number of council apprenticeships by 7,500 to ensure that people are given practical skills that will stand them in good stead for years to come."

Mounting Redundancies

BBC business correspondent Nils Blythe said figures on the wider measure of unemployment—which also included people not claiming benefits—only covered the three months up to December 2008, so did not include the most recent job losses. The total was expected to rise above two million once the latest redundancy programs were taken in official statistics.

The sector with the largest fall in jobs was finance and business services, which shed 72,000 positions. As employers sought to cut costs, the number of jobs available fell.

Vacancies for the three-month period fell to 504,000, down 76,000 from the period to October 2008. In the same period a year earlier, vacancies had been 684,000. A TUC study said that while unemployment in the UK was lower than the European average, it was now increasing twice as fast as the average across Europe. The UK's unemployment rate remained below the European average, which was 7.7 per cent. TUC General Secretary Brendan Barber said: "The UK began the global recession with a relatively strong jobs position, but our advantage is beginning to disappear as redundancies mount."

Swiss Bank UBS to Cut 8,700 Jobs

Switzerland's biggest bank, UBS, has said it will seek to cut costs by shedding 8,700 jobs by next year. The news came as the bank announced it had lost about 2 billion Swiss francs ($1.75 billion; £1.2 billion) in the first three months of 2009.

UBS has been one of the biggest banks hit by exposure to the subprime loans crisis in the US and ensuing turmoil. "Unfortunately I am not able, as yet, to offer you any good news," said chief executive Oswald Gruebel. UBS has recently replaced both its chairman and chief executive. The Swiss President told the BBC that the former UBS management had taken too many risks, but that he was confident the new team would restore the bank's reputation as the backbone of Swiss financing.

Gruebel painted a bleak picture of the short-term outlook for the bank to the assembled shareholders. "I am forced to present you with another round of unsatisfactory performance figures and to announce further drastic measures," he told nearly 5,000 UBS investors attending the bank's annual shareholder meeting. "Our outlook remains cautious and we face many uncertainties. We have to prepare ourselves for this, even though we are entitled to be very optimistic about the longer-term prospects for our bank," he said. The bank, which is also being investigated by the US authorities over alleged fraud and tax evasion involving US citizens, said major job cuts were unfortunately unavoidable. The bank, which employed 76,200 people at the end of March, expects to reduce the number of its employees to about 67,500 in 2010.

Forecasters See Higher Unemployment in 2009

The current recession is projected to worsen during 2009. America stands to lose a sizable chunk of economic activity in 2009 as consumers at home and abroad retrench in the face of persistent economic troubles. And the US unemployment rate—now at 7.6 per cent, the highest in more than 16 years—is expected hit a peak of 9 per cent during 2009. That gloomy outlook came from leading forecasters in the latest survey by the National Association for Business Economics (NABE) released in February 2009. The new estimates are roughly in line with other recent projections, including those released by the Federal Reserve. "The steady drumbeat of weak economic and financial market data have made business economists decidedly more pessimistic on the economic outlook for the next several quarters," said NABE President Chris Varvares, head of Macroeconomic Advisers.

Varvares and his fellow forecasters now expect the economy to shrink by 1.9 per cent during 2009, a much deeper contraction than the 0.2 per cent dip projected in the fall. If the new forecast is correct, it would mark the first time since 1991 the economy actually contracted over a full year and would be the worst showing since 1982, when the country had suffered through a severe recession. Vanishing jobs, rising foreclosures and tanking home values have forced American consumers to cut back, which in turn has caused businesses to lay off workers and slash costs in other ways, feeding a vicious downward cycle for the economy.

"As the news on the economy has darkened, so too, have the forecasts," said Ken Mayland, President of ClearView Economics. "We are suffering a period of maximum stress on the economy." The economy is expected to remain feeble this year—even with new efforts by the administration and Congress to provide relief. After the $787 billion recovery package of increased Government spending and tax cuts was signed into law, the President unveiled a $75 billion plan to stem home foreclosures and Treasury Secretary Timothy Geithner said as much as $2 trillion could be plowed into the financial system to jumpstart lending. In terms of lost economic activity in 2009, the biggest hit will come in the first six months, the forecasters warned.

NABE forecasters predicted that when all is said and done the recession will have caused GDP to decline 2.8 per cent. That would be "slightly less than the 3.1 per cent during the early '70s," according to the survey of 47 forecasters taken between January 29 and February 12, 2009. Even in the best-case scenario, with the recession ending sometime in the second half of 2009, employment conditions will be tough. Some of the forecasters said the nation's unemployment rate could rise as high as 9 per cent for all of 2009 and may hit 10 per cent next year. In 2008, the jobless rate averaged 5.8 per cent, the highest since 2003. The survey's median forecast—or middle point—called for the unemployment rate to rise to 8.4 per cent in 2009 and 8.8 per cent in 2010. Companies touching every part of the economy have already announced thousands of layoffs. Goodyear Tire & Rubber Co. said it will cut nearly 5,000 jobs, or almost 7 per cent of its work force, during 2009, following the elimination of about 4,000 jobs in the second half of 2008. General Motors Corp. and Chrysler, which are asking the Government for billions more in aid to remain viable, announced plans to cut 50,000 more jobs, of which 47,000 would be at GM.

The Fed said the unemployment rate could stay elevated into 2011. Some analysts think the jobless rate won't drift down to a more normal range of around 5 per cent until 2013—at the earliest. Companies won't ramp up hiring until they feel confident that any recovery has staying power. That's why employment is usually the last piece of the economy to reap the benefits of a recovery. "A meaningful recovery is not expected to take hold until next year," said Varvares. NABE predicts GDP will rebound in 2010, averaging 2.4 per cent over the course of the year. The Fed, too, is forecasting that the economy will grow again in 2010 and will pick up momentum in 2011. Even so, the Fed is still guarded about any turnaround. Given all the negative forces weighing on consumers and businesses, the economic recovery "would be unusually gradual and prolonged," the Fed said.

Peugeot Citroen Cuts 11,000 Jobs

France's biggest carmaker, Peugeot Citroen, has announced it will slash more than 11,000 jobs in 2009, starting with European plants outside France. The news came just days after French President Nicolas Sarkozy unveiled a three-billion-euro (£2.7 billion; $3.9 billion) loan for the company.

Peugeot Citroen cut 2,700 jobs worldwide at the end of 2008. The company has reported an unexpected 2008 net loss of €343 million ($433 million; £308 million) after its sales slumped. Peugeot Citroen said it will make the job cuts through a series of voluntary redundancies and non-renewal of contracts, starting in its non-French European plants. "France is, of course, our biggest country in terms of employment," said Peugeot Citroen chairman Christian Streiff, "but we have lots of staff in other countries which we are currently reducing quickly." The news fanned flames of discontent in the Czech Republic and Slovakia, which accused President Sarkozy of protectionism.

China Trebles Jobless Estimate to Twenty Million

The Chinese Government has more than trebled its earlier estimates on joblessness caused by the financial crisis. It has now released a fresh survey saying that 20 million migrant workers have lost jobs while revealing that the world's factory is suffering from a much deeper malaise than what was suggested earlier. Government agencies had earlier suggested that the extent of job loss caused by reduction in export orders and production cutbacks was six million. The Ministry of Agriculture has now released the results of the survey suggesting that 20 million workers have returned to their villages after city-based factories threw them out. The new estimate is based on data collected in a survey covering 50 villages in 15 provinces in the country. It has emerged immediately after the end of the Chinese New Year celebrations when millions of people—who still have jobs—are returning to work after spending a week or more at their rural homes.

Some of the provincial Governments had feared protests and demonstrations by unemployed workers returning home from the cities. They had made elaborate arrangements like distribution of discount coupons for purchase of goodies during the Spring Festival to keep the people happy and avoid unrest. Local Governments fear possible unrest if companies might try to replace existing employees with the better skilled workers returning from the more industrialized cities.

The Chinese Government has asked the forces to be loyal to the Government in curbing upheaval if such a situation develops. China's economic growth slowed to 6.8 per cent in the last quarter of 2008. This resulted in a sharp fall in the annual rate of growth to a seven-year low of 9 per cent in 2008.

The Government had earlier warned that 2009 would "possibly the toughest year" since the turn of the century in terms of economic growth. It foresaw serious challenges in consolidating the "sound development momentum" achieved in agriculture and rural areas. Chen Xiwen, director of the office of the central leading group on rural work, said joblessness has affected 15.3 per cent of the 130 million migrant workers, who have returned to the countryside. A document issued by his office advised official agencies to create jobs and increase rural incomes. It also asked companies to give rural migrant workers favourable treatment when it came to re-employment. They have been advised to adopt flexible employment policies and create re-training facilities for the jobless. The central Government has also advised provincial Governments to offer tax relief to the jobless besides working out measures for providing pension insurance that are suitable for rural conditions.

Pioneer Announces 10,000 Job Cuts

Japanese electronics maker Pioneer is to further cut 10,000 jobs as it warned it expected to report an annual loss of 130 billion yen ($1.4 billion; £1 billion). The struggling company also announced that it is to close its loss-making flat-screen television business. Hit by the sharp fall in global consumer spending, Pioneer had shed 5,900 jobs in 2008. Pioneer described the decision to pull out of making flat TVs—a sector it once led—as "extremely painful". The job cuts will involve 6,000 full-time workers, both in Japan and abroad. The additional 4,000 reductions will hit contract staff also, both in its home nation and worldwide. Pioneer currently has a global workforce of 36,900. "Since the US financial crisis and ensuing global downturn, our sales of car electronics products and flat-screen TVs plunged worldwide," said Pioneer spokeswoman Michiko Kadoi. "We were severely hit by battered consumer sentiment," he added.

Despite being one of the first firms to sell flat-screen televisions, Pioneer never managed to build up a significant market share. Instead, industry figures show that it only held a 6 per cent share of the worldwide market in the first nine months of 2008. This compared with 37 per cent at Japanese rival Panasonic, and 23 per cent at South Korea's Samsung. Most of Japan's main electronics firms are now suffering as consumers around the world cut back on their spending.

Another electronics major, Sony has warned that it expects to make its first annual loss in 14 years, and is continuing work to trim its global workforce by 8,000 positions. The Japanese company, Toshiba has also said it is due to make a loss for 2008.

Nissan to Cut Jobs

Nissan is slashing 20,000 jobs, or 8.5 per cent of its global work force, to cope with what Japan's third-largest automaker expects will be its first annual loss in nine years. "The global auto industry is in turmoil, and Nissan is no exception," CEO Carlos Ghosn said.

Nissan now expects a 265 billion yen ($2.9 billion) net loss for 2008-09 joining a raft of other Japanese corporate giants, including Toyota, Toshiba and Sony, in slashing jobs and projecting annual losses. The last time Nissan racked up an annual net loss was for the fiscal year ending March 2000, during the start of its alliance with Renault SA of France.

The economic growth and change in unemployment—world and regions—is given in Table 4. The unemployment rate in various regions and in the world (total) in given in Table 5, while Table 6 shows total unemployment in the world—from 1998 to 2008.

Table 4: Economic Growth and Change in Unemployment—World and Regions

World/Regions	Year							Change in unemployment rate (% point)	
	2003	2004	2005	2006	2007	2008*	2009p	98-08*	03-08*
World	3.6	4.9	4.5	5.1	5.0	3.8	2.2	–0.1	–0.3
Developed Economies and European Union	1.9	3.1	2.5	3.0	2.6	1.4	–0.3	–0.7	–0.9
Central and South Eastern Europe (non-EU) & CIS	7.0	8.3	7.0	7.7	7.6	6.0	3.3	-3.3	–1.1
East Asia	8.1	8.9	8.9	10.0	10.4	8.4	7.0	–0.5	0.0
South-East Asia and the Pacific	5.7	6.4	5.9	6.1	6.4	5.1	4.2	0.8	-0.6

South Asia	6.6	7.6	8.7	9.2	8.8	7.5	5.8	1.7	0.9
Latin America and the Caribbean	2.2	6.1	4.7	5.5	5.6	4.5	2.5	–0.9	–1.2
Middle East	7.8	6.3	5.8	5.5	5.7	6.0	5.1	–1.4	–2.5
North Africa	5.7	4.7	5.0	6.1	6.1	6.2	5.1	–2.9	–2.9
Sub-Saharan Africa	4.9	7.0	6.2	6.3	6.6	5.3	5.0	0.1	–0.6

*2008 are preliminary estimates

Source: IMF, *World Economic Outlook*

Note: Differences from earlier estimates are due to revisions of World Bank and IMF estimates of GDP

Table 5: Unemployment Rate, World and Regions (Per Cent)

Both sexes	1998	1999	2000	2001	2002	2003	2004	2005	2006	2007	2008*
World Developed Economies and	6.1	6.2	6.1	6.1	6.1	6.3	6.3	6.2	6.0	5.7	6.0
European Union	7.1	6.9	6.7	6.7	7.4	7.3	7.2	6.9	6.3	5.7	6.4
Central and South Eastern Europe (non-EU) & CIS	12.1	12.4	10.5	10.2	9.9	9.9	9.7	9.2	9.1	8.5	8.8
East Asia	4.3	4.3	4.1	4.1	4.0	3.8	3.8	3.8	3.6	3.5	3.8
South-East Asia and the Pacific	4.8	5.1	5.0	5.8	6.1	6.2	6.4	6.1	6.2	5.5	5.7
South Asia	3.7	4.0	4.5	3.8	3.3	4.5	5.3	5.4	5.3	5.3	5.4
Latin America and the Caribbean	8.2	8.5	8.3	8.3	8.6	8.5	8.2	7.9	7.4	7.2	7.3
Middle East	10.8	10.3	9.8	11.4	11.4	11.8	9.2	9.8	9.8	9.4	9.4
North Africa	13.1	13.6	14.2	13.7	13.6	13.2	11.9	11.6	10.5	10.4	10.3
Sub-Saharan Africa	7.7	8.1	8.2	8.3	8.4	8.5	8.2	8.1	8.1	7.9	7.9

*2008 are preliminary estimates

Source: ILO, Global Employment Trends January 2009

Table 6: Unemployment in the World (Million)

	1998	1999	2000	2001	2002	2003	2004	2005	2006	2007	2008
Total	165.9	171.8	170.4	172.7	175.7	185.2	188.0	187.7	183.8	179.5	190.2

Source: ILO, Global Employment Trends January 2009

Five Lakh Workers Lost Jobs in 3 Months: Government Survey

Here's proof that the slowdown is taking away lakhs of jobs across India. A survey conducted by the Ministry of Labour and Employment states that in the quarter—October to December 2008—five lakh workers lost jobs. The revelation came a day after the commerce ministry said about 15 lakh people in the export sector will be jobless by March 2009. "Though we are asking the support of the banks and taking related measures, it is becoming difficult for the industry to cope up with the slowdown," Minister for Labour and Employment said.

The survey conducted by the labour bureau is based on a sample of 2,581 units across six sectors and 11 states. "Employment in the six sectors went down from 16.2 million during September 2008 to 15.7 million during December 2008," the report said. Labour Secretary Sudha Pillai said the affected workers belonged to 20 sectors in 11 states and UTs. "These sectors included textiles, metals, gems and jewellery, automobiles, transport and IT/BPO," she said. "These sectors contribute more than 65 per cent of the country's GDP," the Labour Secretary added, saying that the ministry was urging state Governments and employers to ensure social security protection to jobless workers.

These sectors contribute to more than 60 per cent of India's GDP. Thus an adverse impact on these sectors is likely to slowdown our industrial growth. "The most affected sectors were gems and jewellery, transport and automobiles," the report said. The data indicates that contract labourers are more vulnerable. In the contract category, those in the automobile sector were most hit with employment decreasing by 12.37 per cent.

The bleak estimate confirms the fear that while, unlike in China's case, exports have not been the loco of India's growth story, its integration with the world economy is deep enough for it to remain unscathed.

Pillai said the labour ministry was prepared to extend work-time by amending the Factory Act to protect employment of workers in the garment industry as the sector was losing export orders. She, however, made it clear that the extension was only for overtime work and it would be allowed after provisions were made for workers' safety and health.

Total employment in the sectors covered by the survey declined from 16.2 million in September 2008 to 15.7 million in December 2008. Exporting units showed a higher decline in employment of which the decrease was highest in gems and jewellery (8.43 per cent), followed by metals (2.6 per cent), textiles (1.29 per cent), automobiles (1.26 per cent) and mining (0.32 per cent). Pillai, who reviewed the situation in Gujarat's diamond industry, where a large number of workers have been laid off, said most were working in small units with only 3-4 workers.

India may Shed 1.5 Million Jobs

As many as 1.5 million people could end up losing their jobs in India, as exports contracted for the third successive month plunging by 1.1 per cent in December 2008 amid the worst slowdown in the world economy in the last 80 years. "If these projections continue...it's quite likely that you can expect another five lakh losses...", Commerce Secretary said. About 1 million jobs have already been lost since August 2008.

Exports for the month of December 2008 stood at $12.69 billion, according to the latest available trade data. It had declined by 12.1 per cent and 9.9 per cent in October and November 2008 respectively. Exporters employ about 150 million people in India and the sector is India's biggest provider of jobs after agriculture. Nervous exporters, smarting under severe earnings erosions, are struggling to ink new contracts as demand shrinks amid growing bankruptcies in the US—India's largest export market. In recent months the Government has taken a slew of fiscal measures, including sharp cuts in excise duties and increased plan spending, to help the economy tide over a recession in the world's developed countries.

Hindustan Motors Cuts Salaries of Managers, Executives

C.K. Birla-group company Hindustan Motors (HM) has cut the salaries of its managers and executives by 10-12.5 per cent to tide over the slump in demand for its passenger cars and auto-component businesses. An HM official told PTI that the company has cut the salaries of executives and managers from November 2008 between 10-12.5 per cent on CTC basis. For the workers, the net salaries had been reduced by Rs. 400 per month which took effect from January 2009. The official said this was one of the measures which HM had adopted in these challenging times. The company has around 2,500 workers on its payroll and 275 executives and managers. The company was also looking for other business avenues, the official said. He said since the auto-component and passenger cars businesses were facing a falling demand, the company is planning to enter non-automotive businesses, like supplying components for railways, power transmission and infrastructure companies, where the slowdown is not as big as the auto-components business.

Government's Plea Accept Pay Cuts to Save Jobs

Accept salary cuts to keep the pink slips away—was the Government's message to the industry and labour unions. "Jobs must be protected even if it means some reduction in compensation," said Pranab Mukherjee speaking at the Indian Labour Conference in New Delhi. His attempt to blunt the impact of the crisis came in the backdrop of an official study that revealed five lakh jobs had been lost during the October to December quarter of 2008. Mukherjee and Oscar Fernandes, speaking at separate venues, also sought to reassure the country's workforce of the Government's earnestness in taking steps to ease the impact of the deepening global crisis.

ILO Estimates on Job Losses

International Labour Organisation has estimated that slowdown may wipe out 50.1 million jobs worldwide by the end of year 2009. This would raise the global unemployment rate to 7.1 per cent. It said that if the economic situation continues to deteriorate, about 200 million workers—mostly in developing economies—could be pushed into extreme poverty. Absence of an evolved social security system could make South Asian countries, including India, feel the pinch further, although their unemployment rate (at 5.4 per cent) is expected to be much lower than those in Europe and the United States, says ILO Report. While workers in richer countries like those in Europe have unemployment benefits, similar benefits are not available in South Asian countries, and as a consequence, workers in the latter countries would face harsh working conditions.

More realistically, the ILO Report says that 30 million more people could lose jobs if the financial turmoil persists through 2009, pushing up the world's unemployment rate to 6.5 per cent compared to 6 per cent in 2008 and 5.7 per cent in 2007. "If the recession deepens in 2009, as many forecasters expect, the global job crisis will worsen sharply." The Report says, "Sub-Saharan Africa and South Asia stand out as regions with extremely harsh labour market conditions and the highest shares of working poor of all regions."

Wages and Employment

Prof. A.C. Pigou diagnosed the ills of depression mainly due to two causes, viz. (1) an improper allocation of people among jobs, and (2) the prevalence of wage-rates above the level warranted by the general demand conditions. He, therefore, advocated a policy of wage cuts to cure unemployment. He held that given flexible wage-rates, the economic system has an automatic tendency towards full employment and the more rigid wages are, the larger would be the fluctuations in employment. He stated:

> With perfectly free competition among work people and labour perfectly mobile, the nature of the relation (i.e., between the real wage-rates for which people stipulate and the demand function for labour) will be very simple. There will always be at work a strong tendency for wage-rates to be so related to demand that everybody is employed. Hence in stable conditions everyone will actually be employed. The implication is that such unemployment as exists at any time is due wholly to the fact that changes in demand conditions are continually taking place and that frictional resistances prevent the appropriate wage adjustments from being made instantaneously.

The process by which the reduction in wage-rates cures unemployment is described by the classical economists as below:

> In a free market economy, a reduction in wage-rates lowers the cost of production and hence prices which lead to an increase in sales. Increase in sales leads to increase in

production which leads to an expansion of employment of the workers. Reduction in costs as a result of lower wages also increases profits of businessmen. Profits increase because it is assumed that the decline in wage-rates is larger than that in prices. The process of declining wages accompanied by rising profits and employment continues till equilibrium is reached at full employment. Thus the classical equilibrium is always at full employment equilibrium.

Keynes' Viewpoint

J.M. Keynes criticized Pigou on the ground that reduction in wages should lead to decline in purchasing power and hence in effective demand. But practical situations have shown that high wage rates increase the cost of production and hence prices, keeping goods beyond the buying capacity of the consumers. This results in decrease in demand leading to unemployment.

There is wide agreement that the world capitalist system is in the midst of its most severe crisis since the Great Depression of 1929. Keynes' *The General Theory of Employment, Interest and Money*, which was published in 1936, recommended massive Government investment that would inject purchasing power into the economic system, which would help resuscitate the economy through the multiplier effect.

Keynes' persuasive power was formidable and among the earliest converts to his thinking—other than a close band of students and select professional colleagues—was President Franklin D. Roosevelt. Roosevelt's "New Deal" ushered in a massive public works program as per the Keynesian prescription. The Keynesian idea of having an interventionist state particularly when economic activity was sluggish remained the cornerstone of economic policymaking in the Western capitalist world in the post-World War II era. For more than three decades the capitalist countries in the West recorded uninterrupted economic growth that was without any historical precedence.

In fact, what we require is a combination of reasonable wages, monetary policy in the form of low interest rates, as well as fiscal policy in the shape of public expenditure on infrastructure, i.e. education, transportation, power supplies, buildings, communication networks etc.

At $30 Billion, FDI Target Set to be Missed

The global financial crisis has added new risks to the world economy, and India is set to miss the $35 billion target for global foreign direct investment (FDI) inflows in 2009.

Commerce and Industry Minister said that India would receive $30 billion FDI inflows, falling short of the target by about 14 per cent. "We will be able to go to $30 billion," he said on the sidelines of MindMine Summit-2009 organised by Hero Corporate Services. India registered 17 per cent increase in FDI inflows during 2008 on the back of robust growth, improved investment environment and further opening up of several sectors. The liquidity crunch will pull down worldwide FDI flows by 10 per cent in 2009, although flows to the developing is expected to remain fairly stable.

The Government had announced major changes in the FDI policy, simplifying the calculation of indirect and direct foreign investment. This would give more elbow room for Indian-promoted companies to raise more foreign funds. The policy review has been going on for the last few months amidst hopes of attracting FDI to $35 billion in the 2008-09. India is, however, still expected to remain a hotspot for global investors. A recent United Nations Conference on Trade and Development (UNCTAD) report said India is second only to China as preferred destination for FDI, ahead of US, UK and Germany.

The Government has brought new FDI guidelines recently. The new norms specified under the Government's Press Notes 2, 3 and 4, 2009 state that an entity that is controlled and owned by an Indian with less than 50 per cent foreign investment can invest downstream in any sector. In an internal note on the recent changes in FDI policy, the ministry has expressed fears that in "one sweep any sectoral gap of

49 per cent and below has become meaningless." "Whether this stance has been approved as such or is it an unintended liberalisation is not clear," the note stated.

The ministry also wants a method to be built in where violation of sectoral caps can be detected through a standard filing system either with the RBI or any sector regulator.

"For downward investment, there is no filing at all done or mandated with the RBI and therefore no violation can be detected," the note said.

While the new norms have been specified and approved by the Cabinet, these will find legal sanctity only after they are notified under the Foreign Exchange Management Act (FEMA). The ministry said contentious issues must be clarified before the notification is issued. In a recent letter to the Government, the RBI has also echoed similar opinion. It said under the new norms many private banks may turn "foreign owned (though Indian controlled)." Among the affected banks are ING Vysya, ICICI Bank, Development Credit Bank, Yes Bank, IndusInd Bank, Federal Bank and HDFC Bank.

The Finance Ministry also feared that the new guidelines could open up the floodgates for foreign investment in several sensitive sectors including gambling, agricultural plantations and multi-brand retail, where FDI is currently prohibited. However, in times of crisis like the present one when there is a severe credit crunch, any policy measure that encourages FDI should be appreciated.

The Issue of Wages and Employment

At a time when companies are looking to bring down their wage bill by cutting jobs to reduce cost, a look into the wage bill of 100 companies in the list of benchmark BSE 100 index shows that majority of the companies have witnessed a decline in their wage bill as a percentage of revenue over the past three years.

It has come down from 5.5 per cent in March 2005 to 5.1 per cent in March 2008. In such a scenario, the question is whether the job cut is really required to bring down costs. Of the 93 companies for which the data is available, 55 companies have witnessed a drop in the salary and wage component as a percentage of revenue.

Between March 2005 and March 2008, the aggregate wages and salaries for the list of companies grew by 74 per cent while in the same period, the revenues of the group of companies grew by 86 per cent and the profits rose by 97 per cent. Even in the nine-month period ending December 2008, the revenues for the list of companies have grown by 29 per cent over the same period of the previous year. But, now as most of the companies are witnessing a decline in their revenues the wages are likely to sea a fall.

Impact of Slowdown on Poverty Situation

About 53 million people in developing countries will remain poor because of the world economic slowdown, the World Bank has said. The Bank says the downturn will reverse many of the gains made in reducing poverty in developing countries. It estimates that 40 per cent of the world's 107 developing countries are "highly exposed" to the global crisis. And it calls on the rich countries to devote 0.7 per cent of their bailout packages to help the poor in the developing nations.

The global crisis is likely to keep 46 million more people below the absolute poverty line of $1.25 per day, and another seven million under $2 per day, compared with previous World Bank forecasts for 2009. An earlier version had incorrectly stated that 100 million more people would remain poor. "The global crisis threatens to become a human crisis in many developing countries unless they can take targeted measures to protect vulnerable people," said World Bank President Robert Zoellick. "While much of the world is focused on bank rescues and stimulus packages, we should not forget that poor people are much more exposed if their economies falter," he added.

The World Bank says the crisis will also delay progress towards reducing infant mortality, which could see 200,000-400,000 more children a year die if the crisis persists. These developments will undermine the plans agreed by the UN to reach the world poverty targets agreed in the Millennium

Development Goals by 2015. The food and fuel price increases in 2008 pushed another 130-150 million poor people into poverty, according to the World Bank estimates.

The World Bank says that three quarters of the developing countries most exposed to the crisis—many of them in sub-Saharan Africa—cannot raise the funds they need to curb the effects of the downturn. The proposed "vulnerability fund" would help by funding safety net programs for the poor, ensuring that investments in vital infrastructure go ahead, and small enterprises get much-needed support. The Bank's private finance arm, the IFC, wants to invest $3 billion in recapitalising distressed banks, and, along with Germany, has just pledged $500 million to support microfinance institutions which lend to the very poor. Mr Zoellick says that "poor people in Africa should not pay the price for a crisis that originated in America".

IMPACT OF CREDIT CRUNCH ON CARBON TRADING

Given the global economic downturn, it is quite natural for the participants at a trading conference to be downbeat.

An alarming 60 per cent of respondents to a recent carbon market survey, all of whom work within companies with carbon trading operations, report having scaled back, delayed or cancelled investments in projects as a consequence of the slowdown. The survey was conducted by Point Carbon, a provider of market intelligence, news, analysis and advisory services, and the organizers of the Carbon Markets Insights 2009 conference in Copenhagen, Denmark. The survey received 3,319 responses from people in 116 countries.

Illustrating how the downturn has resulted in real reductions in industrial activity, the respondents reported a 'reduced need', as compared to 'buy' European Union Allowances (EUAs) in addition to their full credit limits. The percentage of respondents reporting they have surplus EUAs to sell has increased to 24 per cent in 2008 from 15 per cent in 2007.

Nearly 90 per cent of participants in the Point Carbon survey say they believe that the US will embark on its own cap-and-trade style emission trading scheme by 2015. And this was repeatedly put forth as a likely outcome in the conference as well.

Several conference speakers pointed to US President Obama's draft budget plan. It has a revenue line item from a federal cap-and-trade scheme amounting to $79 billion in 2012 and $646 billion by 2019. Such a proposed allocation is good news for market participants even if there are some disagreements. "This must surely be one of the first instances in which there is a revenue line item in a budget plan for a scheme that still needs to have legislation developed and passed." wrote Barclays Capital analysts in their Monthly Carbon Standard report of March 2009.

The hopes for a long-term recovery are high, with participants at the conference believing that carbon trading markets are behaving just like the debt and equity markets, where a rebound is inevitable.

STIMULUS MEASURES

Governments all over the world have taken stimulus measures to mitigate the adverse effects of financial crisis and put their respective economies back on track. These measures are briefly discussed below.

India

In October 2008, the supplementary demand for grants provided for a gross expenditure amounting to Rs. 2,37,286 crore with net cash outgo of Rs. 1,05,613 crore mainly to finance schemes/plans announced in the Union Budget for 2008-09. However, no provisions were made for the same.

On 7 December 2008, the three major *ad valorem* rates of central excise duty, viz. 14 per cent, 12 per cent and 8 per cent applicable to non-petroleum products were reduced by 4 percentage points each.

For promoting exports, pre-shipment and post-shipment export credit for labour intensive exports, i.e. textiles (including handlooms, carpets and handicrafts), leather, gems and jewellery, marine products and Small & Medium Enterprise (SME) sector was made more attractive by providing an interest subvention of 2 per cent up to March 31, 2009 subject to minimum rate of interest of 7 per cent per annum. An additional fund of Rs. 1,100 crore to ensure full refund of terminal excise duty/central sales tax (CST) was announced. Furthermore, an additional allocation of Rs. 350 crore for export incentive schemes was announced.

In order to provide a contra-cyclical stimulus via Plan expenditure, an additional Plan expenditure of up to Rs. 20,000 crore in the current 2008-09 was allocated. In the textile sector, an additional allocation of Rs. 1,400 crore was made to clear the entire backlog of Technology Up-gradation Fund (TUF) scheme. In order to support the infrastructure schemes under Public Private partnership mode, India Infrastructure Finance Company Limited (IIFCL) was authorised to raise Rs. 10,000 crore through tax-free bonds by March 31, 2009.

On 19 December 2008, the second supplementary demand for grants provided for a gross expenditure amounting to Rs. 55,605 crore with net cash outgo of Rs. 42,480 crore.

In December 2008, the Government announced an economic stimulus package of $4 billion to shield its economy from recession. A substantial increase in Government expenditure coupled with a cut in interest rates by Reserve Bank of India aimed towards raising aggregate demand.

A number of incentives were announced in economic stimulus package of India. These have been drawn up by Government to infuse a sense of optimism in the minds of investors as well as industrialists. Incentive schemes in Indian economic stimulus package amounting to $70 million have been allocated to boost exports. Measures have been taken to boost exports of labor intensive commodities like textiles and handicrafts to provide stimulus to Indian economic revival. Lending rates on housing loans for low- and middle-income segments have been reduced. Medium and small businesses are being provided tax exemptions and tax holidays. Value Added Tax has been cut at different levels and across products to increase spending. Reserve Bank of India reduced its lending rate to 6.5 per cent and its borrowing rate to 5 per cent on

4 March 2009. With inflation falling below 1 per cent in mid-March, more reductions in interest rates can be expected.

Central Value Added Tax (CENVAT) reduced by 4 per cent, has already brought down prices of cement, textiles, and cars. CENVAT on non-petroleum products has been slashed by up to ten per cent to bring economic recovery. Customs duty on naphtha—an intermediary product for power industry—has been completely revoked. To provide an impetus to export, duty on export of iron ore fines has been removed and levy on iron lump exports has been cut from 15 per cent to 5 per cent.

A 10-point India economic stimulus package program, charted by the Prime Minister was targeted at reviving most badly affected sectors of Indian economy like housing, automobiles, infrastructure, power and medium and small industries. A funding of Rs. 300 billion was earmarked for this. An additional funding of Rs. 100 billion in the form of tax free bonds was earmarked for India Infrastructure Finance Company Limited. Deputy Chairman of Planning Commission commented that this 10-point package was set to force manufacturers to operate in a competitive environment and pass on the benefits to end users.

Three stimulus packages in three months have been announced with fanfare. In the quarter ended 31 March 2009, the Pay Commission award boosted community services growth by a whopping 17 per cent. Before this, stimulus to expenditure was provided by farm loan waiver and spiraling subsidies for petroleum products, fertilizers and food. Despite this illusory boost, overall GDP growth only touched 5.3 per cent. Agriculture declined by an unexpected 2.2 per cent in this period as poor harvests of sugarcane, cotton, pulses and oilseeds overwhelmed gains in rice, horticulture and animal husbandry. This lends credence to the IMF's forecast of 5.1 per cent GDP growth for the calendar year 2009. This should correct the illusion that stimulus packages will lift the economy out of recession.

India's 9 per cent growth in the preceding five years was due to an unprecedented global boom, not great reforms or efforts by the Government. A sharp global boom raised growth rates in many countries; even Africa grew at an unprecedented 6 per cent.

We must accept that we are part and parcel of the global economy. The global boom drove up our growth to 9 per cent and the global slump has lowered it to 5 per cent. We must abandon the illusion that we can somehow grow fast again while the rest of the world stagnates. We must learn to live with the global downswing. We cannot end or mitigate the recession in isolation by our own efforts. At best the so-called stimulus packages are actually pain relievers.

India's Interim Budget 2009-10

Pranab Mukherjee presented United Progressive Alliance (UPA) Government's interim budget 2009-10 on 16 February 2009. Apart from highlighting the initiatives taken by the Government and achievements made in agriculture, rural development, education, social sector and public sector enterprises, the Finance Minister drew attention to the global financial crisis. A few excepts from his speech, pertinent to the topic are reproduced below:

> The global financial crisis which began in 2007 took a turn for the worse in September 2008 with the collapse of several international financial institutions, including investment banks, mortgage lenders and insurance companies. There has been a severe choking of credit since then and a global crash in stock markets. The slowdown intensified with the US, Europe and Japan sliding into recession. Current indications of the global situation are not encouraging. Forecasts indicate that the World economy in 2009 may fare worse than in 2008.
>
> A crisis of such magnitude in developed countries is bound to have an impact around the world. Most emerging market economies have slowed down significantly. India too has been affected. For the first nine months of the current year, the growth rate of exports has come down to 17.1 per cent. According to the latest figures available, the industrial production has fallen by 2 per cent year-on-year basis in December 2008. In these difficult times, when

most economies are struggling to stay afloat, a healthy 7.1 per cent rate of GDP growth still makes India the second fastest growing economy in the world.

To counter the negative fallout of the global slowdown on the Indian economy, our Government took prompt action by providing substantial fiscal stimulus. The two packages announced on December 7, 2008 and January 2, 2009, provide tax relief to boost demand and aim at increasing expenditure on public projects to create employment and public assets. In this context, the Government renewed its efforts to increase infrastructure investments. In the period from August 2008 to January 2009 alone, the Government accorded approval for 37 infrastructure projects worth Rs. 70,000 crore.

In addition to expanding public sector investment in infrastructure, our Government has also taken steps to encourage private investment in infrastructure through Public Private Partnership (PPP). I am happy to say that the Government of India has been successful in attracting private investment in infrastructure sectors such as telecommunications, power generation, airports, ports, roads and railways. Under the PPP mode, 54 Central Sector infrastructure projects with a total project cost of Rs. 67,700 crore have been given in-principle or final approval by the PPP Appraisal Committee and 23 projects amounting to Rs. 27,900 crore have been approved for viability gap funding in 2008-09.

To ensure that such projects do not face financing difficulties arising from the current downturn, we have taken a new initiative for providing refinance to the banks for long term credit extended to these projects. Accordingly, the Government has decided that India Infrastructure Finance Company Ltd. (IIFCL) will refinance 60 per cent of commercial bank loans for PPP projects in critical sectors over the next eighteen months or so. For this purpose, IIFCL has been authorized to raise Rs. 10,000 crore in the market by the end of March 2009. An additional Rs. 30,000 crore can be raised if required.

With this, IIFCL and banks will be able to support projects involving a total investment of Rs. 100,000 crore in infrastructure. Combined with the steps we are taking to increase public investment in infrastructure, this will provide a big boost to such investment.

The RBI took a number of monetary easing and liquidity enhancing measures including reduction in cash reserve ratio, statutory liquidity ratio and key policy rates. The objective was to facilitate flow of funds from the financial system to meet the needs of productive sectors. Our Government has also announced specific measures to address the impact of global slowdown on India's exports. These include extension of export credit for labour intensive exports, improving the pre- and post- shipment credit availability, additional allocations for refund of Terminal Excise Duty/CST and export incentive schemes, and removal of export duty and export ban on certain items. A Committee of Secretaries has been set up to address, on continuing basis, procedural problems being faced by exporters.

The budget provided 2 per cent cut in excise duty and service tax to give boost to the country's economy. Starting December 2008, this is the third stimulus package announced by the Government to counter the crisis faced due to the global economic downturn.

Industry chambers welcomed the move. "It is another stimulus," Pranab Mukherjee told reporters after the passage of the Interim Budget in the Lok Sabha. The tax concessions would entail a revenue sacrifice of about Rs. 30,000 crore. Mukherjee said, "It will have its desired impact because we have given some concessions to the export sector, particularly those which are employment-generating ones, like gems and jewellery, garments and handicraft." "With the strong export linkages India has with these economies it is unlikely India will not feel the impact. Despite the constitutional constraints, I have some flexibility which I want to use to provide a further stimulus to the economy," he added.

The announcements in the budget included 4 per cent across-the-board excise duty cut to be continued beyond March 31, 2009, an additional 2 per cent cut in excise duty, 2 per cent cut in service tax, while excise duty on bulk cement is to be 8 per cent (instead of 10 per cent) or Rs. 230 per metric tonne, whichever is higher. Naptha has been exempted from customs duty to provide relief to the power sector. These duty reductions are likely to cost the Treasury nearly Rs. 30,000 crore. This is above the 4 per cent cut in CENVAT announced in December 2008, which has now been extended to beyond 31 March 2009.

The Government expects the Indian economy to grow nearly 7 per cent in the financial year ending 31 March, the slowest pace in six years. So far, Government has announced two stimulus packages, one on December 7, 2008 and the other on January 2, 2009 besides the several monetary policy measures undertaken by the Reserve Bank of India, like reductions in repo rate and reverse repo rate. However, it has been felt that these reductions are far too little considering the magnitude of the economic slowdown. Moreover, most of the banks are too hesitant to pass on the benefit of reduced RBI rates to the customers. The offtake of bank credit is showing a continuous declining trend since January 2009, which is not a healthy sign for the economy.

Lack of Stimulus Package Disappoints Industry

The lack of any populist announcement in the interim Union budget has gone down well with both the industry and trade circles. Yet, the same circles also felt cheated that there was no mention of new measures to boost the economy, since they had been expecting some such steps.

Despite the fact that the stimulus package to boost the economy had been taken in the past, the industry circles expected something more on that front. "Some reliefs and measures to boost the economy and purchasing power of people were expected, but it was not there," Bihar Industries Association Director C.S. Saxena said. GISCO MD Sunil Kumar Singh, in fact, was disappointed: "There is nothing for industry in the budget. We were expecting some relief for infrastructure and housing sectors. That, too, is not there," he said.

The industrialists were worried that all the taxes had been allowed to continue. They noted the increase in allotments for defence, education, agriculture, NREGA, drinking water, rural roads and health, but there was virtually nothing for the industry, Saxena explained, "The Government makes allotments, but there is no efficient delivery system." The Bihar Chamber of Commerce President P.K. Agrawal said, "...our economy may plunge further. Ethically, this may be a justified decision of...present Government, but it would have been proper for the Government to give a definite direction to the economy," he said.

Job Creation

There is a plan to make huge investments for petroleum, chemicals & petrochem investment regions (PCPIRs). The cabinet approval to set up the first three petroleum, chemicals and petrochemical investment regions (PCPIR) in the country would bring in investments to the tune of Rs. 4,86,180 crore while generating employment for 30 lakh people.

The regions which would be spread over 1,307 sq kms in Andhra Pradesh, Gujarat and West Bengal are being anchored by companies like Indian Oil Corporation, Hindustan Petroleum Corporation, GMR, CALS Refinery and ONGC Petro Additions Ltd.

A PCPIR is a specifically delineated investment region of approximately 250 sq kms for manufacturing facilities for domestic and export led production.

Table 7: Proposed PCPIRs at Andhra Pradesh, Gujarat and West Bengal

Projects	State	Cumulative Investment (Rs. crore)	Committed Investment (Rs. crore)	Employment (lakh)	Area (sq kms)
Vizag-Kakinada-Rajahmundry	AP	3,43,000	1,63,890	11.98	603.58
Vagra-Bharuch	Gujarat	50,000	22,938	8.0	453
Haidia	W. Bengal	93,180	48,180		250.19
Total		4,86,180	235,000		13,06.77

Source: Ministry of Chemicals and Fertilisers

"The Government will provide necessary viability gap funding through existing schemes to ensure availability of external physical infrastructure linkages including rail, road, ports, airports and telecom in a time-bound manner," said Ramvilas Paswan, Minister for Chemicals and Fertilisers. "States will be required to identify and select developers to build and develop internal infrastructure," he said.

The policy was notified in April 2007. PCPIR includes SEZs, free trade and warehousing zones and industrial parks and the state Government is required not to acquire but notify the area. The developers will then negotiate and buy land at existing rates.

Measures in the United States

The Federal Reserve, Treasury, and Securities and Exchange Commission took several steps on 19 September 2008 to intervene in the crisis. To stop the potential run on money market mutual funds, the Treasury also announced a new $50 billion program to insure the investments, similar to the Federal Deposit Insurance Corporation (FDIC) program. Part of the announcements included temporary exceptions to section 23A and 23B (Regulation W), allowing financial groups to more easily share funds within their group. The exceptions were to expire on 30 January 2009, but many of them have been further extended by the Federal Reserve Board. The Securities and Exchange Commission announced termination of short-selling of 799 financial stocks, as well as action against naked short-selling, as part of its reaction to the mortgage crisis.

In United States of America, economic stimulus package has been given shape of a legislation by making it an act. World financial crisis has affected United States most and a number of reputed financial organizations like Lehman Brothers have gone out of business. In a nutshell, American economy is in significantly poor shape and a radical economic overhaul is necessary in order to bring things back to order. This economic stimulus law is being thought of as a step in that direction.

Market Volatility and Retirement Plans

The Pension Protection Act of 2006 included a provision which changed the definition of Qualified Default Investments (QDI) for retirement plans from stable value investments, money market funds, and cash investments to investments which expose an individual to appropriate levels of stock and bond risk based on the years left to retirement. The Act required that plan sponsors move the assets of individuals who had never actively elected their investments and had their contributions in the default investment option. This meant that individuals who had defaulted into a cash fund with little fluctuation or growth would soon have their account balances moved to much more aggressive investments.

Starting in early 2008, most employer sponsored plans sent notices to their employees informing them that the plan default investment was changing from a cash/stable option to something new, like a retirement date fund which had significant market exposure. Most participants ignored these notices until September and October 2008 when the market crash was on every news station and media outlet. It was then that participants called their 401(k) and retirement plan providers and discovered losses in excess of 30 per cent in some cases. Call centers for 401(k) providers experienced record call volume and wait times, as millions of inexperienced investors struggled to understand how their investments had been changed so fundamentally without their explicit consent, and reacted in a panic by liquidating everything with any stock or bond exposure, locking in huge losses in their accounts.

Due to the speculation and uncertainty in the market, discussion forums were faced with the questions about whether or not to liquidate assets and financial gurus were swamped with questions about the right steps to take to protect what remained of their retirement accounts. During the third quarter of 2008, over $72 billion left mutual fund investments that invested in stocks or bonds and rushed into stable value investments in the month of October 2008. Against the advice of financial experts, and ignoring historical data illustrating that long-term balanced investing has produced positive returns in all types of markets, investors with decades to retirement instead sold their holdings during one of the largest drops in stock market history.

During the week ending 19 September 2008, money market mutual funds had begun to experience significant withdrawals of funds by investors. This created a significant risk because money market funds are integral to the ongoing financing of corporations of all types. Individual investors lend money to money market funds, which then provide the funds to corporations in exchange for corporate short-term securities called asset-backed commercial paper (ABCP). However, a potential bank run had begun on certain money market funds. If this situation had worsened, the ability of major corporations to secure needed short-term financing through ABCP issuance would have been significantly affected. To assist with liquidity throughout the system, the Treasury and Federal Reserve Bank announced that banks could obtain funds via the Federal Reserve's Discount Window using ABCP as collateral.

Table 8: Federal Reserve Rate Changes Since January 2008

Date	Discount rate	Discount rate	Discount rate	Fed funds	Fed funds rate
		Primary	Secondary		
	rate change	new interest rate	new interest rate	rate change	new interest rate
Oct 8, 2008*	–.50%	1.75%	2.25%	–.50%	1.50%
Apr 30, 2008	–.25%	2.25%	2.75%	–.25%	2.00%
Mar 18, 2008	–.75%	2.50%	3.00%	–.75%	2.25%
Mar 16, 2008	-.25%	3.25%	3.75%		
Jan 30, 2008	–.50%	3.50%	4.00%	–.50%	3.00%
Jan 22, 2008	–.75%	4.00%	4.50%	–.75%	3.50%

* Part of a coordinated global rate cut of 50 basis point by main central banks

Stimulus Package—I

In September 2008, the then Secretary of the United States Treasury, Henry Paulson and President George W. Bush proposed legislation for the Government to purchase up to US$700 billion of "troubled mortgage-related assets" from financial firms in hopes of improving confidence in the mortgage-backed securities markets and the financial firms participating in it. Discussions, hearings and meetings among legislative leaders were held, and the administration made clear that the proposal would undergo significant change before it could be approved by Congress. On 1 October 2008, a revised compromise version was approved by the Senate with a 74-25 vote. The bill, HR1424, was passed by the House on 3 October 2008 and signed into law. The first half of the bailout money was primarily used to buy preferred stock in banks instead of troubled mortgage assets.

Federal Reserve Response

In an effort to increase available funds for commercial banks and lower the fed funds rate, the US Federal Reserve announced on 29 September 2008, plans to double its Term Auction Facility to $300 billion. Because there appeared to be a shortage of US dollars in Europe at that time, the Federal Reserve also announced it would increase its swap facilities with foreign central banks from $290 billion to $620 billion.

As of 24 December 2008, the Federal Reserve had used its independent authority to spend $1.2 trillion on purchasing various financial assets and making emergency loans to address the financial crisis, above and beyond the $700 billion authorized by Congress from the federal budget. This included emergency loans to banks, credit card companies, and general businesses, temporary swaps of Treasury bills for mortgage-backed securities, the sale of Bear Stearns, and the bailouts of American International Group (AIG), Fannie Mae and Freddie Mac, and Citigroup.

Stimulus Package—II

Members of both houses of Congress reached a deal in February 2009 over US President Barack Obama's economic stimulus plan.

Senate majority leader Harry Reid said the deal "bridged differences" between an $820 billion House version of the bill and a $838 billion Senate version. "The package, now worth $789 billion (£549 billion), includes tax cuts and spending aimed at rescuing the US economy. The middle ground we have reached creates more jobs than the original Senate bill and costs less than the original House bill," said Senate majority leader Harry Reid. He said the stimulus bill should create 3.5 million jobs. He added that more than one-third of it would be dedicated to tax cuts and incentives for middle-class Americans.

The House approved its $825 billion version of the package without any Republican support. The Senate voted 61-37 to approve a different $838 billion version with few Republicans opting to back it. The bill included help for victims of the recession in the form of unemployment benefits, food stamps, health coverage as well as billions for states that face the prospect of making deep cuts in their own public spending.

The BBC's Richard Lister, in Washington, said it is one of the most expensive pieces of legislation ever to come before the US Congress and it has caused bitter partisan divisions.

Vice President Joe Biden said the passage of the bill would be an important psychological moment for the country as it grapples with the economic downturn. "It is the thing that will kick-start the confidence, the psychology that we can climb out of this," he said. Senator Max Baucus, a Democrat from Montana and one of the negotiators, said that 35 per cent of the total would be in the form of tax cuts.

Provisions of the Final Bill

The final $787 billion version signed by President Obama on February 17, 2009 specifies that 34 per cent of the package is to be devoted to tax cuts equaling $286 billion, and a further $120 billion will be used to fund infrastructure projects. Sixty-four per cent of the package will be allocated for money for social programs and spending. The following details some of the spending:

Department of Defense Facilities

Total: $7.03 billion

$4.2 billion to repair and modernize Department of Defense facilities;

$1.3 billion for medical care for service members and their families;

$890 million to improve housing for service members;

$240 million for new child development centers;

$150 million for the construction of state extended-care facilities;

$150 million for an increase of claims processing staff;

$100 million to improve facilities of the National Guard.

Education

Total: $92 billion

$15.6 billion to increase Pell Grants by $4,731 to $5,350;

$13 billion for low-income public schoolchildren;

$12.2 billion for IDEA special education;

$2.1 billion for Head Start;

$2 billion for childcare services;

$650 million for educational technology;

$300 million for increased teacher salaries;

$250 million for states to analyze student performance;

$200 million to support working college students;

$70 million for the education of homeless children;

$45 billion minimum for education under the State Equalization Fund [35].

Energy

Total: $40.75 billion

$11 billion funding for an electric smart grid;

$6.3 billion for state and local Governments to make investments in energy efficiency;

$6 billion for renewable energy power generation loans;

$5 billion for weatherizing modest-income homes;

$4.5 billion for state and local Governments to increase energy efficiency in federal buildings;

$3.4 billion for carbon capture experiments;

$2.5 billion for energy efficiency research;

$2 billion for car battery (traction) research;

$500 million for training of green-collar workers;

$400 million for electric vehicle technologies;

$300 million to buy energy efficient appliances;

$300 million for reducing diesel fuel emissions;

$300 million for state and local Governments to purchase energy efficient vehicles;

$250 million to increase energy efficiency in low-income housing.

Environmental Cleanup

Total: $6.9 billion

$6 billion for the cleanup of radioactive waste;

$600 million to cleanup hazardous waste that threatens health and the environment;

$200 million to cleanup petroleum leaks from underground storage tanks;

$100 million to evaluate and cleanup brownfield land.

Government Technology Improvements

Total: $864 million

$500 million to update the computer center at the Social Security Administration;

$290 million to upgrade IT platforms at the State Department;

$50 million for IT improvements at the Farm Service Agency;

$24 million to improve security systems at the Department of Agriculture headquarters.

Healthcare

Total: $24.1 billion

$19 billion for health information technology;

$2 billion for Community Health Centers;

$1.1 billion to research the effectiveness of certain healthcare treatments;

$1 billion to fight preventable chronic diseases;

$500 million to train healthcare personnel;

$500 million for healthcare services on Indian reservations.

Housing

Total: $12.69 billion

$4 billion for repairing and modernizing public housing;

$2.25 billion in tax credits for financing low-income housing construction;

$2 billion for Section 8 housing rental assistance;

$2 billion to help communities purchase and repair foreclosed housing;

$1.5 billion for rental assistance and housing relocation;

$510 million for the rehabilitation of Native American housing;

$200 million for helping rural Americans buy homes;

$130 million for rural community facilities;

$100 million to help remove lead paint from public housing.

Hunger Assistance

Total: $20.25 billion

$19.9 billion for the Food Stamp Program;

$150 million to help refill food banks;

$100 million for meals programs for seniors, such as Meals on Wheels;

$100 million for free school lunch programs.

Job Assistance

Total: $4.97 billion

$3.95 billion for job training;

$500 million for vocational training for the disabled;

$400 million for employment services;

$120 million for subsidized community service jobs for older Americans.

Other Infrastructure Projects

Total: $17.355 billion

$4.6 billion for the Army Corps of Engineers for environmental restoration, flood protection, hydropower, and navigation infrastructure projects;

$4 billion for the Clean Water State Revolving Fund (wastewater treatment infrastructure improvements);

$2 billion for the Drinking Water State Revolving Fund (drinking water infrastructure improvements);

$1.38 billion for rural drinking water and waste disposal projects;

$1 billion to the Bureau of Reclamation for drinking water projects for rural or drought-likely areas;

$750 million to the National Park Service;

$650 million to the Forest Service;

$515 million for wildfire prevention projects;

$500 million for Bureau of Indian Affairs infrastructure projects;

$340 million to the Natural Resources Conservation Service for watershed infrastructure projects;

$320 million to the Bureau of Land Management;

$280 million for National Wildlife Refuges;

$280 million for the National Fish Hatchery System;

$250 million to improve Job Corps training facilities;

$220 million to the International Boundary and Water Commission to repair flood control systems along the Rio Grande;

$220 million for other public lands management agencies;

$50 million for the National Endowment for the Arts to support artists.

Other Job Programs

Total: $5.51 billion

$4 billion for state and local law enforcement agencies;

$1 billion in preparation for the 2010 census;

$210 million to build and upgrade fire stations;

$150 million for the security of transit systems;

$150 million for the security of ports.

Other Worker Assistance Programs

Total: $7.27 billion

$4.2 billion to provide an additional Supplemental Security Income and Social Security Disability Insurance payment in 2009;

$1 billion to community action agencies;

$1 billion for community and economic development projects;

$500 million to help the Social Security Administration process, disability and retirement claims;

$200 million for AmeriCorps programs;

$140 million for independent living communities;

$100 million for food, shelter and support services;

$80 million to the Department of Labor Worker Protection and Oversight agency to enforce worker protection laws;

$50 million in grants for community "safety net" organizations.

Scientific Research

Total: $17.55 billion

$8.7 billion to the National Institutes of Health;

$3 billion to the National Science Foundation;

$2 billion to the United States Department of Energy;

$1.3 billion for university research facilities;

$1 billion to NASA;

$600 million to the National Oceanic and Atmospheric Administration (NOAA);

$580 million to the National Institute of Standards and Technology;

$230 million for NOAA operations, research and facilities;

$140 million to the United States Geological Survey.

Telecommunications and Digital TV

Total: $7.85 billion

$7.2 billion for complete broadband and wireless Internet access;

$650 million for DTV conversion coupons and DTV education.

Transportation Projects

Total: $48.76 billion

$27.5 billion for highway and bridge construction projects

$8 billion for high-speed rail projects;

$6.9 billion for new equipment for public transportation projects;

$1.5 billion for competitive grants to state and local Governments for transportation investments;

$1.3 billion for Amtrak;

$1.1 billion for improving airport security;

$750 million for the construction of new public rail transportation systems;

$750 million for the maintenance of existing public transportation systems;

$720 million for improving security at the border and ports of entry;

$240 million for the maintenance of United States Coast Guard facilities.

Veterans Affairs Facilities

Total: $1.05 billion

$1 billion for the Veterans Health Administration;

$50 million for the National Cemetery Administration.

Criticism of Stimulus Plan

Lynn Jenkins, a Republican, said that the recent economic stimulus bill that President Barack Obama has signed into law did not do enough to help states and local Governments with infrastructure improvements. "Less than 3.5 per cent will be spent on roads and bridges, and I think that's unfortunate," Jenkins said, "It looks just like a big spending bill to me, and I'm thinking that's not the direction we should be going right now, given the national debt is already $12 trillion," he added.

Jenkins, the former state treasurer who defeated Democrat Nancy Boyda for the seat in November 2008, said she supported a bill by the Republican leadership that included deeper tax cuts and more spending on roads and bridges. The Kansas Democratic Party sent out a statement criticizing Jenkins and calling her the "Herbert Hoover of 2009." "By opposing the economic recovery act, Lynn Jenkins voted against creating 33,000 Kansas jobs," said Chris Harris, communications director for the Kansas Democratic Party. "It doesn't take a Certified Public Accountant to understand the beneficial impact it will have on our Kansas economy," Harrio added.

President Obama has not ruled out a second stimulus package, his Press Secretary, Robert Gibbs, said just before Mr Obama signed his $787 billion recovery package into law with a statement that it would "set our economy on a firmer foundation." The President said he would not pretend "that today marks the end of our economic problems. Nor does it constitute all of what we have to do to turn our economy around," Mr Obama said at the signing ceremony in the Denver Museum of Nature and Science. "But today does mark the beginning of the end, the beginning of what we need to do to create jobs for Americans scrambling in the way of layoffs," he added.

Mr Gibbs, speaking to reporters aboard Air Force One on the way to Denver, said, "I think the President is going to do what's necessary to grow this economy." While "there are no particular plans at this point for a second stimulus package," he added, "I wouldn't foreclose it."

Stopping Stimulus Waste

Lawmakers have passed a nearly $800 billion stimulus plan—roughly the equivalent of an entire year's discretionary Government spending—in just over a month. When signing the bill, President Obama made big promises. "It's a plan that will be implemented with an unprecedented level of transparency and accountability," Obama told a crowd in Denver. "With a recovery package of this size comes a responsibility to assure every taxpayer that we are being careful with the money they worked so hard to earn." While nearly everyone acknowledges there will be some waste, others are maintaining a cautious if skeptical approach as they wait to see how the spending unfolds.

Perhaps the most novel idea put forth by the White House is a website that is supposed to show where all the money is being spent. The White House, again leveraging an online savvy that helped get them elected, created http://www.recovery.gov/—a site where anyone can go and supposedly see exactly who is getting what. The site currently contains an overview of the stimulus plan, a chart breaking down where the money is going in broad terms and a handy timeline tracking stimulus milestones and alerting users to upcoming announcements, among other things.

The site promises that "within days after the signing of the legislation, Federal agencies will start distributing funds and you will be able to see which states, Congressional districts, and even Federal contractors are receiving them. As soon as we are able to, we'll display that information visually, through maps, charts and graphics." It goes on to say: "You'll be able to send in comments, thoughts, ideas, questions and any responses you have to what you find."

The stimulus plan also increases the budget for the Office of Inspector General in the various federal departments responsible for distributing stimulus money. Each department has an Office of Inspector General charged with investigating and auditing various federal programs. The bill allocates an additional $253 million for these offices to do their work, according to a spokesperson for Senator Claire McCaskill, a Democrat from Missouri, who fought to secure the increased funding.

The administration is also creating a special board to oversee stimulus spending. The board is supposed to be headed by the Deputy Director for Management of the Office of Management and Budget and includes various Inspector Generals. It is slated to get $84 million in funding, has the power to subpoena and is charged with issuing periodic reports on the stimulus spending. Projects would presumably be cancelled or criminal charges pursued if the board uncovered wrongdoing.

The bill also extends protection for private workers who report fraud or corruption to authorities. Current law gives protections—which basically attempt to ensure the whistle-blowers do not lose their jobs—to federal employees and certain private employees, like those in the defense sector. The bill expands those protections to any worker at a company receiving stimulus money.

In addition to audits by the federal departments, the Government Accountability Office—which audits federal programs for abuse and fraud—is charged with various oversight tasks in the stimulus bill.

Republicans in Congress, who generally wanted a much smaller stimulus package (if any at all), criticized the oversight provisions for giving too much power to the President. Mike Steel, a spokesman for House Minority Leader John Boehner, a Republican form Ohio, called the website "a great way of displaying whatever information is put into it." Steel said Congress had very little oversight capacity now that the bill has become law. "We can't rely solely on the administration to self-police," he said. But others dismissed the idea that Congress would actually do anything even if it was given the tools for the job. "Generally, Congress had no record of ever actually doing anything with the oversight reports they get," said Brian Riedl, a federal budget analyst at the conservative

Heritage Foundation. Riedl said there will likely be lots of waste in the bill and recommended making all contract awards subject to competitive bidding. Audits, he said, were ineffective because they are done after the fact. But others said audits are an effective tool for deterring waste. "The knowledge that somebody could be checking will increase accountability," said Maya MacGuineas, President of the Committee for a Responsible Federal Budget, a non-partisan watchdog group.

MacGuineas said there's bound to be waste, but also acknowledged the difficult balancing act between passing a robust bill with lots of oversight protections and passing a bill quickly—a requirement most economists say is essential if stimulus is to actually help the economy. "We're striving for as good as we can get," she said.

Critical Evaluation of Stimulus Package

Professor Porter concedes that America does need something to stimulate its ailing economy. But he is not impressed with the shape of the package presented to the US Congress—leaving aside the controversy over the "Buy America" clause.

The current package includes almost $300 billion (£205 billion) of tax-cuts and twice that in extra Government spending, which would extend unemployment benefits, and increase spending in some areas of healthcare, education and transport. It is all meant to give a short-term jolt to the economy and set in motion projects that will create jobs over the longer term.

The plan has left Professor Porter frustrated. In his opinion, much of it displays "the usual pork-barrel, favourite projects" and he insists that America ought to be identifying the fundamental challenges facing its economy and the country and investing in those. The country, he says, ought to focus on "issues which would be critical constraints to our future". He accepts that some parts of the stimulus package addresses those subjects, but not enough. He believes that much of it is about the politics of local self-interest. In Professor Porter's view, those include the problem of access to higher education, and a dearth of spending on research and development.

Asked why the plan from the Obama team is being rushed through, Professor Porter considers for a moment, before saying: "I don't think it's so much their plan. "It's a plan that's come out of the political process in Washington," he adds. That's the trouble. In his view "Washington is broken". "It's not good at strategic thinking and it's become a circus that jumps from issue to issue and soundbite to soundbite." Professor Porter believes the US has never dealt with any of the real issues that affect its competitiveness, such as healthcare and public education. Any suggestion that these are major problems that need time and thought for wholesale reform—time that America's economy does not have—are met with a reminder that there are short-term things that could be done immediately. One example would be providing better access to higher education. Increasingly, Professor Porter insists, university is unaffordable. America's educational attainment in terms of university education has "not gone anywhere in 20 years". The stimulus could provide student loans and grants to support kids going to college, and grants to allow people to re-train, he suggests. "This kind of activity does put money into the economy. It helps the short-term problem, but it's investing behind a fundamental priority, and if we don't address that priority, the country's not going anywhere," he said.

Professor Porter's is not the only voice raised in criticism of the existing stimulus package. Any number of politicians and economists have expressed a range of concerns, but his centre on America's long-term competitiveness. He still hopes though, that the plan may yet be adjusted. "President Obama has an ability to break the pattern", he muses. "It will be interesting to see if he can use his tremendous, amazing popularity to start to nip and tuck on this stimulus package and get more of it aligned with the nation's real agenda." He professes to have enormous respect for President Obama's economic team, but tempers that with a concern that he "would like to see some more business expertise and credentials in his people".

But could the United States manage to re-invent itself? Professor Porter sighs and talks about his tremendous faith in the resiliency and dynamism of the US economy "which over and over again, takes its hits and moves on". People across the world should not be pessimistic about the US, he insists, though there is a "but".

With the current stimulus plan, he says, "we're falling into the trap of taking an enormous amount of money that we really don't have right now, and not necessarily spending it well".

The Obama stimulus plan is certainly more ambitious and costlier than many expected, especially in its use of Fannie Mae and Freddie Mac to influence the mortgage market. But will it all work? An analysis by IHS Global Insight concludes that it will help prevent some number of "preventable" foreclosures. So that's something. But between 10 million and 15 million homeowners are underwater and that number is growing. Who knows how many will walk away from their homes and to what extent the Obama plan will help? IHS Global just shrugs. Me, too, especially since the plan, while potentially lowering mortgage interest rates, doesn't make a clear provision for reduction in the principal. That's the real killer.

But it is certainly debatable whether we should even be trying a savior-based plan to prevent foreclosures. Do we need Uncle Sam to "save" homeowners who have sinned against the gods of financial prudence? Here's how the folks at Weiss Research see things after examining the Obama plan: "Foreclosures are actually resulting in overpriced homes burdened with too much debt being moved into the hands of new buyers, who are paying drastically reduced prices. They can therefore purchase using a traditional mortgage.... Delaying and dragging out the downturn by artificially propping up home prices will arguably work against the market healing."

In the same vein, former Bush economic adviser Lawrence Lindsey has suggested an immigration program that would give a provisional green card to anyone who invested at least $10 million in residential property and held it for five years.

And bond guru David Goldman of the Inner Workings blog relates that he's been getting inquiries from Chinese investors interested in the US housing market. He also highlights what is easily the worst aspect of the Obama plan, the "cramdown" provision which would allow judges to modify mortgages. "Allowing judges to show generosity to homeowners...and keep them in their homes makes the core assets of the banking system uncertain.... Cramdown probably is responsible for the deterioration of subprime...." That's what happens when you toss 1,000 years of contract law out of the window in the middle of a global financial crisis.

But the plan falls short of what some experts were pushing for, in both elegance and scope. For instance, Alan Blinder, the former Fed vice chairman, wanted a $400 billion, 21st-century version of the New Deal-era Home Owners' Loan Corp, which bought mortgages from banks and then issued more affordable new loans to struggling homeowners. Then there's Glenn Hubbard and Christopher Mayer of the Columbia Business School who advocated a $338 billion plan to allow all mortgages on primary residences to be refinanced into low 30-year, fixed-rate mortgages. And independent investment strategist Ed Yardeni and Carl Goldsmith of Delta Asset Management proposed fully nationalizing Fannie Mae and Freddie Mac and then offering a trillion bucks worth of 30-year, fixed-rate mortgages at 4 per cent to all qualified borrowers to buy a new or existing home.

Maybe one of these pricey plans could have turned around the housing, the market and the economy. Maybe not. But Obama's surely won't. And that's not really the intent, apparently. It's all about stabilization. As the President himself said, "If we act boldly and swiftly to arrest this downward spiral, then every American will benefit. It will prevent the worst consequences of this crisis from wreaking even greater havoc on the economy.... And by bringing down the foreclosure rate, it will help to shore up housing prices for everybody."

"Arresting downward spirals." "Preventing the worst." "Shoring up prices." Well, you can't exactly accuse Obama of overhyping the benefits of this proposal. Nor should he—given the pessimism found in current economic forecasts. The Fed now thinks that the unemployment rate could climb to over 9 per cent in 2009 and 2010 and still be above 8 per cent in 2011—some four years after the recession began. And the Philadelphia Fed surveyed 43 forecasters who predicted that the unemployment rate will rise from 7.8 per cent in the first quarter of 2009 to 8.9 per cent in the fourth quarter. Unemployment is expected to average 8.4 per cent in 2009 and 8.8 per cent in 2010.

So there are no miracles in any of this. No quick turnarounds. No light at what appears to be a very long and treacherous tunnel. As Bill Murray's weatherman character put it in Groundhog Day, "I'll give you a winter prediction: It's gonna be cold, it's gonna be grey, and it's gonna last you for the rest of your life." At least, it kind of feels like that. This is probably a good time to point out that just over a year after President Reagan signed his revolutionary economic plan, the economy shifted into high gear and never looked back.

America's Sector-Specific Bailout Plans

Auto Bailout

GM and Chrysler say they need $21.6 billion more in loans. But that won't be enough to save Detroit. Here's a rundown of all the auto bailout proposals.

General Motors and Chrysler LLC have asked the Government for $21.6 billion in additional loans, but the final cost of a bailout of the auto industry could be significantly higher. The two struggling auto giants have already received a total of $17.4 billion in loans. If they get the new loans they want, the price tag of the bailout would climb to $39 billion.

Funds amounting to $7.5 billion in loans have already been approved for the financing arms of GM and Chrysler. Congress also approved in 2008, a funding of $25 billion in loans to help automakers convert their plants to produce more fuel efficient cars. But dealers and suppliers are also asking for federal aid. And consumers may eventually get further incentives from the Government to buy new cars. All told, it could take up to $130 billion to save Detroit. A breakdown of the rest of the money that might be needed is explained below.

Loan guarantees requested by auto parts suppliers is $18.5 billion. The trade groups for parts suppliers are asking loan guarantees for the amount that domestic automakers owe to them. They are also seeking guarantees on other types of commercial loans and help so that General Motors and Chrysler pay their suppliers more quickly. Loan guarantees being requested by auto dealers: $5 billion to $20 billion. But the National Automobile Dealers Association is working on a request for federal loan guarantees to make sure they can get the cash they need to finance their inventories. NADA Vice President and general counsel Andrew Koblenz said it is likely to be in the range of $5 billion to $20 billion.

Line of credit being requested by Ford is $9 billion. Ford Motor continues to insist that it shouldn't need federal help, primarily because it locked up financing years before the credit markets dried up. But in December 2008, the automaker asked Congress to approve a $9 billion line of credit for the company in case sales were worse than expected or a rival's bankruptcy caused widespread failures in its own supplier or dealership base. Since that request, car sales have plunged further and forecasts for 2009 have grown increasingly bleak.

Tax credit for "Cash for Clunkers" program is $16 billion. There are a couple of different proposals floating around Capitol Hill to have the federal Government give buyers of new, fuel-efficient vehicles a tax credit of up to $10,000 if they turn in an old, fuel-inefficient vehicle to be scrapped. One version of the proposal, which would have been available for 1.6 million buyers, was briefly included in the economic stimulus package before it was stripped out. But stand-alone versions of the bill are still alive in Congress, and they have support of both the auto industry and environmentalists.

Allowing car buyers to deduct interest on auto loans amounts to $9 billion. This proposal from Senator Barbara Mikulski, easily passed the Senate during debate on the stimulus bill. But it was stripped out of the final version, leaving a far more modest tax credit that allowed buyers to deduct only the sales and excise tax they pay on a new car purchase. Auto dealers and automakers were strong supporters of making interest deductible as a way to spur demand.

If the Obama administration had decided to move ahead with additional loans for GM and Chrysler, it may have wrapped various proposals into one auto bailout bill. Still, there would be questions about where future funding will come from. Much of the money for Detroit so far has come from the Troubled Asset Relief Program, the $700 bailout of the nation's financial system approved in 2008.

But much, if not all, of the additional money will probably have to be approved by Congress, rather than just Treasury. That could prove to be easier in this Congress though. The House passed a $34 billion bailout for GM, Chrysler and Ford in December 2008 but it failed to win approval from enough Republicans in the Senate. But the Democratic majority of both houses has grown significantly since then. So it is likely that a similar bailout measure would find the 60 votes needed to advance in the Senate, assuming all Democrats support it as they did the recently passed stimulus bill. The automakers' strongest argument for getting the help to get the industry back on its feet is that it could cost the Government far more if they fail. GM and Chrysler both included estimates in viability plans submitted to the Treasury about how much they would need to fund their operations if they went through a bankruptcy reorganization. GM said it could cost up to $100 billion in loans over two years, while Chrysler estimated it would cost between $20 billion and $25 billion. Both companies said that if they went bankrupt, they would be forced to halt operations and liquidate if they did not receive the loans. And if they were to go out of business, lost federal tax revenue would reach into the hundreds of billions of dollars, according to company estimates.

Experts agreed that a bankruptcy at either company would be far more expensive for taxpayers than the amount of money they are asking for. "There would be nothing standard about a bankruptcy filing at GM," said Michigan bankruptcy attorney Douglas Bernstein. "You don't normally have the Government as your lender. And I don't think anybody has been through a bankruptcy of this magnitude."

Obama Housing Plan

The Obama administration's housing rescue plan committed up to $275 billion in funds to help reduce mortgage payments for up to 9 million families and arrest the devastating fall in US home prices. According to the plan, $50 billion to modify mortgages will come from the $700 billion financial bailout fund approved by Congress in 2008; up to $25 billion in direct costs to finance firms Fannie Mae and Freddie Mac to modify mortgages. Up to $200 billion from the US Treasury to increase capital for Fannie and Freddie if necessary, authorized under a housing bill passed in 2008. Fannie and Freddie would increase their mortgage portfolios by $50 billion each.

The plan enables refinancing for 4 million to 5 million "responsible" homeowners who took out conforming 30-year fixed mortgages with a down payment of 20 per cent or more and are current on payments. The decline in home values means many of these families cannot qualify for conventional refinancing because their loan-to-value ratio now exceeds 80 per cent. The program would allow mortgages owned or guaranteed by Fannie Mae and Freddie Mac to be refinanced through private lenders, reducing monthly payments, as long as the amount owed on a first mortgage does not exceed 105 per cent of the property's current market value. Refinancing rates will be based on market rates in effect at the time of the refinance plus any associated points and fees quoted by the lender. All of the refinanced loans under the plan will be 30-year or 15-year fixed-rate notes. Mortgage lenders started accepting applications after program details were announced on 4 March 2009.

Initiative intended to reach 3 million to 4 million "at risk" homeowners who are struggling to meet their mortgage payments. It aims to bring payments down to 31 per cent of a borrower's monthly income through modifications at no cost to the borrower. Program targets owner-occupants with high mortgage debt compared to income or those with "underwater" mortgages that exceed the value of their homes.

Borrowers don't have to miss payments to qualify. Borrowers with high total debt obligations exceeding 55 per cent of their income must enter consumer debt counseling to help reduce car, credit card and other debt to receive mortgage modifications. The US Treasury will share the cost of reducing payments with mortgage lenders and servicers. Lenders must agree to cut interest rates so that monthly payments are no more than 38 per cent of a borrower's income. The Treasury will match those reductions dollar-for-dollar to bring down payments to 31 per cent of income. Lenders must agree to keep the modified payments in place for five years. The Obama administration will seek "careful" changes to bankruptcy law to allow judges to rewrite mortgage terms on loans originated in the past few years. This will apply only to existing mortgages under the GSE conforming loan limits "so that millionaire homes don't clog the bankruptcy courts."

Lenders participate in the "at risk" loan modifications on a voluntary basis, but will receive substantial incentives to do so. The administration anticipates that most major lenders will participate. Mortgage servicers will get $1,000 for each successful modification under the program, and up to $3,000 over three years if the borrower stays current on payments. Mortgage holders also will receive $1,500 and servicers will receive $500 if the modifications are made before a borrower defaults. Borrowers will receive up to $5,000 in loan principal reductions over five years if they stay current on payments. The Treasury will fund a $10 billion insurance fund to protect lenders against home value declines as a means to discourage foreclosures based on anticipation of falling home prices. Holders of modified mortgages could receive payments from the fund if a home price index falls more than expected, and these could be used as reserves to offset potential increases in foreclosure losses.

The Treasury will double its capital funding commitments to Fannie Mae and Freddie Mac to $200 billion each under a preferred stock purchase mechanism launched in 2008. The increased backstop does not anticipate increased cash draws or a change in financial position, but is aimed at strengthening investor confidence in the two firms, helping to lower their funding costs and reduce mortgage rates. Fannie's and Freddie's retained mortgage portfolios will be allowed to increase under the agreements by $50 billion each to $900 billion each. This will be accompanied by corresponding increases in allowable outstanding debt. The Obama administration also will work with Fannie and Freddie to support state housing finance agencies to help homebuyers.

Recapitalisation of the Financial System

Fannie Mae and Freddie Mac and American International Group (AIG) were taken over by the US Government. Emergency Economic Stabilisation Act was passed on October 3, 2008. Troubled Assets Relief Program, authorising the US Government to purchase troubled assets of US$ 700 billion was introduced. Limit on deposit insurance was raised at banks and credit unions from US$ 100,000 to US$ 250,000 per account. The US Treasury Department of the Treasury announced voluntary Capital Purchase Program. Under the program, the US Treasury would purchase up to US$ 250 billion of senior preferred shares on standardised terms as described in the program's term sheet. Restructuring of Government's financial support to AIG was announced. The US Government entered into an agreement with Citigroup to provide a package of guarantees, liquidity access, and capital. A program to purchase the direct obligations of housing-related Government-sponsored enterprises and mortgage-backed securities (MBS) was initiated.

Buyback of Banks' Troubled Assets

The Obama administration's new plan to liberate the nation's banks from a toxic stew of bad home loans and mortgage-related securities is bigger and more generous to private investors than expected, but it also puts taxpayers at great risk. Taken together, the three programs unveiled in the third week of March 2009 by the Treasury Secretary, Timothy F. Geithner, could buy up to $2 trillion in real estate assets that have been weighing down banks, paralyzing credit markets and delaying the economic recovery. Investors reacted ecstatically, with all of the major stock indexes soaring as soon as the markets opened. The Dow Jones Industrial Average ended the day up nearly 500 points, or 6.84 per cent, to 7,775.86. The thundering response was in sharp contrast with the bitter disappointment by investors when the plan was first vaguely described on 10 February 2009. "For the first time in seven months, I can say they've done it right," said T. Timothy Ryan Jr., President of the Securities Industry and Financial Markets Association.

Despite lingering worries that Congress would add new pay restrictions or make other changes in the rules, several major investment firms, including BlackRock and Pimco, said they would participate as buyers of bank assets. Banks, which would sell mortgage assets in auctions, were less enthusiastic, though no major bank publicly said it would not participate. Administration officials outlined a three-part Public-Private Investment Program that offers private investors vast amounts of cheap, taxpayer-supported financing for every dollar they put up of their own money. In essence, the Treasury and the Federal Reserve will be offering at least "a tablespoon of financial sugar for every teaspoon of risk that investors agree to swallow." "There is no doubt the Government is taking a risk," Mr Geithner acknowledged at a briefing for reporters. "The question is how best to do it."

Under one main component of the plan, the Federal Deposit Insurance Corporation (FDIC) would oversee a program in which banks offer bundles of whole mortgages for sale to investors. The FDIC would set up an auction for each bank portfolio, allowing a bank to sell the mortgages to the investor that offered the highest bid. But the crucial incentive for investors—traditional fund managers, hedge funds, private equity funds, pension funds and possibly even banks—is that the Government would lend as much as 85 per cent of the purchase price for each portfolio of mortgages. On top of that, the Treasury would invest one dollar of taxpayer money for every dollar of private equity capital to cover the remaining 15 per cent of the portfolio's purchase price.

The arrangement is similar to some of the distressed-asset sales arranged by the Resolution Trust Corporation, the federal agency that was responsible for cleaning up the savings-and-loan debacle of the early 1990s. But the scale of the new program is much bigger. In addition to the FDIC's program, the Treasury would help finance a series of public-private investment funds to buy up unwanted mortgage-backed securities, or pools of mortgages that have been packaged into bonds with a credit rating. Those two programs alone could buy $500 billion to $1 trillion worth of troubled assets, according to Mr Geithner. The Treasury would kick in $75 billion to $100 billion from the Troubled Asset Relief Program as equity. But the Treasury could pump almost $1 trillion more into the toxic-asset effort through a program called the Term Asset-Backed Securities Loan Facility (TALF), a joint venture with the Federal Reserve.

That program, which became operational in the middle of March 2009 was originally created to help finance mostly new consumer loans and also some new business lending. But in a major expansion, Treasury and Fed officials said that they would expand the program to finance the purchase of existing troubled mortgage-backed securities, including those backed by commercial real estate loans.

The biggest inducement in all the programs is the Government's willingness to provide "nonrecourse" loans to institutions that buy up the unwanted assets. A nonrecourse loan is secured only by the underlying home or building. If the borrower defaults, the Government would only be able to seize the real estate. If the mortgages or the securities generate bigger losses than expected, the Government and not the private investors would have to absorb the brunt of those losses.

Some analysts and fund managers were surprised that the Treasury was offering to lend up to $6 for every $1 of investors' own money. Several said that those terms appeared more generous than what Merrill Lynch had offered when it sold a portfolio of mortgage securities to Lone Star Funds in July 2008. In that deal, Lone Star bought Merrill's assets for only 22 cents on the dollar and Merrill lent Lone Star only $3 for every $1 the investor put up. "This is a better deal than

Lone Star got," said Barry Ritholtz, chief executive of FusionIQ, an investment research firm.

It is too early to tell whether the inducements amount to a huge taxpayer giveaway or a shrewdly designed package that returns a profit to taxpayers and stimulates the financial system. Taxpayers could profit from the interest paid by the public-private partnerships on the Government loans if the troubled assets rise in value above the prices paid to acquire them.

In the short term, the big question is whether the inducements are enough to overcome both rising political anxiety among investors and reluctance by banks to sell mortgages. Mr Geithner said there were no restrictions on compensation on the participating investors. Still, investors are worried about attracting the wrath of Congress if they appear to reap big profits. After the Treasury acknowledged that employees at American International Group were getting $165 million in bonuses, the House voted to impose a retroactive 90 per cent tax on those bonuses.

The other potential obstacle could be on the side of the sellers, i.e. the banks. Because banks would probably have to sell their mortgages at a substantial discount to their original value, they would also have to write down the value of the mortgages and book a loss in the process. In turn, that could force many banks to raise more capital. Bill Gross, chairman of Pimco, said in a statement that the Treasury plan was a "win-win-win policy" and that his firm was "intrigued by the potential double-digit returns" that it offered.

Laurence D. Fink, BlackRock's chairman and chief executive, said his firm would invest in a broad range of mortgages and related securities through the Treasury plan. BlackRock is also exploring ways to set up mutual funds that would allow individual investors to participate. The combined impact of all the Treasury and Fed bailout programs, he added, could start to stabilize the economy sooner than many expect.

At the core of the plan is a new $500 billion fund to absorb toxic bank assets. Analysts say there is scepticism over whether the proposal will work, and worries over both a perceived lack of detail and the sums of money involved. "This is not a clear-cut plan," said analyst Bucky Hellwig.

Mr Hellwig, who works for Morgan Asset Management, added that it wasn't "what investors are looking for", and that the package was "convoluted".

Mr Geithner said the new bank bailout package was vital as "critical parts of our financial system are damaged". "Instead of catalyzing recovery, the financial system is working against recovery, and that's the dangerous dynamic we need to change," he added.

The new plan is aimed at restoring confidence in the damaged financial system and restarting bank lending. The key question now is how eager the private sector will be to participate both in the new fund to absorb toxic assets and the new Federal Reserve lending program, which will be expanded to $1 trillion from $200 billion to help banks lend more. Mr Geithner said the new bank bailout plan should unfreeze the credit market, strengthen banks and "provide critical aid for homeowners and for small businesses". "And as we do each of these things, we will impose new higher standards for transparency and accountability," he added. Analyst James Ellman of Seacliff Capital said investors were disappointed, as they had wanted "clarity, simplicity and resolution". "This plan is seen as convoluted, obfuscating, and clouded," he added. Others say that the plan is not perfect, but in general they agree with many of its proposals. "I think the idea of more or less buying back some of the debt, monetizing it, is a good idea. I think that's probably a good move," said Carl Birkelbach, head of Birkelbach Management.

European Bank Resists Printing Money

The European Union's current President labelled President Obama's emergency stimulus package "a way to hell" that will "undermine the stability of the global financial market." The blunt comments by the Czech Prime Minister, Mirek Topolanek, whose country holds the rotating presidency of the union, came just a week before a crucial meeting of the Group of 20 that was called to show global solidarity in fighting the recession. The comments were greeted with embarrassment by many Europeans who believe that the Czech leader does not represent a European consensus.

Despite widespread fears that European nations could prolong the current recession unless they act in concert with one another and the United States, the slump has highlighted differences over deficit spending, interest rates and possible bailouts for new union members in the East. There are few signs that the alliance is developing the political leadership to match its economic weight. Britain, like the United States, has undertaken an aggressive fiscal stimulus and slashed interest rates. But Germany and France have opposed calls for further large stimulus packages and even greater deficit spending, while the European Central Bank has kept interest rates higher than they are in the United States and Britain. Germany and even some Central European countries opposed calls by Hungary for the creation of a single rescue fund for heavily indebted countries in Eastern Europe.

Gordon Brown, the British Prime Minister, said there was "far more agreement" among world leaders than recent reports suggested. "I believe that now, for the first time, global leaders recognize the need to cooperate," he said during a question-and-answer session at New York University. Even so, Mr Topolanek's comments during a speech to the European Parliament underscored unresolved differences between the members. The country holding the revolving presidency is supposed to speak for Europe as a whole, and Mr Topolanek went to the Group of 20 meeting on 2 April 2009 in London as the European President. The Group of 20 comprises 19 industrialized and emerging countries and the European Union. Numerous other European nations that attended, included the head of the European Commission, José Manuel Barroso, and the leaders of individual countries like France, Germany, Britain, Italy and Spain.

Jiri Paroubek, the leader of the Social Democrats in the Czech Parliament, who called a vote of no confidence against Mr Topolanek, accused him of making an undiplomatic gaffe. "In my view, it is extremely impolite and undiplomatic towards President Obama...," he said. Europeans themselves are well aware of the leadership problem, having painfully negotiated a new Constitution, which European voters rejected. They then forged the Lisbon Treaty, which will create a permanent European President and foreign minister, and which was supposed to go into effect on 1 January 2009. But the Lisbon Treaty, which requires the votes of all member states, was rejected by Irish voters in June 2008, giving the Czechs their turn in the six-month rotating presidency.

Mr Topolanek's remarks were considered impolite, with the German leader of the Socialist group in the European Parliament, Martin Schulz, telling him, "You have not understood what the task of the EU presidency is," and describing his comments as "not the level on which the EU ought to be operating with the United States." A Czech spokesman said that Mr Topolanek meant to say that the European Union would be on the way to hell if it increased its own spending too much, rather than predicting that the United States was doomed.

Mr Topolanek is not alone in his concern that Mr Obama's stimulus package, which will push the United States budget deficit this year to 10 per cent or more of gross domestic product, will put a huge strain on global financial markets. German officials have also criticized the evolving American program, and many other European nations have declined to create fiscal stimulus programs anywhere near as large as that of the United States, arguing that too much extra money will lead quickly to inflation. There are also disagreements between the United States and the Europeans about how much emphasis to place on fiscal stimulus as opposed to enhanced regulation of finance and tax havens. Even so, participants have been making progress on a communiqué that signaled a rough consensus on principles the in London G20 meeting. They expect that there will be enough in the final communiqué about the need for fiscal stimulus to satisfy Washington, with Europe ready to do more if its first package of spending does not do enough, and that there will be enough about the need to beef up regulation and international oversight to satisfy the Europeans.

A senior European Union official said everyone hoped to de-emphasize the trans-Atlantic dispute over fiscal policy. "We don't think we need it, we don't think the world needs it and we don't think it makes sense," the official said. Katinka Barysch, deputy director of the London-based Center for European Reform, said that Mr Topolanek had undermined a consensus that was carefully forged at last week's European Union summit meeting in Brussels. "The EU had made some progress towards a coherent position," Ms Barysch said. "He has undermined that," she added.

Analysts in Prague said that Mr Topolanek was eager to show that he was still politically relevant. They noted that some countries, like the Czech Republic, which emerged from decades of communism, were deeply suspicious of state intervention in the economy.

Overhaul of Financial Regulation

The Obama administration has called for a sweeping overhaul of financial regulation. The hedge funds, private equity firms and derivative markets are likely to come under Government supervision for the first time. According to Treasury Secretary Timothy Geithner the regulatory changes were essential to restore confidence to the financial markets: "We need much stronger standards for openness, transparency, and plain, common sense language throughout the financial system. And we need strong and uniform supervision for all financial products marketed to consumers and investors, and tough enforcement of the rules to ensure full accountability for those who violate the public trust."

The plan would give the Government vast powers over systemically important banks and other financial institutions that are so big that their collapse would jeopardize the economy as a whole. The Government will have the power to pear into the inner working of companies that are currently outside the scope of federal supervision. They include insurance companies like the AIG, multi-billion-dollar hedge funds like the Citadel Group, and PE firms like Carlyle Group and Kohlberg, Kravis & Roberts. The big companies would be subjected to much stricter capital requirement. The most striking new proposals that may provoke the most heated opposition would be regarding the regulation of so-called private pools of capital—hedge funds, private equity funds and venture capital funds—and the colossal market in financial derivatives, including instruments like credit-default swaps, the insurance-like instruments that allow investors to hedge against bond defaults.

It is believed that the ongoing economic crisis was triggered by a dramatic rise in mortgage delinquencies and foreclosures in the US with adverse consequences for banks and financial markets around the world. The crisis "has exposed the pervasive weakness in financial industry regulation and the global financial system." Overhauling of financial regulator is therefore a step in the right direction.

Financial-Rescue Plan: Nationalization in Disguise?

The Financial Stability Plan (FSP), presented by Treasury Secretary Timothy Geithner, like the Troubled Assets Relief Program (TARP) before it, is a simple swap of assets and risk between the private and the public sector, albeit on a massive scale. In effect, the federal Government is nationalizing the banks' assets, even as it declines to nationalize the banks themselves. Under the FSP, commercial banks, hedge funds and other investors will spring clean their balance sheets by selling the worst assets to the Federal Reserve, or to an off-balance sheet public-private "trust fund" financed with a mixture of public and private capital and a large quantity of cheap loans from the central bank. In return, the Fed will credit their accounts at the central bank with hundreds of billions of dollars of new reserve funds (in essence cash). And the Treasury will issue trillions of dollars of new debt, of which some of the proceeds will be deposited with the Fed to fund its asset purchases and lending activities. Much of this new Government debt will be bought by the banks and other investors. Once the operation is complete, private sector's portfolio will become significantly less risky in aggregate because it will hold a reduced proportion of private sector loans and securities (such as mortgage backed bonds) and an increased proportion of Government debt and Fed balances.

The balance sheet of the Fed and the Treasury, on the other hand, will become significantly more risky because the combined Fed/Treasury will own (or have extended loans against) private securities backed by household mortgages, credit card payments, auto loans and commercial lending. The cost of defaults will ultimately be shouldered by the taxpayers rather than the banks.

The basis of the plan is a huge balance sheet swap between the private sector and the combined Fed/Treasury. In some instances, the risk of losses will pass to the public sector, even as the assets themselves will remain with the private sector, or are parked in the trust-fund—which looks very much like an off-balance sheet special investment vehicle (SIV) sponsored by the Fed. The Treasury argues that a public-private trust fund will enable it to harness private sector expertise in valuing the assets to be bought (though the argument seems a bit specious, since it was precisely the private sector's failure to value assets correctly that created the crisis in the first place). In any event, the Fed/Treasury/SIV will have to pay a valuation above the current market price for the assets (otherwise the commercial banks will derive no benefit from selling them). It can only afford to do so if it has access to subsidised funding from the central bank and ultimately the taxpayer. Once again, the risk is being transferred from the private sector to the Government's own balance sheet.

Government as Banker and Insurer

The basic strategy is a sound one. Only the federal Government, backed by a steady stream of tax revenues, has the financial strength to absorb the worsening losses on bank lending. The asset swap (private debts for US Treasury bonds) shifts the risk assets to the strongest hands capable of holding them during the crisis.

The US banking system has less than $1 trillion worth of equity remaining. Losses under some scenarios could easily wipe it out. The Government on the other hand can absorb the losses, and also has the strength to restructure troubled loans, refinance them, or hold them to maturity in the hope they become current again in future.

In some sense, the federal Government is entering the banking business. The characteristic function which distinguishes the banker from the money lender is that the banker interposes its own promise to repay between savers and borrowers, substituting its own creditworthiness for the creditworthiness of the borrowers. The money lender merely gathers cash and distributes it. In this sense, the Geithner plan takes the US Government into the banking business. It swaps claims based on household mortgages, credit card repayments and commercial loans for a promise to repay based on tax revenue and the full faith and credit of the United States. Investors may not be certain about the repayment capacity of households and firms, but no one has yet expressed serious concern about the repayment ability of US taxpayers collectively. The other way of viewing the plan is as a giant reinsurance pool. Normally, loan losses would be spread across the pool of bank shareholders and absorbed by the banks' regulatory and equity capital. But in the current crisis, the prospective losses under some scenarios are so large that the capital pool is not wide or deep enough to absorb them safely. By transferring the risks from the banks to the Treasury, the loss-sharing pool is being broadened from bank shareholders to the much wider pool of taxpayers. Eventual losses will be spread more widely and thinly.

In the meantime, by leaving the banks themselves in private ownership, rather than nationalising them, the Government hopes to protect the basic commercial infrastructure (loan officers, risks systems, management expertise and technology) needed to resume providing banking services in the private sector two or three years down the line, once the crisis has passed. Like the original rationale for the TARP, before it became a scheme to inject capital into the banks, the basic strategy is sound but it has been marred by poor presentation and execution.

Learning a Costly Lesson

The US effort to detoxify its economy is the costliest clean-up in history. By now the world has committed a fifth of its yearly income to bringing its financial market back to normalcy. But, as an International Monetary Fund paper presented at a meeting of Finance Ministers and central bank governors from the G20 pointed out, the attempt to restructure afflicted banks has been ad hoc, responding to "market pressure rather than being based on a full diagnosis of the underlying soundness of institutions". Targeted protection for creditors yields bizarre side-effects. The case in point is the popular outrage US President Barack Obama faced over the million-dollar bonuses that the bosses of the seriously ailing American International Group paid themselves out of taxpayers' money.

The IMF has warned that in "countries where banking sectors still appear resilient, the deepening global financial crisis is likely to imply greater stresses". At $10 trillion the stimulus packages have reached an enormous amount. Now it is time to make proper use of it so that positive results could be in sight.

Wall Street CEOs Scolded by US Lawmakers

Wall Street bank executives squirmed under a public scolding in Congress over how they used $176 billion in bailout money without noticeably improving the battered economy. "America doesn't trust you anymore," Massachusetts Democratic Representative Michael Capuano told eight bank CEOs during a congressional hearing on the troubled bank bailout plan. They demanded to know what the banks have done with the bailout money, given an ongoing credit crisis that has added to the country's deteriorating economy. The CEOs, representing the titans of the once seemingly invincible capitalist society, argued that they had responsibly used billions in taxpayer dollars to increase lending, not to pay executives, lobbyists or shareholder dividends. They all said they had received 2008 salaries ranging from $600,000 to $1.5 million and had not received bonuses. All but one reported that their companies own or leased airplanes, prompting California Democratic Representative Brad Sherman to advise them to give up the expensive aircraft.

Prodded by New York Democratic Representative Gregory Meeks on whether Americans deserved an apology for lax loan standards that fueled the now-collapsed debt bubble, only Morgan Stanley CEO John Mack spoke up. "I think the entire industry bears responsibility, and I'm sorry for it," Mack said.

"I feel more like corporal of the universe, not captain of the universe at this moment," said Ken Lewis, CEO of Bank of America, as he came under intense questioning from California Democratic Representative Maxine Waters.

Barney Frank, chairman of the House Financial Services Committee, opened the proceedings by telling the CEOs they needed to understand Americans' anger and frustration and cooperate with lawmakers willingly, "not grudgingly, not doing the minimum." New York Democratic Representative Gary Ackerman said that in "the real world," people cannot get loans to buy cars or homes or send children to college. "It seems to me and some of us that this money hasn't reached the street, that you haven't loaned it out," he said. Paul Kanjorski of Pennsylvania was equally baffled, telling the executives that if their banks did not use the money, "please find a way to return that money before you leave town." South Carolina Republican Representative Gresham Barrett said his constituents "simply have not seen the evidence that the money you were given is working or making their lives better."

The CEOs reported they had forsworn bonuses for now. "I've told my board of directors that my salary should be $1 per year with no bonus until we return to profitability," said Vikram Pandit of Citigroup. But Frank demanded why they needed bonuses at all when a good salary would do. New York state officials say financial companies doled out $18.4 billion in bonuses last year. "At your level, why do you need bonuses?" Frank asked.

"This notion that you need some special incentive to do the right thing troubles people," replied Pandit. "It's complicated," Mack replied, citing the risks involved, the global nature of the banking business and the size of the companies. "If you gave me no bonus for the best year, I'd still be here." The executives also said they are embracing some of the reforms proposed for the badly crippled US financial system.

Jamie Dimon, head of JPMorgan Chase, said he is endorsing a proposal to create a systemic risk regulator to help oversee US markets. "This would allow us to begin to address some of the underlying weaknesses in our system and fill the gaps in regulation that contributed to the current situation," he said. "We stand ready to work with you on the range of issues confronting the financial services sector and our economy." The United States' economy, already in recession for a year, is facing its worst crisis in generations as banks struggle to absorb losses and resume lending.

Obama Unveils Executive Pay Cap

President Barack Obama announced a $500,000 (£355,000) limit on executive pay at US firms that need substantial fresh Government aid. The move followed widespread public anger over the levels of pay on Wall Street, but was not expected to be applied retrospectively. Obama said it was "shameful" that top bankers had awarded themselves giant bonuses last year. He added that taxpayers should not be "subsidising excessive compensation".

In addition to the limit on basic pay, Mr Obama said if affected executives receive any further bonuses, they "will come in the form of stock that can't be paid up until taxpayers are paid back for their assistance". Firms will also have to publicly disclose "all the perks and luxuries bestowed upon senior executives, and provide an explanation to taxpayers and to shareholders as to why these expenses are justified". "We're asking these firms to take responsibility, to recognise the nature of this crisis and their role in it," said the President.

Analysts said the plan could raise the likelihood of senior executives moving from firms who need Government aid to those that don't. "There is certainly a possibility of talent flight from the big firms to the smaller investment banks," said Lauren Smith, analyst at Keefe, Bruyette & Woods.

Mark Poerio, an analyst at law firm Paul Hastings also agreed. "If you have someone who was making well over

$1 million, and now they are capped at $500,000, it is very conceivable that they are going to look to go to a company that is not subject to those limitations," he said.

"We all need to take responsibility," said President Obama. "And this includes executives at major financial firms who turned to the American people, hat in hand, when they were in trouble, even as they paid themselves their customary lavish bonuses. "We're asking these firms to take responsibility, to recognise the nature of this crisis and their role in it." According to the available figures, US banking bosses received bonuses of more than $18.4 billion during 2007. However, Citigroup, which has received $45 billion of Government aid, has already said its bosses, including chief executive Vikram Pandit, would forgo their 2008 bonuses.

Mr Pandit earned more than $3 million in 2007, including bonuses. Republicans have supported the move to limit the pay of executives at firms that secure fresh Government money. BBC business editor Robert Peston said President Obama's move will inevitably increase pressure on the UK Government to introduce something similar for British banks that have received state support, such as Royal Bank of Scotland and Lloyds.

Curbs on Pay and Perquisites in the United States

The public outcry over sky-high compensation appears to have shaken some corporate boardrooms enough that changes are being made to curb pay, redefine appropriate practices and give shareholders more influence over compensation.

Wall Street has been the target of criticism for paying executives exorbitant amounts, while allowing them to take excessive risks. Those firms now have been forced to alter their pay practices by the Government under the taxpayer-funded bailout.

The investors charged that executives were rewarded for short-term results rather than sustained profitability but CEO compensation never came back down to earth, and the big rewards for taking big risks only ballooned. That's why investors are demanding change. They don't want to see executives being pampered, overpaid and oblivious to shareholders.

It turns out that some directors at technology, retail, energy companies, etc. are listening. They recognize they can't just rubber-stamp CEO pay anymore, and then try to defend its size by saying it has to be that way to keep up with competitors.

Huddled in boardrooms nationwide right now, compensation committees and executives are pulling apart their pay programs. They are dissecting what they did, why they did it and what needs to be done going forward. "There is a heightened awareness of power, accountability and stewardship in the compensation committee," said Myrna Hellerman, Senior Vice President at Sibson Consulting in Chicago who works with boards on executive pay.

GE Makes Rare Cut in Dividend

US conglomerate General Electric has made a rare cut in its shareholder dividend as it seeks to conserve cash to see out the recession. GE said it would cut its quarterly dividend to \$0.10 (£0.07) per share from an originally planned \$0.30—a 68 per cent reduction. GE, which had long resisted cutting its divided, said the move would save it \$9 billion a year. The news hit the company's share price, with stocks sinking 6.5 per cent to \$8.51.

"We recognise the importance of the dividend to our shareholders and the significance of this decision," said GE Chief Executive Jeff Immelt. "The revised dividend is competitive and reflects what we believe is an appropriate payout in today's market," Mr Immelt said. GE's problems mainly stem from its finance unit GE Capital, which makes a wide variety of loans including mortgages.

However, the wider economic downturn has also hit its industrial unit, which makes aircraft engines, home appliances, light bulbs and wind turbines. Several US blue-chip firms, including JPMorgan and Textron, have cut dividend payments to preserve capital. GE has paid a divided to shareholders for more than 100 years.

Capital Shore-up of Banks in India

The Indian Government has also considered a stimulus package for ailing banks. The Cabinet has approved the infusion of Rs. 3,800 crore to strengthen the balance sheets of three public sector banks—UCO Bank, Central Bank of India and Vijaya Bank. The fund would help these banks to shore up their capital adequacy ratio (CAR).

Of the total amount, Rs. 1400 crore would go to Central Bank of India, while UCO Bank and Vijaya Bank will get Rs. 1,200 crore each. This capital infusion would be done in two tranches. While the first tranche was to be made available in 2009-10 year, the remaining will be given in 2008-09.

UCO Bank was to get Rs. 450 crore, while Central Bank of India and Vijaya Bank would get Rs. 700 and Rs. 500 crore, respectively, in the first tranche. P. Chidambaram said that the move would enable banks raise their CAR over the 12 per cent mark, which is well above the Basel norms which mandates banks to have a capital adequacy of 9 per cent. Chidambaram added that the infusion of funds would be a part of Tier I capital. The Government holding in these three banks would also increase. The state holds 80.20 per cent in Central Bank of India, 75.98 per cent in UCO and 53.87 per cent in Vijaya Bank.

Chidambaram also said that tapping the capital market to raise funds is not a viable option at this stage. Banks are allowed to raise capital as equity and innovative instruments such as perpetual non-cumulative preference shares and perpetual bonds under the Tier I category.

China

China launched an economic stimulus package worth nearly $600 billion, in November 2008 which included more Government investment in infrastructure, tax deductions for exporters, and bigger subsidies to the poor and farmers. Asian markets soared in response. One analyst described the massive package, which was bigger than expected, as a "new deal with Chinese characteristics." China's economy is weakening faster than expected. Growth slid to 9 per cent in the third quarter, the slowest pace in five years. Andy Rothman, of the brokerage CLSA, said that China is going further than the developed economies by spending more and spending faster on its package. He noted that the stimulus was equal to 8 per cent of China's Gross Domestic Product, compared with US and German packages that are about 1 per cent of those countries' GDP. China is likely to spend money on low-cost housing, social welfare and rural infrastructure, aimed at stimulating domestic spending. But analysts warned that China's billions are unlikely to turn around the county's economic slowdown, though they might put a floor under it.

China is ready to face greater economic difficulties and has an emergency stimulus plan in place if the impact of the global financial crisis gets worse, said Premier Wen Jiabao. Wen told the press after the annual parliament session that China has sufficient "ammunition" to combat the crisis. China had rolled out a 4-trillion-yuan, two-year stimulus package in 2008, for which the central Government has now pledged 1.18 trillion yuan. Wen said that 1.18 trillion yuan from the central Government was new investment. He said the stimulus package included housing for seven and a half million low-income Chinese over three years, and would provide better shelter for 2.4 million Chinese who still live in shacks. The premier admitted that some projects in the package, such as roads and railways, were already in the country's 11th five-year plan. Wen called for confidence in the plans. He said it "produced courage and strength, and only with those can we overcome difficulties."

Premier Wen Jiabao said China still has much room to make new economic stimulus package to revive the economy, but did not say when the Government would release it. "China has prepared policies for future contingencies," he said. "We have ample choices and can make...at any time," he added. It is believed that Premier Wen Jiabao would soon announce new stimulus measures, adding to the earlier stimulus package. Some economists, however, did suggest that the Government would expand the stimulus plan if it failed to revive the economy as expected in the second half of 2009.

Chinese Economy: Government's Role in Economic Stimulus

The past decade of rapid development of the economy and the urban system is the result of interaction between economic reforms and the open policy. Because of the locational advantage of the Eastern Coastal region, the open policy has made it grow faster than the Central and Western regions. Urban growth and urbanization, especially rural urbanization, are also most rapid in the Eastern Coastal region. With continued economic development as a result of the open policy, more towns in the Eastern Coastal region will be upgraded to become cities in the future, reversing the pre-1978 trend of decentralizing cities to the Central and Western regions.

The open policy has also favoured the development of cities that have better accessibility and an economic base for foreign investment. It has opened the highly centrally controlled economy to a mixture of central and market economies. More and more people do not rely on the state for income and housing. The pre-1978 mechanisms and state resource allocation are becoming less effective in controlling urban development.

With these developments now China can implement economic policy more easily and quickly than other large economies like the US, Japan, or European economies can due to its central, communist structure. This makes it easier to dictate the country's direction in times of economic need or crisis, without the back-and-forth debates and indecision seen elsewhere.

In the US, the action taken in the wake of the financial crisis was slow, full of heated debate and just highlighted the uncertainty of both lawmakers and financial institutions. However, some people believe that democracies are nice, and it is healthy to view all angles of an issue and stress-test each one instead of blindly jump into how to spend $700 billion.

China's ability to implement instant, blanket law might be nice at times too, but has resulted in exactly what happens in most communist and dictatorial Governments: restrictions of freedom of press, religion, political beliefs and other violations of basic human rights, as viewed by the West. "China is like a big kid on the playground that doesn't quite fit in with the cool crowd and nobody really trusts.... As a result, China seems to be constantly vying to earn the trust of the world."

Ever since China's free market reforms began in 1978, the nation has gradually and successfully emerged as a global economic power. China phased out old communist standards, such as collectivized agriculture and a lack of autonomy for state enterprises. Reforms in the financial system, privatization, and relaxation in FDI followed with this liberalization.

It has been done slowly and carefully to avoid any of the shocks associated with overnight changes in an economic system. Massive and sudden introduction of foreign funds and a total relaxation of policy would obviously have spelled disaster. China even started (much before 1978) with 5-year plans, as seen also in India. These are remnants of Soviet-style development strategies.

Throughout this massive growth period, the Communist Party has sought to portray a climate of progress, stability, and an overall smooth transition into the market economy China is becoming. And without bipartisan debate or dispute, it has been very easy to project whatever figures to the world it wanted.

Indeed, GDP growth in China has been impressive in the past years. China's robust financial system, high per capita savings, and export-led, manufacturing-based economy have contributed to its growth and long-term potential. Between 1990 and 2004 the Chinese economy grew at an average annual rate of 10 per cent. This is despite the many bureaucratic and unproductive state-owned enterprises which weigh it down, as well as the masses of non-performing (unpaid) loans the financial system has to absorb.

While the Government has far less say in the economy now than it did in communist times, it still guides the nation's economic development, as per the State Constitution of 1982. Almost all of the 100-plus ministries, commissions, and corporations in the Chinese Government are structured around economic matters.

However, the Government's involvement in the economy has been limited by the huge volume of economic activity and trade, moving more towards a role of indirect guidance. Nevertheless, that did not stop it from swiftly authorizing an introduction of US$586 billion into infrastructure and social welfare programs in early November. The funds will be spent over the next two years and was called a "massive infrastructure spending program".

This injection came as fears of a slowing economy set in. China grew at almost 12 per cent last year; some analysts forecast a growth of only 6 per cent next year, if no fiscal action is taken. International pressure has been put on China to accelerate its economy to help offset the recessions elsewhere. Hong Kong, Singapore, Japan, the eurozone, New Zealand, India, and some in the US all announced they were in recession.

Beijing's recent interest rate cuts (three of them), removal of bank lending quotas, homebuyer help, and aids to exports were not enough to restore confidence. Domestic demand could be revived, however, through infrastructure spending.

The ease—and lack of public debate—with which this stimulus package has been passed is remarkable.

Major Economies Need Immediate Cash Boost: Japan Ex-PM

Japan's former Prime Minister Shinzo Abe urged leading nations to inject cash into their economies to stimulate the global economy and also warned against rising protectionism.

"An extraordinary economic situation requires an extraordinary response," Abe told the Global Competitiveness Forum in the Saudi capital. "Major economies must immediately make fiscal injections to stimulate the economy."

Abe, premier from 2006 to 2007, and now a special Government envoy, cited Japan's experience during a long downturn in the 1990s as evidence of the need for increased Government spending to overcome the world financial crisis.

He said this was also necessary to fend off protectionist moves by countries seeking to shore up their economies. "We should not yield to the temptation of protectionism, but take financial action to stimulate the economy," he said. He added that Japan needed to stimulate domestic demand to help the world recover growth. "It is important for our country to lead the world with a will to be the first to get out of this depression by launching bold countermeasures one after another, with a sense of alacrity."

Japan PM Unveils $150 Billion Stimulus Package

Japan formally unveiled its record $150 billion (£105 billion) stimulus package as it sought to revive its flagging economy. Prime Minister Taro Aso said the plan—worth about 3 per cent of its Gross Domestic Product—aimed to protect livelihoods and to foster future growth. The 15.4 trillion yen package included measures to boost fuel-efficient vehicles and consumer electronics. Japan's economy has been battered by a collapse in exports and is facing its deepest recession since World War II. "We are implementing a resolute policy in the form of economic crisis measures in order to protect the livelihoods of the people," Mr Aso told a news conference. "The first of our objectives is to prevent the economy from falling through the floor. Another objective is to give a sense of security to the people," he said.

This was the Government's third stimulus plan and come on top of 12 trillion yen of spending in earlier packages, as well as tax breaks and cash handouts. It aimed to create a financial safety net for temporary workers, boost struggling firms and support regional economies. Mr Aso said the new steps would be partially funded by issuing new Government bonds. Japan has been worst-hit among advanced nations by the global economic downturn. Its exports have halved amid an unprecedented collapse in worldwide demand for the cars and electronic gadgets the country produces. The Government has a long-term goal to shift the economy's focus from exports to domestic sectors poised for major growth. It wants to be a world leader in energy efficient technology and to bolster care for its huge and growing elderly population. The aim is to create as many as two million jobs in the next three years.

United Kingdom

In UK, short selling in specific stocks in stock exchanges was temporarily banned and market-to-market rules were eased.

Official bank rate was cut thrice by 300 bps during October-December 2008 and further by 50 bps to 1.5 per cent on January 8, 2009. The collateral eligible for the long-term repo operations was extended on October 3, 2008.

After Northern Rock, Bradford and Bingley became the second mortgage lender to get nationalized. Government rescue plan of UK£400 billion for financial institutions was introduced.

The Government invested £50 billion in the banking industry, offered guarantees over £250 billion of new bank debt and further added £100 billion to the existing Bank of England short-term loan scheme.

The Government took control of Royal Bank of Scotland (RBS) and Halifax Bank of Scotland (HBOS).

France

France economic stimulus package was declared in December 2008 to cushion the impact of global economic crisis and ease undesirable effects of increasing layoffs. An economic stimulus package for France worth $33 billion—spread over two years—was mainly directed at increasing investments in infrastructure development and help recover the country's ailing automobile industry.

Automobile industry in France is a predominant economic activity since it engages over ten per cent of France's total workforce and hence there was a need for an economic stimulus package for France.

This particular France economic stimulus package was different from ones that have been announced previously by French Government. Those packages tried to increase consumption in order to deal with economic crises but this one focused more on automobile industry of France.

This economic stimulus package of France was designed to accelerate tax rebates and credits owed to companies, thereby speeding up investments in infrastructure. In a televised address, French President Nicolas Sarkozy declared that France economic stimulus package was an effort of massive investment in response to a crisis and best way to do this was to support present-day competitiveness and invest in future projects. He had taken this opportunity to caution managerial segment in taking this as an excuse to reduce their work force and restructure their organizations.

As per European Commission guidelines, not more than 1.5 per cent of a nation's Gross Domestic Product is to be allocated for growth. This stimulus package was as per guidelines of European Commission. According to President Sarkozy's plans, budget deficit of France was expected to rise to 4 per cent of GDP as against 3 per cent limit of European Union.

In this France economic stimulus package, \$13.7 billion was earmarked for infrastructure development, \$5.25 billion towards investment in state owned postal, rail and energy projects, and \$1.31 billion for mobilizing their car credit market. An additional \$2.36 billion was allocated for building 100,000 homes to be made available to low income earners at zero interest loans. This package further aimed at hastening payment of \$15 billion towards investment credits.

Sarkozy Defends Plans for Economy

French President Nicolas Sarkozy has defended his plans to revive the French economy, saying state intervention with banks has so far cost people nothing. Mr Sarkozy also said there would be no bonuses for executives of failing banks that have been bailed out by the state. The Government would scrap a local business tax in 2010 and was ready to consider cutting income tax, he added. He made the comments in a TV interview, a week after nationwide protests and strikes at his handling of the economy. A million workers downed tools to protest against what they said was an inadequate response to the global financial crisis, and to call on the Government to do more to protect jobs and wages.

The Prime Minister Francois Fillon announced a 26 billion euro ($33.1 billion; £23.5 billion) initiative designed to "revitalize" the economy. The package comprised 11 billion euros to help businesses improve their cash flows; 11 billion euros of direct state investment; and 4 billion euros of investment by state-owned firms in modernisation programs. Mr Sarkozy ruled out the provision of direct aid to struggling consumers.

Speaking in a live 90-minute television interview, Mr Sarkozy defended his Government's handling of the economic crisis but acknowledged that the French people had every right to be concerned about the situation. "It's normal that the French are worried. It's a crisis the like of which the world has not seen for a century," he said. "I must ensure that France enters the crisis as late as possible and gets out of it as early as possible. Naturally, I will continue to reform the country. It is the only way for France to emerge from the crisis stronger than going into it," he added.

The President then defended his decision to set aside billions of euros to recapitalise banks, saying it would cost taxpayers nothing. "The money loaned to the banks will not only cost the French people not one cent, but will bring in money," he stated. Mr Sarkozy announced that there should be no bonus payments in 2009 for executives of the banks which have been bailed out. However, he said he was "more shocked by the system of pay" for lower-level bank traders and wanted it to be changed.

The revenue from the loans to failing banks would be spent on social measures, Sarkozy said, such as increases in family welfare and short-term unemployment benefits, or a possible reduction in income tax. He also pledged to scrap in 2010 the local "professional tax" at a cost of some 8 billion euros ($10.25 billion; £7 billion), which he said penalised French companies and encouraged outsourcing. But he ruled out an increase in the minimum wage or any provision of direct aid to struggling consumers, saying his priority was to protect jobs. "If consumers don't spend, it's because they are fearful for their jobs," he said. He added that he wanted company profits to be shared in future, saying he would like to see a third of profits handed out to employees, a third to the investors and a third going on investments.

Huge crowds took to the streets to protest at the Government's policies. But despite these protests, he said he would press ahead with his reform program, which includes cutting taxes and slimming down the public sector. "Naturally, I will continue to reform the country. This is the mandate I received, it is my duty," he said. "It is the only way for France to emerge from the crisis stronger than going into it." The union leaders said they had been disappointed with the lack of "concrete or immediate action" presented by the President and warned that they were ready to launch new protests.

Portugal

Portugal economic stimulus package was announced on 13th December 2008. This stimulus package was worth 2 billion euros and amounted to 1.25 per cent of the country's GDP.

This package was supposed to be provided to medium sized business enterprises. However, smaller business enterprises of Portugal would also be beneficiaries. The package aimed at improving condition of infrastructure facilities available at Portugal.

Money from Portugal economic stimulus package would also be provided for improving technological scenario in this Iberian nation. As per reports, education sector is also in radar of Portugal economic surplus package. Fifty per cent of surplus package would be provided by members of European Union and remaining amount is supposed to come from Portugal itself.

Bank of Portugal has predicted that in 2009, the economy of Portugal would decrease by 0.8 per cent. In 2008 however, Portuguese economy had grown by 0.3 per cent. Previously, Bank of Portugal had predicted that in 2009 Portuguese economy would grow by 1.3 per cent.

Bank of Portugal has also predicted that GDP of Portugal would be able to sustain itself in such an environment of economic instability. It has also predicted that the country's GDP would be able to grow in 2010 fiscal by 0.3 per cent.

Bank of Portugal has also opined that rate of inflation would be lower in 2009 than the previous years. It has predicted a rate of 1 per cent, which is lower than 2.7 per cent of the previous year, i.e. 2008.

Even though Portuguese economy has been able to adjust to changing times and economic downturn till now, it is beginning to crack up as an after effect of global financial recession. This scenario made Portugal economic stimulus package even more necessary as weaker sectors of Portuguese economy would now need all the support that they can get.

Italy Economic Stimulus Package

Italy's economy has witnessed a recessive trend, especially from beginning of 2008 when whole world came under the menacing effect of financial downturn. National Government has declared an Italy economic stimulus package to curb this regressive fiscal status and to counter this country's worst economic slump after World War II. This comprehensive economic stimulus package of Italy, formulated by economists, was declared by Italian economy minister Giulio Tremonti.

The stimulus package was designed after identifying loop-holes in various sectors of Italian economy and vulnerable areas dampening steady monetary growth. Main focus of economic stimulus package to Italy is to opt for tax breaks for companies and poorer households to ensure that banks continue to lend to businesses. It is inclusive of tax deductions worth almost 2.4 billion euros. Economic stimulus package in Italy also includes some other features like delayed payment of VAT, reduction in advance tax payments and speedy reimbursements of excess tax payments.

According to Tremonti, total value of Italy's economic stimulus package is worth 80 billion euros. Some economists are of the opinion that a significant percentage of this amount will be in the form of recycling of funds that are already existing. Economic stimulus package also covers domain of mortgage rates which are lowered down to 4 per cent. This well-conceived package also emphasizes state's responsibility of underwriting special convertible bonds issued by banks. In another attempt to solve problem of funding underwriting of bonds, Italy's economic stimulus package states that funds for covering underwriting of bonds will be derived from spending cuts and new public debt issues. Moreover, funds for each case will be allocated on individual basis.

Italian economic stimulus package also contains additional measures including state help for Italian banks worth up to 20 billion euros to ensure their continuous support by lending. This policy is adopted in compliance with a motive of boosting Italy's weak unemployment benefit system. According to Berlusconi, Italian Government is not able to cut taxes and its ability to raise spending is limited. The amount of Italy's economic stimulus package was lower than in other European counterparts like Germany and France owing to country's large public debt. Italy's lower house of parliament has approved this economic stimulus package and final approval from Senate is expected to be provided by February 2009.

Netherlands

Netherlands economic stimulus package was announced by their Prime Minister Jan Peter Balkenende in November 2008. This Dutch economic stimulus package of €6 billion equalled one per cent of the country's GDP. The package primarily included fiscal measures directed at improving corporate liquidity.

The economic stimulus package of Netherlands of $7.5 billion was drawn up in agreement with joint regional economic plan of European Union. Global financial crisis has forced Dutch Government to nationalize two major banks ABN Amro, and Fortis in order to prevent them from collapsing triggered by delinquent funding. In addition, this economic stimulus package included €20 billion, which was injected into Dutch money market to guarantee interbank transfers and thereby restore confidence of investors and consumers. Aegon, an insurance company, received a sum of

€3 billion as a part of economic stimulus package to Netherlands. ING, a commercial bank, has received €10 billion as booster funds. Inflation has been projected at 1.8 per cent in 2009 and at 1.4 per cent in 2010. GDP is expected to grow at 1.8 per cent in 2009. This low growth rate is a reflection of consumer and business pessimism.

Lower growth in exports and high commodity prices led to a fall in GDP growth from 3.5 per cent in 2007 to 2 per cent in 2008 and is estimated at 0.6 per cent in 2009. GDP calculated on the basis of purchasing power parity (ppp) worked out to $687.5 billion in 2008. This estimate in terms of official exchange rate amounts to $909.5 billion. Per capita GDP calculated on ppp basis for corresponding period was estimated at $41,300. Nearly 74 per cent of GDP was contributed by services or tertiary sector, followed by over 24 per cent contribution from secondary or industrial sector and remaining 2 per cent contribution came from primary or agricultural sector. Investments in Netherlands, as per estimates of 2008 data, accounted for 20.3 per cent of GDP, while public debt worked out to 57.3 per cent of GDP in corresponding time.

National budget of Holland for 2008 recorded revenue of $408.5 billion and an expenditure of almost $399 billion. Exports comprising mainly of chemicals, foodstuff, machineries and equipments, and fuels amounted to $573.5 billion compared to its import of $485 billion for 2008. Holland economic stimulus package made provisions for foreign direct investments. In 2008 this was worth $730 billion. Dutch exchequer has a gold and foreign exchange reserve of $27 billion approximately.

Netherlands Weighs Extra Spending

The Dutch Government may boost spending by 16 billion euros ($22 billion) over three years to tackle the recession. The plan includes increasing Government expenditure by 4 billion euros in 2009 from the 179 billion euros budgeted for in September 2008. The extra money would be directed to speeding up infrastructure projects, investments in energy-efficient housing and helping more people to find work.

The Dutch Government is seeking to revive the euro region's fifth-largest economy, which is set to suffer the worst recession since 1931. The Government forecasts a contraction of 3.5 per cent in 2009 and 0.25 per cent in 2010, leading to the first budget deficit since 2005. Spending would be reduced in 2011 if economic growth is forecast to reach 0.5 per cent or more the sources say. The Netherlands increased its budget-deficit forecast for 2009 to 5.6 per cent from an earlier estimate of 5.4 per cent as income declined from taxes and natural-gas sales, exceeding the European Union's 3 per cent deficit ceiling for the first time since the euro was introduced a decade ago.

The Cabinet plans to raise the state-pension age to 67 years from 65 years to "fill a future budgetary gap," Agnes Jongerius, who heads the largest Dutch union FNV, said at a press conference. "We ask the Cabinet to refrain from raising the state-pension age; we will provide a better alternative," he said.

Romania Gets 20 Billion-Euro Bailout Aid from IMF, EU

Romania got a 20 billion-euro ($27 billion) loan from the International Monetary Fund, European Union and other lenders. It is the sixth eastern European nation to be bailed out as the region's economies struggle to stay afloat.

About 13 billion euros will come from the IMF and the rest from the EU, World Bank and the European Bank for Reconstruction and Development, the Washington-based fund said in a statement. The "package should more than cover Romania's financing needs...," said Ozgur Yasar Guyuldar, an emerging markets strategist in Vienna at Raiffeisen Centrobank. "The IMF deal will certainly bring some discipline to the budget. I view this aid package as a big relief," he added. The Balkan nation, which had the fastest-growing economy in the EU during 2008, is plunging into a recession and the central bank has little scope to lower interest rates to revive growth. The loan brings to more than $60 billion the total handed out to eastern Europe. Hungary, Ukraine, Belarus, Latvia and Serbia have also sought bailouts to prevent defaults and aid banks.

"The objective of the policy package is to cushion the effects of the sharp drop in private capital inflows," IMF Managing Director Dominique Strauss-Kahn said in the statement.

The Government will target a budget deficit of 4.5 per cent of GDP in 2009, compared with 4.8 per cent in the previous year, even as the economic contraction cuts revenue, Jeffrey Franks, head of the IMF negotiating team said. The budget approved in December 2008 would have led to a deficit of about 9 per cent of GDP, he said. The country, which had a record current account deficit of about 13 per cent of GDP in 2008, has predicted it will narrow to less than 10 per cent in a few months as a weaker leu trims imports.

Romania requested talks with international organizations as exports suffered from waning demand in its key Western European trading partners. "Core measures under the program are designed to strengthen fiscal policy to reduce the Government's financing needs and improve long-term fiscal sustainability, thus preparing Romania for Eurozone entry," the IMF release said. The country aims to adopt the European common currency in 2014.

Sweden

A Sweden economic stimulus package of $1 billion was announced on 5 December 2008 to overcome global financial crisis by ways of infrastructure development and investment in human capital. It was devised to stabilize itself in an environment of global export scarcity.

Sweden being an export-oriented economy is greatly dependent on global market conditions and is urgently in need for an economic stimulus package. With dwindling exports it became necessary to create alternative avenues of revenue and an economic stimulus package could come in handy for Sweden in this regard.

Human capital empowerment is not only a worthy investment but also an effective form of investment. Investment in human capital is done in forms of on-the-job training, vocational workshops, and restructuring at workplace. As part of an economic stimulus package to Sweden, social welfare benefits are also extended to individuals facing short- or long-term unemployment. As part of this social benefit program, Swedish economic stimulus package has set a target of training about 59,000 individuals in 2009, 72,000 in 2010 and 34,000 in 2011.

Calculated monetary regulations have been implemented in economic stimulus package in Sweden with an aim to stabilize money supply. Commercial banks' borrowing rates from Swedish central bank has been reduced to 2 per cent. These commercial banks extend a wide gamut of credit instruments to private business houses. Domestic as well as overseas investors have access to these commercial banks for their respective capital needs. Commercial banking in Sweden is concentrated among four banks controlling over 80 per cent of total banking operations in the country.

Foreign countries are permitted to invest in most sectors and activities except for sales of alcoholic beverages and pharmaceuticals, which are monopolized by Swedish Government. Though the processes acquiring licenses and permits for setting up industries are complex, efficient bureaucracy and effective laws make procedures convenient.

Private enterprises account for 90 per cent of total industrial output out of which 50 per cent are from engineering sector. This industrial sector contributes 29 per cent of Sweden's GDP and provides employment to 22 per cent of available labor force. Services or tertiary sector is Sweden's largest contributor to GDP and labor market with shares of 69 per cent and 76 per cent respectively. Real growth rate of GDP in 2008 was 0.9 per cent and inflation stood around 1.6 per cent. Gross fixed investment was calculated at 19.6 per cent of GDP in 2008. Sweden's stimulus package has been augmented by its foreign exchange and gold reserves amounting to $31 billion approximately. This has helped the country to implement stimulus package in right earnest.

Belgium

The economic stimulus package for Belgium falls within European Union's economy package outlined at €200 billion. This package is equivalent to 1.5 per cent of aggregated Gross Domestic Product of 27 member nations of European Union. Foreign direct investment and growth rate dropped in 2008 after a moderate growth phase from 2004 to 2007.

Subsequently, falling consumer expenditure, pessimistic investment environment and tightened credit facilities contributed to a decline in national income. GDP calculated with purchasing power parity (ppp) as basis was estimated at $398.7 billion in 2008 which when calculated at official exchange rate worked out to $530.6 billion. Such an environment made an economic stimulus package for Belgium very necessary.

Real growth rate of GDP was estimated at 1.5 per cent in 2008 whereas per capita GDP calculated on ppp terms was $38,300. Services sector with nearly 75 per cent share was greatest contributor towards GDP, followed by industrial sector's 24 per cent and agricultural sector's 1 per cent. Implementation of economic stimulus package in Belgium became even more important in view of Belgian economy's shrinkage at a rate of 1.7 per cent. Belgian economy stimulus package, if put in place, can bring down inflation to 1 per cent in 2009 as compared to 4.6 per cent in 2008.

Exports are likely to fall by about 4.5 per cent and aggregate demand by 0.3 per cent. An economic stimulus package can prove to be handy for Belgium in such an adverse economic scenario. A reduction is aggregate demand and exports would result in fall in work force, thus demand, raising unemployment level to more than 8 per cent as compared to 2008's 7.1 per cent. Effects of such economic fallouts could be averted with the help of an economic stimulus package.

In 2008 budget, Belgian Government had earned revenue of $251.3 billion and incurred expenses of $254.2 billion, thereby yielding a deficit of $2.9 billion. Public debt calculated in 2008 worked out to almost 81 per cent of GDP. Balance of payments reflected a negative figure with exports amounting to $373 billion and imports $375 billion. As 80 per cent of Belgium exports comprise of industrial products, a worldwide decline in demand for industrial commodities has adversely affected overseas trade of this European industrial economy. Belgium economy stimulus package has allowed for open participation of foreign investors in domestic investments, specially in infrastructural projects.

Ireland Economic Stimulus Package

As per noted economists and economic analysts in Ireland, an Ireland economic stimulus package would not be a suitable answer to woes being faced by national economy. Irish Government is experiencing a crisis in the wake of global financial meltdown. The issues would not be solved by an economic stimulus package in Ireland only.

As per these experts, financial problems being experienced by Irish Government are not causes but are rather results of world financial downturn and they have opined that it would take more than an economic stimulus package of Ireland to set things right. As per their opinions, Irish Government would not be heading in right the direction if they depended solely on an economic stimulus package to Ireland to make matters right as problems lie much deeper. Ireland, like most other countries, has been affected by global financial crisis but its degree has been greater as is shown by its economy, which is on the verge of collapsing.

As per statements made by Irish exchequer in November 2008, budget deficit of Ireland national Government would be 6.5 per cent of its Gross Domestic Product. Irish Government has adopted certain measures regarding public expenditure and taxation and it is being assumed that in 2009 budget deficit faced by Ireland would be 8.5 per cent of its GDP. Economists are of the view that a change in Governmental attitude, and not Irish economic stimulus package, would be a probable answer to questions being posed by financial crises.

An Irish economic stimulus package is necessary, however, as economists predict that in years to come both output as well as employment in Ireland's economy are set to decrease. As per calculations of economists in Ireland, structural budget deficit for Ireland in 2009 would be 9 billion euros. This would be equivalent to 5 per cent of its GDP and it may be assumed that in such a scenario an economic stimulus package is necessary for the country.

Germany Economic Stimulus Package

A Germany economic stimulus package of €50 billion, biggest since its formation in 1949, was announced in December 2008. This economic stimulus package is spread over a period of two years and was agreed upon by German coalition Government led by Chancellor Angela Merkel. It broadly included infrastructural investments, social benefits, tax concessions and soft loans. The Germany economic stimulus package worth $66.8 billion was approved by national Government on 27th January 2009. This package was approved by Social Democrats, Christian Democratic Union, headed by Angela Merkel and the Christian Social Union. Angela Merkel reiterated that German Government would make sure that policies formulated in the package were put to use in the shortest time possible.

A substantial portion of this German economic stimulus package, of about €17 billion, is in the form of investments to be made in highway construction, educational spending, and tax cuts for individuals and businesses. To increase disposable income among consumers health insurance rates have been cut, thereby releasing an additional sum of €9 billion in their hands. A further amount of €9 billion would be realized by process of reducing corporate and personal income tax from 15 per cent to 14 per cent.

German Government has allocated €100 billion towards loan for sick and recovering industries. This credit and guarantee fund would inspire upgrading of old manufacturing processes with updated technologies. A one-time bonus of €100 per child was provided to families. Another lucrative bonus was planned for drivers who replace their old automobiles with new environment friendly ones.

To implement economic stimulus package in Germany effectively, some regulations have been simplified for creation of temporary employment opportunities. Subsidies are being paid for growth of human capital and contribution towards social benefits. Construction of highways is another priority area in this package.

German economy is expected to shrink three per cent in 2009 and unemployment might cross three million. Budget deficit, because of this stimulus package, is likely to be 4.5 per cent in 2010 as compared to stipulated limit of 3 per cent in Euro Growth and Stability Pact.

Spain Stimulus Package

On 18 April 2008, Spanish Government decided on a stimulus package worth about 18 billion euros. Primary aim of this stimulus package was to maintain a certain semblance of economic expansion, which has been hit hard by credit crunch and declining housing market of Spain.

On 14 August 2008, Spanish Government pledged a stimulus package worth 20 billion euros. Main purpose behind this was to deal with problems of an economy that was cooling down due to global financial crisis.

This Spain stimulus package was supposed to be providing tax cuts on an emergency basis. According to this package, there would be a provision of tax rebate worth 400 euros to every pensioner and worker. This amount was a part of outlays worth 10 billion euros provided in financial year 2008-09. Remaining 8 billion euros would be spent in the financial year 2009-10.

Jose Luis Rodriguez Zapatero, Prime Minister of Spain has been making provisions for a budget surplus that would be employed as a buffer against impact of global meltdown on Spanish economy that had suffering a downturn. As per International Monetary Fund, rate of economic growth came down to 1.8 per cent in 2008. This was more than 50 per cent less compared to financial year 2007.

Situation of housing sector in Spanish economy has been extremely deplorable of late, as prices of housing properties have been falling in real terms. This was first time in a span of ten years that Spain's housing sector has been in such a plight. In the previous decade, housing sector of Spain had been in a better situation as it had grown to become three times as large.

Deputy Prime Minister of Spain, Maria Teresa Fernandez de la Vega opined that Spain's national Government had followed a fiscal and budgetary policy that enabled them to collect a surplus from public accounts. As a result of this, Spanish Government was now able to introduce stimulus packages like this, that would help to boost economy, assist households and individuals in times of financial crisis and revive job market.

Australian Stimulus Plan Approved

Australia's Senate has passed the Labor Government's A$42 billion ($27 billion; £19 billion) stimulus plan after the bill was blocked during an earlier vote. It was approved after the Government reached a deal with an independent senator who had earlier joined the Liberal Party-led opposition. Prime Minister Kevin Rudd said the bill was vital to boost the economy amid a global economic slowdown.

The approval came after the Government agreed to A$1 billion in extra funding for water projects. "I'm pleased to say I believe we have been able to reach a compromise, which while not giving everybody what they want, may give everyone what they need," said independent senator Nick Xenophon, who had blocked the plan a day earlier.

Treasurer Wayne Swan, who led the negotiations with Mr Xenophon, said, "We are prepared to act in the national interest. That's what governs the fiscal stimulus package in the first place." The bill had already passed once through the House of Representatives, the Senate's lower chamber, where Labor has a large majority.

The plan proposed spending A$28.8 billion on schools, housing and roads over four years. In addition, it wants to dedicate A$12.7 billion on tax breaks for small firms, and cash handouts for eligible workers and students.

Opposition leader Malcolm Turnbull had said the Government was treating parliament with "disingenuous contempt", accusing it of refusing to negotiate a less expensive package. But business leaders had expressed their frustration at the Senate's earlier rejection of the stimulus plan. "No other nation's parliament has refused a major stimulus package in the current environment of unprecedented global economic downturn," said the Australian Chamber of Commerce and Industry.

Mexico Economic Stimulus Package

In January 2009, President Calderon, in order to prevent layoffs, added $150 million in Mexican economic stimulus package. Mexican central bank cut its lending rates from 8.25 per cent to 7.75 per cent. Inflation which was around 6.5 per cent in 2008 is expected to reduce to around 5.4 per cent in 2009 and down to 3 per cent in 2010. Mexican 'peso' has been badly affected because of decreased oil exports to United States, the main trading partner of Mexico.

A Mexico economic stimulus package of $5.6 billion had been announced by their President Felipe Calderon in March 2008. This economic stimulus package in Mexico is being provided in form of utility rates discounts, tax breaks and spending programs. In its efforts to strengthen domestic economy, national Government planned new investments in infrastructure development, housing, agriculture and diversification of exports in the stimulus package.

Agustin Carstens, Finance Minister of Mexico had estimated a growth rate of 2.8 per cent in 2008 as compared to 3.7 per cent in 2007. This reduced estimate was due to a devastating money market and economic slowdown of neighboring United States. The situation in Mexico called for an economic stimulus package for Mexico to be provided immediately. Accordingly, companies were given an income tax relief of 3 per cent and a reduction of 20 per cent in electricity rates as part of economic stimulus package. These companies were also provided with certain compulsory payroll benefit options. Mexican state owned oil company, Pemex Oil said it would increase spending by $935 million through repairing its old pipeline network.

While declaring Mexico economic stimulus package Felipe Calderon said that economic performance of United States of America, its major trading partner has been well nigh unimpressive. Housing sector and financial sector of United States of America have been hit hard by global financial recession and this has in turn affected Mexico as well.

Nigeria Economic Stimulus Package

Nigeria economic stimulus package has been provided mainly in the shape of economic assistance and foreign direct investments to ailing sectors of the economy.

This west African country has received an economic stimulus package worth $1.87 billion from World Bank FDIs. A significant amount of economic stimulus package to Nigeria, amounting to $5.2 billion, is being spent mostly in finance and energy sectors.

Fossil fuel or oil is Nigeria's main export revenue earner. Out of total revenue earned from oil exports by Nigeria, 80 per cent is earned by Nigerian Government, 16 per cent is spent on operational costs, and 4 per cent goes to investors. Beyond oil, economy of Nigeria is inefficient and requires adequate attention. Economic stimulus package in Nigeria is also being provided by way of National Economic Empowerment Development Strategy (NEEDS).

Liberalization, deregulation, privatization and stability are primary concerns of Nigerian economic stimulus package. NEEDS focuses on developing infrastructural facilities like setting up of adequate power supply facilities, supply of drinking water, and provision of irrigation facilities. NEEDS also aims at diversification of Nigerian economy, creating 7 million jobs, maximizing utilization of industrial capacity, encouraging exports of non-energy commodities, and removing corruption and obstacles to formation of new enterprises. A corresponding State Economic Empowerment Development Strategy (SEEDS) has been framed for developmental programs at state level.

To strengthen this economic stimulus package of Nigeria till 2015, a National Millennium Goals program has been sponsored by United Nations. Under this program Nigeria is committed to eradication of poverty, ensure universal primary level education for all, combat diseases like malaria and HIV/AIDS, reduce child and maternal mortality, and protect environment.

In view of current global meltdown, Nigerian budget has been drawn to boost agricultural sector, unlock rural assets, and mobilize rural assets for increasing agricultural productivity. Provisions for steady flow of foreign direct investments have been incorporated for strengthening Nigerian economy.

South Africa Economic Stimulus Package

South African Government is implementing an economic surplus package, in the form of an infrastructural expenditure plan. It is supposed to be worth $69 billion. Kgalema Motlanthe, President of South Africa hopes that this would help South African economy achieve a growth rate of 4 per cent.

A South Africa economic stimulus package had been announced in February 2008. Main purpose of this economic surplus package was to make business establishments spend more by way of introducing attractive incentives.

Economic stimulus package in South Africa was more of a legislation. It is expected to provide business entities in South Africa with rewards that are necessary to increase spending of financial resources.

As per this package, companies were to be rewarded if they bought assets. However, in order to be eligible to receive this benefit companies needed to buy an asset that would have helped them improve aspects of their business such as a software.

It was expected that as a result of this South Africa economic stimulus package business establishments would be taking right steps to ensure that they made full use of that particular benefit. This package would also help these business establishments to save various costs, incurred in their regular business procedures, such as expenses for qualifying properties by way of using them after having bought them.

Various financial institutions within South Africa are also providing help to business establishments. In January 2009, Development Bank of Southern Africa provided Airports Company South Africa with financial assistance worth 1.5 billion rands. This money would be used by Airports Company South Africa for an infrastructural program that would be executed at ten airports across the country. This project would run for five years and is worth 22 billion rands.

Russia Economic Stimulus Package

Russia economic stimulus package was announced by Prime Minister Vladimir Putin in November 2008. Putin assured his countrymen that the package would be successful in guiding them through global economic crisis to a better economic future.

The package worth $20 billion has been earmarked for cushioning Russian economy from unfavorable impacts of global recession. A number of fiscal measures have been undertaken in this package for increasing disposable income for consumers and business houses. As per this package, profit tax has been decreased from 24 per cent to 20 per cent, which allows funds for investments. Russia's foreign exchange, earned from oil, and gold reserves are large enough for tiding over this global economic crisis. According to Finance Minister Alexei Kudrin, deficit in national budget would be one per cent of the GDP.

Russian economy, which had grown at an annual rate of 7.5 per cent in 2007, fell to 6.5 per cent in 2008, and in projected to grow only by 3.5 per cent in 2009. Production cutbacks, job losses and pay cuts have been announced across various segments of Russia's economy. Instances of 50 per cent reduction in production are not unusual. Employee payments have been reduced from anywhere between 1.5 per cent and 10 per cent. Lack of liquidity and reduction in bank lending rates have forced consumption expenditure to diminish.

Oil and metals are primary export revenue earners for Russia. These minerals are accountable for nearly 80 per cent of export earnings. A shift in overseas demand for these commodities can influence foreign revenues to a considerable extent. A decrease in international oil prices has drastically affected foreign exchange earnings of this nation. A reduction in export earnings coupled with a rise in social security costs has diminished foreign exchange reserves of Russia from $590 billion to $460 billion. To control money market behavior Russian central bank has widened its 'rubles' trading. This is an important part of an effort to strengthen Russia's economy.

Brazil Economic Stimulus Package

Brazil economic stimulus package is based on its 'accelerated growth program'. Economic stimulus package to Brazil is aimed at higher investment levels and sustained economic growth. Fiscal reforms together with a higher revenue realization approach has ensured a growth of 4.1 per cent in 2008 and projected a growth of 3.8 per cent in 2009. These financial reforms share a close relation with economic stimulus package for Brazil.

Brazil Government has adopted a number of monetary policies for effectuating Brazilian economic stimulus package. Rebates and tax deductions amounting to $3.1 billion in 2007 have been set to increase to $5.05 billion by 2011. These tax deductions would be funded by reducing budget surplus and are being provided by means of exemptions of industrial and wealth taxes. To enlarge this tax exemption cover, indirect taxes on commonly used items have also been cut. A good example is that of personal computers. Expenditure tax is exempted for all personal computers upto $1750. Fiscal surplus target has been upwardly revised to 4.3 per cent of GDP.

Monetary tightening has restricted consumption expenditure, which, coupled with diminished exports to United States, has projected a reduced economic growth rate from 3.8 per cent to 3.6 per cent in 2009. To keep inflation within controllable limits under an environment of strong demand, it became imperative for a stricter monetary policy and an economic stimulus package in Brazil. The country's central bank has set its lending rate at 14.25 per cent. National Government of Brazil has announced an infusion of approximately $44 billion into National Development Bank of Brazil as a fiscal policy measure contributing to the stimulus package.

Building up of infrastructure is another important aspect of Brazil economic stimulus package. An investment of $221.4 billion has been earmarked for infrastructure building, focusing on transport system and energy segment. Though most of public transport and communication services have been privatized, prices are determined by regulatory agencies. Brazilian Government controls airfares while oil prices are regulated by National Petroleum Agency. Government spending in Brazil is high—often reaching 41 per cent of GDP—whereas public debt remains around 50 per cent of GDP. In addition to debt service, Government spending includes pensions, and monetary transfers to bureaucracy and local Governments.

Indonesia Economic Stimulus Package

Indonesia economic stimulus package was set at $6.31 billion to cushion existing crisis. In Indonesian currency, this amounted to Rp 71.3 trillion, which included a previous Indonesian economic stimulus package of Rp 27.5 trillion. The package was declared by President Susilo Bambang Yudhoyono. This enhanced package was worth Rp 71.3 trillion and included tax savings of Rp 43 trillion, Government spending and subsidies of Rp 15 trillion and waived import duties and taxes amounting to Rp 13.3 trillion.

This stimulus package, in monetary terms, can be broken down into several independent parts. Rp 13.3 trillion and Rp 43 trillion have been set aside for waived taxes for consumers and businesses and tax savings respectively in economic stimulus package of Indonesia. In this stimulus package, Rp 10.2 trillion have been allotted for infrastructure spending with Rp 2.8 trillion as diesel subsidy and Rp 1.4 trillion in the form of discounted electricity rates for industries.

Rp 0.6 trillion have been earmarked for developmental expenses for rural areas.

According to Finance Minister Sri Mulyani Indrawati, these economic stimulus packages are aimed at strengthening consumers' purchasing power, increasing spending on labor-intensive infrastructure, and raising sturdiness and competitiveness among businesses. In brief, this Indonesian economic stimulus package is targeted at cutting costs borne by business houses and consumers. Consequently, infrastructure spending has been projected to increase by Rp 10.2 trillion, tax incentives raised to Rp 6.5 trillion and subsidizing diesel prices have been increased by Rp 2.8 trillion. The entire amount of package worth Rp 71.3 trillion accounts for 1.4 per cent of the country's Gross Domestic Product.

These economic stimulus packages in Indonesia have been devised to counter slowing down of investments, weakening of exports and diminished consumption expenditure. Government spending has been increased by 10.4 per cent which is expected to achieve an overall growth of 5 per cent.

Taiwan Economic Stimulus Package

The Taiwanese economic stimulus package amounting to US $5.6 billion was declared by Chen Tian Jy, Chairman of Council for Economic Planning and Development, in September 2008. It aimed at stabilizing money market, encourage consumer spending, and stimulate industrial growth in general and infrastructure development in particular.

This economic stimulus package of Taiwan was worth Taiwanese dollars (Taiwan $) 180 billion or US$5.6 billion and was expected to help Taiwan achieve a growth of approximately 4.3 per cent for domestic economy in 2008 current year and revive their ailing stock market.

President Ma Ying Jeou after assuming office in May 2008 made concerted efforts in providing financial incentives for business, increase exports, and introduce tax breaks. The stimulus package earmarked an expenditure of 58.3 billion Taiwanese dollars in infrastructure development, 20.5 billion Taiwanese dollars as financial incentive for small and medium scale businesses, 37.5 billion Taiwanese dollars towards tax holidays for new investments and 13.5 billion Taiwanese dollars as subsidies for low income households.

The Taiwanese economic stimulus package has targeted streamlining exports, which is an important component of national revenue. To boost shipments to new overseas markets like Russia, Brazil and Middle East, this Taiwan economic stimulus package allotted Taiwanese dollars 1.5 billion for exports. Exports from Taiwan are expected to grow by 10 per cent towards later phase of this package. An aggregate growth of 4.3 per cent was projected for Taiwanese economy in 2009 as compared to 5.7 per cent in 2008.

Taiwan economic stimulus package also set aside 1.81 billion Taiwanese dollars to be provided in the form of interest subsidies and its beneficiaries would be home buyers. This package was part of a preferential mortgage program, worth 200 billion Taiwanese dollars.

As part of this Taiwan economic stimulus package 37.5 billion Taiwanese dollars would be provided as five year tax breaks. This benefit would be provided on investments made by technical service and manufacturing companies. It would last till end of 2009.

Singapore Economic Stimulus Package

A record Singapore economic stimulus package of $13.7 billion was unveiled to provide a safety cordon for worst recession in recent years. According to their Finance Minister Tharman Shanmugaratnam, the primary objective of economic stimulus package in Singapore was to save jobs and prevent unemployment rate from going beyond the rate of 2.2 per cent prevailing in December 2008. A sharp increase in unemployment might lead to political unrest against People's Action Party, which would be celebrating its 50th anniversary of being in Governmental power.

Singapore, known for its thrifty nature, has a rare budget deficit of $5.8 billion for 2008. Amounting to roughly 6 per cent of its GDP, this deficit would be financed by Singapore Government's reserves of $300 billion. This particular financial aid has been likened to a economic stimulus package of Singapore. Economic growth is expected at a modest 5 per cent for 2009 and could be heralded, to a significant extent by economic stimulus package for Singapore.

To prevent unemployment from increasing and encourage hiring, corporate tax has been reduced by one per cent for 2009. Investments in infrastructure have been planned to create new job opportunities. Subsidies and tax rebates have been planned for income earners and households. A substantial economic stimulus package to Singapore would also be needed in order to supplement these measures.

Singapore, being an open economy in Asia, is susceptible to global economic changes. Exports, which are main revenue-earners of Singapore, have received a substantial setback due to global fall in demand. Consumer spending has been curbed by introducing a forced savings option into state-operated pension fund. According to Credit Suisse, greatest impact of this recession would fall on about 200,000 overseas workers who would have their work permits exhausted by 2010.

In 2009, needy families would be provided a support amounting to $1.7 billion in the form of tax rebates and cash handouts. The next few months would be most trying for Singapore economy.

Thailand Economic Stimulus Package

Thailand economic stimulus package of $3.33 billion was largely built along social-welfare segment. Some other segments targeted were consumption, real estate, tourism, and medium and small enterprises. Thai central bank, Bank of Thailand, eased monetary policies as part of an economic stimulus package to Thailand to boost growth.

An initial economic stimulus package of Thailand, consisting of 17 programs—aim mainly towards curbing recession—was declared in January 2009. Kobak Sabhavasu, deputy premier in charge of economic affairs, in an effort to provide economic stimulus package for Thailand, declared a monthly allowance of Baht 2000 per individual for 9 million low-income earners. Further, electricity and water were made available to small households free of cost.

School education was subsidized till 1st May 2009, and included books, uniforms and tuition fees. In addition to the aforesaid, Kobak Sabhavasu announced financial assistance to individuals earning less than Baht 14,000 a month to make his economic stimulus package a success. This assistance would be provided to all eligible members of Social Security Fund.

Most of these Thai economic stimulus package instruments were an impetus for increasing consumer expenditure. For this reason small and rural enterprises are also being promoted aggressively. A rise in domestic consumption would, to a substantial extent, make up for loss in export earnings. In an effort to encourage growth in real estate, new home purchasers would have their tax deduction increased from Baht 100,000 to 200,000. These newly devised mortgage insurance schemes would motivate low-income earners to buy homes at low deposits.

As additional Thai economic stimulus packages, their Government declared Baht 15 billion for community-based enterprises, Baht 9 billion for senior citizens over 60 years, Baht 6.9 billion for retraining idle workforce, and Baht 3 billion for community-based health workers. To boost tourism and services industries, Government injected Baht 500 million in the form of easy loans. Thailand, like most other countries of the world, has been hit hard for financial crisis and finds itself in great economic peril, which is why a Thailand economic stimulus package was extremely necessary.

Malaysia Economic Stimulus Package

Malaysia economic stimulus package was announced in November 2008. Their Deputy Prime Minister and Finance Minister Datuk Seri Najib Razak announced a package of Ringgit 7 billion to maintain economic growth, reinforce Malaysian economy, and strengthen resilience against economic recession. Budget deficit for 2009 has been projected at 4.8 per cent of GDP, and growth rate has come down to

3.5 per cent in 2008 as compared to 5.4 per cent in the previous year.

The stimulus packages in Malaysia is in the form of housing benefits, entrepreneurial credit facilities, and reduction in compulsory deposit options. An amount of MYR 1.2 billion has been earmarked for construction of 25,000 homes for low and medium income groups. The Government has further set aside an amount of MYR 7 billion—saved from fuel subsidy—to be channelized for housing development and promotion. As regards reduction in compulsory deposit options, Malaysian Government has reduced employees' contribution to provident fund from 11 per cent to 8 per cent. Universal participation by all beneficiaries can increase consumption expenditure by MYR 4.8 billion.

For encouraging infrastructure development the Malaysian Government has worked on reducing import duties on iron and steel products and cement. Coupled with a reduction in import duties, national Government is offering benefits for setting up industries in the construction sector. This is an opportunity for setting up healthy competition in construction materials market. Its benefit would pass on to consumers. In its endeavor to further develop infrastructure in Malaysia, its Government has allowed foreign entities to buy properties worth MYR 500,000 without approval from Foreign Investment Committee. However, such properties can be put to personal use only.

Malaysia's Second Economic Stimulus Package

Malaysia announced an unprecedented second economic stimulus package of $16 billion as it said the export oriented economy was in danger of sinking into deep recession.

Malaysian Finance Minister Najib Razak said state spending will equal 9 per cent of the country's GDP, even as the Government warned that the economy could shrink by 1 per cent, instead of growing at 3.5 per cent as expected earlier. Malaysian exports crashed by 28 per cent in January 2009.

The following are salient points in the mini-budget announced by Deputy Prime Minister Najib Razak Malaysiakini:

GDP growth is expected to be in the range of –1 per cent to 1 per cent for 2009. Without the two stimulus packages, the economy faces the prospect of a deep recession.

RM60 billion stimulus package—RM15 billion is fiscal injection, RM25 billion guarantee funds, RM10 billion equity investments, RM7 billion private finance initiative (PFI) and off-budget projects, as well as RM3 billion is in tax incentives.

According to the Government, the budget deficit, which is likely to shoot up from 4.8 per cent to 7.6 per cent in 2009, can be financed from domestic sources. It added that the financing of the deficit will not crowd out the private sector in sourcing funds.

The RM60 billion is allocated to achieve four aims:

1. *RM2 Billion to Reduce Unemployment, Increase Employment*

(i) To create a total of 163,000 training and job placement opportunities in the public and private sectors.

(ii) To establish 22 JobsMalaysia Centres and upgrade 109 existing centres to facilitate access for workers and employers to obtain job placements, career counselling and information on training opportunities.

(iii) Employers who employ workers retrenched from 1 July 2008 will be given double tax deduction on the amount of remuneration paid.

(iv) Government will recruit 63,000 persons to fill vacancies and serve as contract officers in various Government agencies

(v) To encourage more Malaysians to pursue Masters and PhD by financing tuition fees and research grants up to RM20,000 for student pursuing PhDs locally and RM10,000 for those taking Masters program.

(vi) Levy on foreign workers will be doubled for all sectors except construction, plantation and for domestic maids; the levy will be paid by the employers and not by the workers.

2. *RM10 Billion to Ease the Burden of the Rakyat*

(i) To assist oil palm and rubber smallholders whose incomes have been affected due to declining commodity prices.

(ii) RM674 million in subsidies to be allocated to avert price increases of necessities, such as sugar, bread and wheat flour.

(iii) To provide RM480 million to ensure that toll rates are not increased. With these above measures, the Government will allocate a sum of RM27.9 billion for subsidies in 2009.

(iv) House buyers to be given tax relief on interest paid on housing loans up to RM10,000 a year for three years.

(v) RM200 million to repair and maintain drains and roads.

(vi) RM150 million for renovation, maintenance and repairs of welfare homes, fire and rescue stations and quarters, as well as public toilets in mosques, surau and tourist spots.

(vii) RM1.95 billion to build and improve facilities in 752 schools, particularly in rural areas as well as Sabah and Sarawak, with RM300 million to be used to improve facilities in Government-aided religious schools, national-type Chinese and Tamil schools as well as mission schools.

(viii) RM230 million will be provided to increase the coverage of electricity and water supply in rural areas, particularly in Sabah and Sarawak.

(ix) RM350 million will be provided for the construction of rural roads.

(x) RM1.2 billion to be allocated in Sarawak and Sabah. This includes the expansion of Sibu Airport, deepening works at Miri Port, repairing and improving infrastructure damaged by floods, upgrading of schools as well as construction of Lawas Training Centre, Kota Samarahan Industrial Estate and tourism facilities.

(xi) In Sabah, among the main programmes and projects to be implemented include building of Giat Mara centres, Kota Kinabalu Electricity Transmission System, as well as upgrading of schools, roads and bridges. The Government to take action to resolve issues related to health services in Queen Elizabeth Hospital, Sabah.

(xii) Existing tax exemption of RM6,000 given on retrenchment benefits to be increased to RM10,000 for each completed year of service. Banks to allow retrenched workers defer the repayment of their housing loans for one year.

3. *RM29 Billion to Assist the Private Sector*

(i) RM5 billion to provide working capital to companies with shareholder equity below RM20 million. The Government to provide guarantee in the ratio of 80:20, that is 80 per cent will be guaranteed by the Government and 20 per cent by the financial institutions.

(ii) To set up an Industry Restructuring Guarantee Fund Scheme totalling RM5 billion for loans to increase productivity and value-added activities, as well as the application of green technology.

(iii) Securities Commission to implement additional measures to reduce time to market commodities to enable companies to raise funds in the capital market in a more efficient and cost-effective manner including doing away with approvals for rights issues by listed companies.

(iv) A new program where permanent resident status would be considered for high-net-worth individuals bringing more than US$2 million for investments or savings in Malaysia.

(v) RM5,000 discount to be given to car owners, who trade in their cars which are at least 10 years old, for the purchase of new Proton and Perodua cars.

(vi) RM2 billion for a new LCCT at Kuala Lumpur International Airport, which is expected to be ready in 2011.

(vii) A rebate of 50 per cent on landing charges will be given for a period of two years effective 1 April 2009 to all airlines that operate from Malaysia. This is likely to result in lower air fares.

(viii) Company's current year losses be allowed to be carried back to the immediate preceding year.

(ix) An Accelerated Capital Allowance will be given to encourage companies to renovate and refurbish their business premises. The allowance is capped at RM100,000.

(x) RM200 million to upgrade infrastructure in tourist spots, diversify tourism products, organise more international conferences and exhibitions in Malaysia as well as improve the homestay program.

4. *RM19 Billion to Build Capacity for the Future*

(i) To promote domestic private investments, the investment funds of Khazanah Nasional Berhad will be increased by RM10 billion.

(ii) Khazanah to invest RM3 billion in the telecommunications sector, which among others, will facilitate its subsidiary to improve broadband infrastructure.

(iii) RM1.7 billion of Khazanah's investment to go into Iskandar project for the building of infrastructure, hotels, theme parks as well as universities.

(iv) RM5 billion for 23 projects implemented on off-budget basis, including LCCT at KLIA and the expansion of Pulau Pinang Airport at an estimated cost of RM2 billion and RM250 million.

(v) RM2.4 billion for the Malaysian Communications and Multimedia Commission to improve telecommunication infrastructure.

(vi) RM100 million to build sky bridges and covered walkways between buildings, especially in the Golden Triangle, Kuala Lumpur.

(vii) RM2 billion for private finance initiative (PFI) and public-private partnerships.

(viii) RM20 million for Radio Televisyen Malaysia to implement several projects to develop the local music industry.

(ix) All Government procurements will be made through open tenders or restricted tenders, except for specific cases.

Pakistan Economic Stimulus Package

Pakistan economic stimulus package is required to be examined very carefully. In October 2008, inflation in Pakistan touched 30 per cent, and their national currency rupee was devalued by 25 per cent. Fiscal deficit was 10 per cent of GDP and foreign exchange reserves were just enough to sustain imports for about six weeks.

It required at least $3 billion in the short run and a further $10 billion to fill in balance of payment gaps. Matters further worsened by terrorist attacks on Islamabad Marriott Hotel when IMF delegates were on a visit to Pakistan. All these factors made an economic stimulus package to Pakistan even more necessary than before.

IMF support could act as an economic stimulus package for Pakistan. It is expected to come with enough preconditions specifically at the cost of budget outlay on defence and development. Economic stimulus of Pakistan in the form of alternative aid could be arranged from Saudi Arabia in the shape of deferred long-term payment for oil. Syed Naveed Qamar, in order to provide Pakistani economic stimulus package to national economy, has withdrawn subsidy on fuel gas. There was also a proposal to remove subsidy on electricity from June 2009 onwards. Gross Domestic Product (GDP) is expected to grow at 4.7 per cent in 2009-10 as compared to 4.2 per cent in 2008-09. Pakistan's economic revival process, initiated by their Finance Minister in September 2008, was essentially designed to raise foreign exchange reserves.

Pakistan's economy is expected to be dependent on textiles and services and primarily be driven by private investments and consumption. Monetary policy is directed towards controlling inflationary pressures. A widening gap between services and trade revenues is, to a considerable extent, countered by growth in foreign remittances. Compared to last five years, depreciation of Pakistan rupee is expected to take place with respect to US dollar.

Since October 2008, Pakistan has been asking for financial assistance from International Monetary Fund in order to keep its economy afloat. These requests have come from higher levels of Pakistani governance. They had asked for an audience from International Monetary Fund in order to find out ways to address critical financial issues in Pakistan. Prices of important items like oil and food have gone up, thus signaling a critical phase in Pakistani economy.

South Korea Unveils Stimulus Package

South Korea announced a 14 trillion won (US$ 11 billion) stimulus package as it faces its worst economic turmoil since it needed an International Monetary Fund bailout a decade ago. Public spending will be increased by 11 trillion won in 2009, and the package's remaining 3 trillion won would go to tax benefits, the Finance Ministry said. Finance Minister Kang Man Soo estimated South Korea's economy would grow only 3 per cent in 2009 because of the global financial crisis but also warned of a further slowdown. "It will be difficult to achieve the growth if global economic conditions further worsen," he said. Kang had earlier forecast a growth rate of below 4 per cent for next year for Asia's fourth-largest economy. The Government further downgraded its economic forecast in July 2008 from 5 per cent to 4.5 per cent growth. Earlier, it had expected 6 per cent. The stimulus package would provide more than 4 trillion won for infrastructure projects, such as roads, schools, universities and hospitals. Small and medium-sized businesses as well as farmers, fishermen and low-income families are also to receive help.

The Government announced another stimulus package of 5 trillion won, which aimed at supporting the construction industry, including buying land. The National Assembly also approved a 130-billion-dollar package at the end of October 2008 aimed at stabilizing the country's financial sector through credit guarantees and the infusion of fresh capital to boost liquidity in the banking and export sector.

Philippines Puts Stimulus Package on Hold

Fearing negative effects from a massive one-time spending to shield the Philippines from the fallout of a possible US recession, Malacañang put on hold a P75-billion stimulus package announced earlier—and replaced it with "performance budgeting" worth P50 billion already in the 2008 national budget. President Arroyo apparently agreed with her economic managers to temper such spending to spur consumer confidence in the economy. In her speech at the National Congress on Education at the Manila Hotel, Mrs. Arroyo said, "Under our fiscal stimulus program to keep us resilient from the anticipated US slowdown, we are scaling up Ahon Pamilyang Pinoy from P50 million to P5 billion this year." She said as a more direct incentive to school attendance, the Government earlier launched the Ahon Pamilyang Pinoy program of conditional cash donations to poor households who comply with rules that enhance learning and health.

Budget Secretary Rolando Andaya Jr. said the Government would enhance its proven move made in 2008, of performance budgeting by adding P50 billion more spending in infrastructure, agriculture, education and health. The amount is already included in the 227-trillion national budget earlier approved by Congress. He said frontloading additional funds in the four sectors during 2008 proved to have worked and it did not derail the Government's deficit reduction schedule. Under performance budgeting, all Government agencies are closely monitored in implementing their project by quarters, and if an agency fails to meet a target for a project in the previous quarter, funding for it would be diverted to priority projects in one of the four sectors, he said.

Joey Salceda, one of Mrs. Arroyo's advisers and proponent of the P75-billion stimulus package, however, refused to concede following a long and heated meeting with economic managers at the Manila Golf Club in Makati City, saying his proposal could bring the country's growth to eight per cent this year despite a looming US recession. "With the 2008 budget set at only six percent growth and the consumer price index at 4.2 per cent, this is a cop-out, the P75 billion is both a hedge against US recession and a fuel additive to domestic growth," Salceda said.

Salceda's proposal included extending discounts on electricity and water as well as education vouchers and tax refunds to individual taxpayers earning below P500,000 a year. The package amounting to P75 billion is equivalent to one per cent of the country's nominal GDP. Economic and finance officials, including Andaya and Bangko Sentral ng Pilipinas Governor Amando Tetangco Jr., opposed such a move, saying it would only trigger high inflation and bring the country back to a high deficit regime. Andaya said when the same move was made during the Estrada administration, the projected deficit of P17 billion swelled to P114 billion. He said the same thing happened early in the Arroyo administration with the target budget shortfall of P40 billion reaching P150 billion. He said the meeting ended with the consensus that the proposal be placed on standby and only be implemented when the US economy indeed hit a recession.

OTHER GLOBAL REMEDIAL MEASURES

Indian Government Relaxes FDI Norms

The Indian Government has relaxed FDI norms in companies. The new guidelines say that foreign investment can cross sectoral caps and in sectors like multi-brand retail, foreign investment has been permitted through investing companies owned by Indians. An investment by a non-resident entity in an Indian company is termed as FDI. Earlier, there were different criteria for calculating FDI in different sectors. For example, in telecom and broadcasting sectors, indirect foreign investments in a company through Indian investing companies is treated as foreign investment. In all sectors except defence, foreign investment in an investing Indian company is not set off against FDI cap.

The new guidelines say that in all sectors equity investments routed through companies in which majority ownership and control is in the hands of Indians would be treated as fully domestic equity. It means that foreign investment in FDI-restricted sectors can cross the set limits. The Indian entities can form multi-layered structures of investment companies in which all companies are owned and controlled by Indian residents. In this manner, foreign equity in sectors like telecom where 74 per cent FDI is permitted, can go up to as high as 98 per cent.

Before 2005, the Government had a similar policy of calculating FDI in the telecom sector. But it was exploited by some companies like Hutch Essar to increase foreign equity beyond the permitted 49 per cent.

The Government says that the adoption of the guidelines will simplify, streamline and rationalise the method of calculating indirect foreign investment across sectors.

The department of industrial policy and promotion (DIPP) has formally issued the new guidelines for calculation of foreign investment in Indian companies. The guidelines issued under two different "Press Notes" lay down norms for calculation of total foreign holding in Indian companies. The new norms stipulate that if a company is owned and controlled by Indians, its investments would be counted as Indian. If foreign holding in a company is less than 50 per cent and foreigners have no other 'beneficial interest' in the company, it will be considered as Indian-controlled.

The guidelines do not state that such a company cannot invest in all sectors, including in sectors where foreign direct investment (FDI) is prohibited, raising questions whether the Government has actually allowed FDI in the retail sector through the backdoor. An Indian company would be considered as controlled by non-resident if the foreign entities have majority holding or have the power to appoint directors in it. In case a joint venture company sets up a wholly-owned subsidiary in India, the foreign holding in the downstream company will be treated as equal to the level of FDI in the parent company. In areas such as broadcasting, defence production and others where there are sectoral caps of 49 per cent or less, the company will have to be owned and controlled by an Indian. It has also been made mandatory for Indian companies to seek Foreign Investment Promotion Board's (FIPB) approval if ownership and control is transferred to a foreign company where there is a ceiling FDI.

It also states that foreign institutional investment (FII) holdings, American and global depository receipts, NRI investment and investment through foreign currency convertible bonds (FCCBs) would now be included while calculating FDI.

India Inc Reduces Health Insurance Benefits to Cut Cost

Rising medical costs, slowdown and rising premium rates on employee health insurance policies are forcing corporates to cut benefits in these covers. According to insurance officials, several companies have cut on these benefits. However, officials refused to share the names of these corporates due to a confidentiality agreement. "Companies are introducing various steps such as co-payment of claims (where the employee pays a part of the claim amount), premium sharing for extending coverage to parents, introducing sub-limits, capping the amount according to diseases, reducing the sum insured of the policy to manage the rising costs," said Kanchana TK, Vice President, Marsh India Insurance Brokers, a leading insurance broker who designs and places employee benefit policies for over 350 corporates.

Healthcare cost is rising annually at 15 per cent in metro cities and health insurance premiums are hardening in a detariffed and deregulated market. Group health insurance business has mostly been a loss-making business for non-life insurers. According to industry data for 2007-08, the premium underwritten was Rs. 2,758 crore while the claims paid by insurers was Rs. 2,904 crore. Non-life insurers had a claims ratio of 105 per cent. Add to it the distribution cost and the total claims ratio for the industry rises to around 120 per cent. According to Sanjay Datta, head (health and personal accident insurance) at ICICI Lombard General Insurance, "Group health insurance premium has increased by 10 to 15 per cent for corporates with a loss ratio. We have suggested several measures to companies such as co-payment, capping room rent and introducing disease specific caps. Some of the companies have introduced a 20 per cent co-payment."

Till 2007, premium rates for property and engineering lines of business were decided by the Tariff Advisory Committee. Since these rates were high and profitable, insurers would underwrite group health at a low premium if the corporate had a property cover. However, with the lifting of price controls from property and engineering lines, insurers have mostly stopped cross subsidising.

RBI Cuts Repo, Reverse Repo Rates by 50 bps

The Reserve Bank of India reduced the repo and reverse repo rates by 50 basis points each, but industry said its effectiveness would depend on how well banks use the cheaper money to provide more credit to an economy rapidly losing steam. While Bank of India said it could take weeks to decide on lowering prime lending rates, UCO Bank announced a reduction in its benchmark by 50 basis points to 12.50 per cent. The money and stock markets had factored in the rate cuts for some time, but they are not expected to sustain a rally. A CII statement said another 50-bps cut would have been more appropriate. Nevertheless, many industrialists are hopeful. Binani Cement MD Vinod Juneja said, "The cut will boost demand for cement as housing loans are now expected to become cheaper and affordable. This will boost housing demand, in turn improving demand for steel and cement."

General Motors India Vice President P. Balendran echoed that sentiment when he said, "Interest rates on auto loans will come down further. This will improve liquidity in the system and consequently volumes are expected to go up further," he said. Sumit Bali, CEO of Kotak Mahindra Prime, which is major player in the auto lending business, said he expected interest rates for autos to be reduced by a minimum of 25 bps. "We will decide on the exact reduction in a day or two."

The Reserve Bank of India made another cut in the repo and reverse repo rates of 25 basis points each in April 2009. The repo rate has been cut from 5 to 4.75 per cent, while the reverse repo rate has been reduced from 3.5 to 3.25 per cent, in the annual credit policy review.

The central bank cut its growth estimate for 2008-09 to 6.5 from 6.7 per cent. The growth forecast for 2009-10 is around 6 per cent. The RBI said that managing large Government borrowing in 2009-10 in a non-disruptive manner would be a major challenge, and that it would use a mix of monetary and debt management tools to ensure this was done smoothly. The central bank's policy statement stated: "Large borrowings also militate against the low interest rate environment that the Reserve Bank is trying to maintain to spur investment demand in keeping with the stance of monetary policy."

The RBI has now cut its short-term lending rate by 425 basis points in six steps since 20 October 2008 as the global economic crisis has hit Asia's third largest economy harder than expected. The central bank said wholesale price-based inflation was expected to turn negative early in the year 2009-10, but this should not be interpreted as deflation for policy purposes. The projected WPI inflation would be around 4 per cent by the end of 2009-10.

Federal Reserve Makes Dramatic Move to Reduce Rates, Unfreeze Credit

In a dramatic attempt to lower long-term interest rates and unfreeze credit markets, the Federal Reserve Board's Open Market Committee (FOMC) announced a major expansion of its program of buying debt securities that injects fresh capital into the system. The move, which is partially aimed at lowering mortgage and consumer rates, could result in the Fed's balance sheet growing to \$3 trillion as it attempts to pump an additional \$1 trillion of capital into the economy. While keeping short-term interest rates near zero, the FOMC announced that it will purchase up to an additional \$750 billion of mortgage-backed securities, an additional $100 billion in debt from Fannie Mae and Freddie Mac, and $300 billion in Treasury securities.

Indonesia Cuts Key Interest Rate

Bank Indonesia (BI) reduced the benchmark rate to 8.25. "The impact on the domestic sector is felt more than before, especially in the trade sector. Sectors outside trade have relatively stable growth," the Bank said. Indonesian exports in December 2008 dropped 20 per cent from the same period of previous year—the steepest decline in seven years. The bank has been able to reduce interest rates as inflation continues to fall due to lower energy and commodity prices. The consumer price index dropped to 9.17 year-on-year in January 2008 from 11.06 per cent in December 2008.

The Bank said inflationary pressures are set to ease in the coming months, opening the way to further rate cuts.

South Korea Cuts Interest Rate to Record Low 2 Per cent

South Korea's central bank slashed interest rates by half a percentage point to a record low of 2 per cent, as expected—the sixth cut in four months aimed at preventing the global crisis tipping the country into recession. The Bank of Korea has now cut interest rates by a total of 3.25 percentage points since early October 2008, including an unprecedented 1 percentage point reduction in December 2008.

"...rate decision was a defensive measure against a rapidly weakening economy," said June Park, an economist at Woori Investment & Securities. "We are nearly at the bottom at this point. The central bank may cut the rate by another 50 basis points, but that's probably about it, as the real effect of the rate cut is limited at this stage."

South Korea's economy shrank a seasonally adjusted 5.6 per cent in the fourth quarter of 2008 from the previous three months, suffering its second-biggest economic contraction on record. The finance ministry cut its GDP growth forecast for 2009 to a fall of 2 per cent from a rise of 3 per cent, the first official acknowledgement that the economy would contract. The IMF has projected a 4 per cent contraction.

The Bank of Korea said that its future monetary policy would focus on improving liquidity and economic conditions. "The (Monetary Policy) Committee will do what is needed to improve liquidity conditions and to ward off the risk of a severe slowdown in economic activity," the BOK said in a statement after slashing the base rate by 50 basis points. The central bank said that despite the latest signs of thawing in the credit crunch, firms still faced considerable difficulty in raising funds due to highly risk-averse financial institutions.

PROTECTIONISM—A FALLOUT OF ECONOMIC MELTDOWN

There has been in the US and UK, a rise of legislation aimed at protecting industries and jobs through some anti-trade measures. The most notable examples of the same have been the insistence by the Democratic congressional leadership in the US to require that the stimulus money come with strings like "Buy America", and strikes by workers in the UK showing slogans "British jobs for British workers" on the placards.

The World Trade Organisation (WTO) Director General, Pascal Lamy, calls such measures catastrophic, and says, "If you start killing imports, you will kill exports." The political impulse to protect domestic economies during times of crisis is understandable, but "that's precisely why we have these rules, to avoid the slippery slope of protectionism,"[1] he adds.

Willem Buter, a noted economist warns that we can "have a global depression if we really continue to work at it." He hopes that the nations do not keep on "beating the protectionist drums" and "foot-dragging that prevents effective qualitative and quantitative monetary policy ensuing in the Eurozone and the UK...and raise the spectre of countries not belonging to the group of usual suspects."[2]

Barack Obama had declared, long before becoming the American President that he "will stop giving tax breaks to corporations that ship our jobs overseas, and...will start giving them to companies that create good jobs right here in America." If Obama indeed does that, it will adversely affect the massive flow of work to Indian IT and BPO firms. It will also hurt the American economy. Nasscom President Som

Mittal points out that "Obama earlier said India and China will help the growth of US. US tech firms have thousands of jobs but not enough talent at home." Mittal added that outsourcing has boosted America's economy by making the US companies competitive. Now if protectionism gets the better of American policymakers, it will serve nobody's cause.

Barack Obama who started his campaign to become America's 44th President with some protectionist statements now finds himself in a dilemma after reaching the White House. Backing those statements could start a trade war, but opposing them could mean a backlash from his supporters. The slogan "Buy America or Bye America" has not gone very well with two of the largest US trading partners. Canadian Prime Minister, Stephen Harper, has already expressed concern. The European Union has also warned that it could not "stand idly by" if such measures are taken. Brazilian President, Luiz Inacio Lula da Silva has also responded critically to the protectionist moves coming from America.

However, there are people who believe that such a policy is necessary under the present conditions. For example, John Judis feels that the US has to do something like this to ensure that its spending does not simply disappear in a flood of imports. Complaints by other countries are immaterial. As things stand today, it seems difficult to hold back the tide of protectionist sentiment.

Obama Ups Ante on Outsourcing

Giving his first speech to a joint session of the US Congress, Obama said, "We will restore a sense of fairness and balance to our tax code by finally ending the tax breaks for corporations that ship our jobs overseas." If Obama follows through with the announcement in the budget, the move may hurt India's BPO sector as without the tax breaks, US companies may find it less attractive to outsource jobs to India.

Protectionist Approach to Hurt US Firms: Mukherjee

In view of the US ban on hiring H-IB visa holders by US firms receiving bailout money, External Affairs Minister

Pranab Mukherjee said, "any protectionist policy would hurt the interest of the US companies the most."

In the wake of US putting restrictions on American companies hiring H-IB visa workers, the Union Government said it is constantly endeavouring to sensitize authorities there that any protectionist policy would hurt the interests of their companies. "In our regular interaction with the US, we have been conveying that employment protectionism does not help the US or any other country, nor it is good for the global economic order," External Affairs Minister Pranab Mukherjee informed the Lok Sabha during a question hour. The minister stated that the Government was "fully committed" to protecting the interests of Indian professionals working in the US. Mukherjee said India has been sensitizing the US authorities to the fact that India happens to be the largest contributor of highly skilled workers to the US economy.

Why Obama cannot Stop Outsourcing

The Indian Information Technology industry has reacted with a mix of hope and caution after President Barack Obama said that he will not allow US companies that send jobs away to enjoy his tax breaks. Obama is presumably talking about industry-specific tax breaks, though the details are not clear yet. But it is obvious that he cannot go very far.

The US plan can affect General Motors, which is getting Government help. The GM is doing advanced design for its next generation of automobiles using aviation-standard materials in Bangalore. The question is: Does Obama's budget mean that GM will stop using India as a base for innovation? If yes, it is difficult to see how General Motors will keep a global edge.

Now, take Accenture, which many think is a US company. It is actually incorporated in Bermuda. Will a US-based retail company (like J.C. Penney, for instance), handing over IT work to Accenture suffer from Obama's moves? If it does, and rival IBM gets a deal that Accenture might have had. It is pertinent to mention that IBM has tens of thousands of employees in India, doing work for US clients. The simple point is that US has itself led efforts in making the world economy in an inter-connected web. And now, it is trying to crunch IT spending. The experts believe this move will adversely impact India as well as America.

US firms have already lost the game of efficiency in automobiles to the Japanese and in overall manufacturing to the Chinese. In pharmaceuticals and services, Indian firms can shake the US in everything except blockbuster product development. If you take new products, IT and distributed global research and development are at the heart of whatever remains of American capital efficiency, innovation and competitiveness.

In other words, US firms are no longer US firms, but effectively global firms. By doing harm to what Americans call outsourcing, Obama may be axing a branch he is sitting on. Which is why many see his speech as little more than symbolic post-election posturing. If the benefits of tax breaks are outweighed by the gains of outsourcing, US firms will do what makes more sense to them.

Cutback on Outsourcing will only Hit US: India Inc

India Inc too has expressed concern over Barack Obama's plans to clamp down on the outsourcing industry. Such a legislation will clearly make outsourcing unattractive to US companies, which is bad news for the Indian tech sector. Reiterating one of his election campaign agenda, in one of his more recent speeches, Obama made it clear that there would not be any tax benefits for American companies that outsource jobs to other countries. It would create/save 3.5 million jobs in the country.

The domestic industry in general said such a move will only hurt US as outsourcing makes a lot of economic and logical sense to the country. Reacting to Obama's statement, Kris Gopalakrishnan, CEO, Infosys, said, "Outsourcing has enhanced the competitiveness of US corporations and has created more jobs within US economy. US is an open economy and a strong proponent of free trade globally. We are confident that US will not take any measures which might hurt its own global competitiveness."

Echoing similar sentiments, MindTree CMD, Ashok Soota said, "Defying logical and economic sense [Obama's] speech was an extension of what he had spoken earlier in his campaigns. The basic economics and logics of outsourcing have not changed, and therefore it will not impact India adversely." Some corporate leaders said American companies which get aid from the US Government can get around the Obama move by outsourcing to US firms not availing of similar assistance and the latter, in turn, could outsource to non-US companies.

CIOs are under tremendous pressure to find best cost structures to support their global trade. "Businesses today are truly global than ever before and such protectionist measures not only restrict innovation but also hamper the progress of globalisation. Global markets are a two-way street to sell and buy products and services," said Sujata Rakhra, Vice President (marketing & communication) APAC Perot Systems. Fieri President Rajeev Chandrashekar said such a move will hurt companies in the US and India alike. "This poses yet another challenge for Indian IT and software companies that are growing in the US. It will also punish American companies, not just Indian firms," said Chandrashekar. However, Nasscom expressed a mild reaction to Obama's statement. "All efforts of Obama are currently focused on the revival of US economy. A turnaround in US economy is good news for India. We need not read much into other details of Obama's speech," said Som Mittal, President, Nasscom. Wipro CFO Suresh Senapaty said, "We endorse Nasscom's view on this and feel that in the current economic environment it is imperative for global corporations to collaborate on technology and innovation. Policies of protectionism will only hinder the revival of the world economy."

France too has demonstrated some protectionist vibes. For example, Mr Sarkozy's loan to Peugeot Citroen and Renault is said to be dependent on assurances they will not shut French plants or cut French jobs. The car manufacturing sector is a stronghold of French industry. "We want to stop factories from relocating abroad and, if possible, bring them back home," said Mr Sarkozy. "If we give money to the auto industry to restructure itself, it's not so we can hear about a new plant moving to the Czech Republic or wherever," he added. The European Commission has warned that France is violating EU laws against protectionism.

'Buy America' Call of Stimulus Upsets China

China is rattled by the 'buy America' call in the $789 stimulus package passed by US Senate because it will severely hit Chinese exports. The move has foreign policy dimensions because it might wipe out a lot of the trade surplus enjoyed by Beijing and affect China's ability to deal with the world. The Xinhua news agency, which is the mouthpiece of the Communist Party of China, described the move to favour American goods as a 'poison' that would hurt efforts to solve the financial crisis. The Xinhua editorial also hinted as possible trade disputes concerning the package between China and the US at WTO. "History and economics have told us, facing a global financial crisis, trade protectionism is not a solution, but a poison to the solution," the news agency said. Official broadcaster CCTV roped in several experts, who criticised the 'buy America' move while reminding audiences that Beijing had avoided opting for a 'buy China' campaign.

Chinese Deputy Commerce Minister Jiang Zengwei recently said Beijing would "treat domestic and foreign goods equally so long as we need them." Recent cancellation of export orders from the US is an important reason why millions of people have lost jobs in the export-oriented factories of South China. China-US bilateral trade rose 10.5 per cent in 2008, which is the lowest growth seen since China joined the WTO seven years back. On the other hand, labour groups in the US accuse China of robbing American jobs by selling goods at extremely cheap rates. In 2008, China accounted for 57 per cent of the total Sino-US trade of $333.74 billion, enjoying a trade surplus of $170.86 billion. The 'buy America' has caused a lot of surprise here because it came at a time when G7 countries decided in Rome to eschew national protectionism to tackle the global crisis. US Treasury Secretary Timothy Geithner, who earlier criticized Beijing of manipulating its currency suddenly changed track to praise China for "playing a very important stabilizing role in the international financial system today". US leaders have said that a managed exchange rate was the reason why China continued to enjoy a significant advantage in its world trade. Xinhua described the US stimulus bill favouring American steel, iron and manufactured goods for Government projects as protectionist measures that could trigger trade disputes.

G7 Pledges to Avoid Protectionism

Leading industrial countries have pledged to avoid protectionism as they battle the global economic crisis. Finance Ministers at a G7 meeting in Italy said raising barriers to free trade would make the downturn worse. The G7 comprises the US, the UK, Japan, Germany, France, Italy and Canada. The US Congress approved an $787 billion economic recovery plan that includes a 'buy America' clause. G7 ministers said stabilising the world economy and financial markets was their priority. They said they would work together to support growth and jobs. The 'buy America' clause has raised fears that protectionism could be growing in the world's largest economy.

But in a statement after the meeting, new US Treasury Secretary Timothy Geithner dismissed such concerns. "All countries need to sustain a commitment to open trade and investment policies which are essential to economic growth and prosperity," he said. Ministers also called for urgent reform to the International Monetary Fund, saying the crisis had shown weaknesses in the world financial system. "We agree that a reformed IMF, endowed with additional resources, is crucial to respond effectively and flexibly to the current crisis," the ministers' statement said.

G20 Leaders Reject Protectionism

World leaders reiterated their rejection of protectionism, and trade barriers that threaten to deepen the global financial crisis.

After meeting in London, the heads of the Group of 20 nations vowed "to do whatever is necessary to promote global trade and investment and reject protectionism." That pledge is almost identical to one made at a November 15, 2008 summit where they decided to "underscore the critical importance of rejecting protectionism and not turning inward in times of financial uncertainly." Since then, 17 of the G20 members have implemented 47 trade restrictions, a 1 March 2009 study by the World Bank showed.

Mounting protectionism will lead to a 9 per cent drop in global trade in 2009, its first decline since 1982, according to the World Trade Organization. Led by the US's $17.4 billion bailout of General Motors Corp. and Chrysler LLC, subsidies for the car industry rose to more than $48 billion worldwide, according to the Washington-based World Bank.

While the developing countries such as Brazil have been outspoken on the issue, with President Luiz Inacio Lula da Silva calling it a "drug," there are few signs their warnings are being heard from world's biggest to the smallest nations.

The G20 leaders reaffirmed "the commitment made in Washington to refrain from raising new barriers to investment or to trade in goods and services, imposing new export restrictions or implementing WTO-inconsistent measures to stimulate exports," the G20 statement said. "In addition, we will rectify promptly any such measures. We extend this pledge to the end of 2010."

History points to the potentially catastrophic impact of protectionism amid an economic slump. The US Smoot-Hawley Tariff Act of 1930 increased duties on more than 20,000 goods, inviting retaliation by other countries. Within two years of the law's enactment, global trade declined 70 per cent.

UN Secretary General Hails G20 Commitment to Resist Protectionism

The UN Secretary-General Ban Ki-moon extended a welcome to the commitment from the Group of 20 leaders at the London Summit "to resist protectionism and to monitor compliance." "I welcome the commitment from G20 leaders to resist protectionism and to monitor compliance," the Secretary-General, who was in London to attend the G20 summit to make joint efforts to tackle the current financial crisis, said in a statement.

"I am pleased that G20 leaders have committed themselves to a 1.1 trillion US dollars package," he said. "But it will be critical that the share of this going to the poorer countries is delivered" he said. "The G20 leaders have reaffirmed previous commitments to increase aid and help countries achieve the Millennium Development Goals," Ban added. "This means that they are promising at least 300 billion US dollars in aid over the next two years. For the poorest countries this will be crucial. The world will be watching," he said in the statement. "In addition to committing significant new resources for the International Monetary Fund (IMF) and World Bank, the G20 also asked the UN to monitor the impacts of this and future crises on poor and vulnerable people—in order to spur action," he further added.

PRESENT GLOBAL ECONOMIC CRISIS AND THE GREAT DEPRESSION OF 1930s

The current global meltdown cannot be compared to the 1929 crash. Some historians believe that the Great Depression set the stage for the Second World War. But we have compelling reasons to believe that the final denouement of the present crisis will not be as grave as in 1930s.

The roots of the current global crisis lie in the interplay of several developments that have radically changed the finance capitalism which existed in 1929 or as recently as just three decades ago. Traditionally, banks were careful to lend only to trusted clients, and carried the debt on their books. These days there is securitization. Lenders pool the loans and resell them as asset-backed securities. These securities are then repackaged, leveraged and resold many times over. Another pertinent development is the emergence of highly sophisticated derivative products, including the credit default snaps (CDSs). The asset-backed securities and derivatives widely spread the risk and prevent catastrophes like GD 1929.

There is no doubt that securitization, derivatives, leveraging and globalisation have made the global economy more volatile and risky than the world of 1930s. In those times, however, the Governments had relatively little understanding of the macroeconomic management. Today, the Government and central banks have several tools to restore confidence and revive the economy. "The pace at which the US subprime loan defaults snowballed into a global financial crisis was quite astonishing, but so was the speed with which G7 countries and the emerging economies responded. In a period of less than two months after the collapse of Lehman Brothers, the advanced countries and emerging economies had all introduced broadly similar measures to deal with the crisis—a remarkable feature of global coordination without a single formal treaty or agreement."[3]

It is said that out of the Great Depression was born Keynesian economics which encourages Government action to increase or decrease demand and output. Keynes' *The General Theory of Employment, Interest and Money,* published in 1936, states that some micro-level actions of individuals and firms can lead to aggregate macroeconomic outcomes in which the economy operates below its potential output and growth. Many classical economists had believed in Say's Law which states that supply creates its own demand, so that a "general glut" would therefore be impossible. Keynes contended that aggregate demand for goods might be insufficient during economic downturns, leading to unnecessarily high unemployment and losses of potential output. Keynes argued that Government policies could be used to increase aggregate demand, thus increasing economic activity and reducing unemployment and deflation.

Keynes argued that the solution to depression was possible by means of "inducement to invest...through some combination of two approaches: a reduction in interest rates, and Government investment in infrastructure. Investment by Government injects income, which results in more spending in the general economy, which in turn stimulates more production and investment involving still more income and spending and so forth. The initial stimulation starts a cascade of events, whose total increase in economic activity is a multiple of the original investment."[4] The nations across the world are therefore making efforts to stimulate their respective economies through packages that will increase spending in various sectors.

Many countries have joined hands to tide over the global financial crisis. Apart from America, the UK has taken a leading role in shaping the international response, and ensuring that China ana other emerging economies are fully involved in international discussions. It has convinced the other European Union members to take action on pressing issues like capital, liquidity, credit guarantees, etc. announced at Eurozone Summit held in Paris in October 2008. The G20 Summit on Financial Markets and the World Economy, in Washington DC in November 2008 also mandated a substantial action plan of measures to support international economy, strengthen financial sector supervision and reform global economic governance. The vein of international cooperation to fight global recession was visible at the London G20 meeting of April 2009 where the member countries pledged to "restore confidence, growth and jobs; repair the financial system to restore lending; strengthen financial regulation to rebuild trust; fund the reform...international financial institutions to overcome this crisis and prevent future one; promote global trade and investment and reject protectionism, to underpin prosperity; and to rebuild an inclusive, green, and sustainable recovery."

American President, Barack Obama brought a recovery package worth US$787 billion in February 2009 with which the US has resumed its leadership of the Keynesian path to global economic revival. With all these efforts, the present crisis is not likely to linger for more than one to two years. The Great Depression of 1930s is said to have lasted upto 1939.

GLOBAL ECONOMIC MELTDOWN AND FUTURE OF CAPITALISM

The leaders of the former bastions of communist bloc have blamed capitalists for dragging the world into a serious economic crisis. In the opening address of the World Economic Forum at Davos, Switzerland, the Russian Prime Minister, Vladimer Putin spoke of a "perfect storm" that has decimated the old system, rendering it obsolete. He said that the fundamental stability and "the investment banks once considered the pride of Wall Street have virtually ceased to exist." But the damage has gone beyond Wall Street. Putin said, "The entire economic growth system where one regional centre prints money without respite and consumer material wealth, while another regional centre manufactures inexpensive goods and saves money printed by other Governments has suffered a major setback." The Chinese premier, Wen Jiabao also blamed the United States for economic slowdown. "Inappropriate macroeconomic policies ...unsustainable model of development characterised by prolonged low savings and high consumption...the blind pursuit of profit and the failure of financial supervision, all have contributed to the present crisis."

The spectre of failure of capitalism is haunting the world. "Suddenly, the invisible hand that is supposed to guide the goods and people in a free market economy has vanished and the visible hand of the Government is back in action."[5] Some economists have called the use of taxpayers' money to cover private losses of mega corporations, big banks—considered to be the backbone of the market system—a strange thing to have happened. It seems that Adam Smith's 'hand' money has vanished into thin air, and the world is returning to the good old days of big Government as recommended by J.M. Keynes. There are even beliefs that Karl Marx's prophecy that "capitalism will be replaced by communism just as feudalism was replaced by capitalism", may come true in the foreseeable future.

Marx saw the power of unbridled capitalism as a kind of myth which became more real than it actually is. In the present era of unchallenged capitalism, the only reality is money and its purchasing power. People want money in their pockets and their accounts, and the liberty to buy what they want to. That is how they understand the system. People believe in capitalism as it talks about profits, incentive and consumers' sovereignty.

According to Paul Krugman, the Nobel laureate for Economics in 2008, communism failed, not because of some technical problem, but because people lost faith in it. But he argues that a market system works whether people believe in it or not: "You may dislike capitalism, even feel that as a system it will eventually fail, yet do your job well because your family needs the money you earn. Capitalism can run, even flourish in a society of selfish cynics. But a non-market economy cannot."[6]

Today people have become cynical about banks, stocks, loans, markets, etc. They may not have stopped believing in the system, but their faith has been visibly shaken. No one knows what the future events may bring for the system, but people are already looking for some alternative. There are calls to reinvent the global system.

"Economists like Joseph Schumpeter adopted nihilism's description of capitalism as 'creative destruction', but argued that this was the system's strength. When firms get greedy and stupid the market wipes them out, making way for more sensible firms."[7] By this yardstick, if a company like Lehman Brothers had survived and prospered, it would have been a failure. The fact that it went bust shows the strength of the system. It can, however, be argued that such a system which allows the bubble to swell before letting it burst is questionable because of the far-reaching adverse impacts it brings on the sector, economy, employees and society.

Alan Greenspan, who inadvertently created two bubbles—the dotcom one in 2001 and the housing one in 2007—is himself in a state of shock. The former chief of US Federal Reserve said, "I could never imagine that the markets would crash like this." The present financial trouble, according to him is "one in a century" kind of crisis. Many have disagreed with Greenspan and blamed his policy of promoting unregulated markets for the present mess. Amartya Sen has pointed towards an "over-reliance on markets" and "absence of regulation" as the main reasons for the global economic downturn. Joseph Stiglitz, another Nobel laureate, opines that market fundamentalism does not work. He finds the idea that the markets are self-correcting, flawed. Stiglitz has compared the collapse of Lehman Brothers with the fall of Berlin Wall. Just as the fall of Berlin Wall symbolised the acceptance of open policies, the failure of Lehman Brothers may bring radical changes in what today capitalism stands for. Some economists believe that Stiglitz has given an ominous warning which the fundamentalists will ignore at their own peril. Those who have become averse to capitalism say that the problem has been caused by greedy bankers and selfish brokers. They have begun to challenge some of the basic precepts of capitalism such as putting profit motive above everything else, availability of cheap money and living on credit. The fact that—from New York to New Delhi—people are slowing down their spending, realizing that there is a tomorrow, bears testimony that they are changing their lifestyle to become more attuned to the present situation.

The first true global economic crisis of modern capitalism occurred in 1857 which involved all major capitalist countries of that time, e.g. England, USA, France and Germany. Karl Marx, who expected a deluge that would wipe out capitalism started writing his long-planned economic work. He was convinced that capitalism would not recover from the deep trauma and it would unleash revolutionary movements. But that first global crisis of capitalism led neither to its collapse nor to any revolutionary movement. As a matter of fact, the crisis was overcome in 1858 and the capitalist system came out of it much stronger. "Marx learnt a lesson: in capitalism crises function as brutal acts of purification. The destruction wreaked by crises removes previous impediments to accumulation and frees up new possibilities for capitalist development."[8]

Marx brought the first volume of *Das Kapital* in 1866. Though he fundamentally broke with the notion of a final crisis of capitalism, he again waited for the end of another crisis that occurred in 1879, before writing a sequel to the first volume of the book. But that crisis again passed and capitalism initiated a new industrial cycle with all its diversified phases of prosperity. Marx bid farewell to the theories of capitalist collapse and for good reason, though many of his followers remained loyal to such theories. For staunch Marxists who believed in social democracy, before the First World War, as well as the communist parties of the 1920s, end of capitalism was a foregone conclusion owing to the increasingly strong crises it generated. "Every recovery was interpreted as a last rearing up before the final and inevitable collapse, which frequently led to grotesque political misjudgments. In the early 1990s, the theory of capital collapse celebrated a joyful resurrection in the newly-united Germany, furnished with the pretence of being a new idea. The crisis that followed—the East Asian crisis of 1997/98, the stock market crash that heralded the collapse of the 'New Economy' bubble in 2000/01, and the crisis in Argentina in 2001/02—were interpreted each and every time as a sure sign of the final crisis of capitalist collapse. But all these crises were over relatively quickly. They led to processes of enormous immiseration (particularly the crises in East Asia and Argentina), but the capitalist system, contrary to all prognostications of collapse, emerged rather strengthened from these crises."[9] Now there is a new crisis and consequently, new predictions about the imminent downfall of capitalism are being made. Only time will tell whether it will overcome this crisis unscathed or at the cost of giving up some of its basic characteristics.

Some experts feel that the present global crisis cannot be attributed to capitalism as much as to the structural changes which have taken place within global capitalism since the economic crisis of mid-1970s, and the neo-liberal policies introduced to combat it. The distribution of wealth in the leading capitalist countries like America, England, France, among others, has shifted to a large extent to the benefit of high-income individuals. Real wages have risen only marginally since then; the increase in social wealth has benefited almost entirely those already possessing a good amount of wealth. A large amount of these gains was invested in the financial markets which wooed the investors with increasingly novel speculative financial instruments like derivatives after the sweeping deregulation of markets in the 1970s.

The pension reforms undertaken in most of the advanced nations also led to strivings by many employees to improve their future pension through pension funds. In this way, even the lower- and middle-income individuals also ended up investing in the financial markets. As a result of these, the volume of financial wealth grew more strongly than the aggregate output. The share prices of several companies skyrocketed as there was a constant search for further investment opportunities due to an enormous increase in financial wealth, which stimulated a high degree of speculation. The bubble had to burst one day, which happened in the second quarter of 2008-09. However, capitalism and its core principles cannot be blamed squarely for this.

The biggest charge being leveled against capitalism these days is that it privatises profits and socializes losses. During good times, the rich get richer while the poor keep waiting for the multiplier effect to percolate down to them, whereas during bad times, the lower-middle classes suffer more because their capacity to absorb economic shock is very low. Some economists have questioned the legitimacy of using taxpayers', money to bail out ill-functioning institutions including banks. America, the leader of the pack, has already brought two stimulus packages—one for US$700 billion signed by George W. Bush in October 2008, and the other for US$787 billion signed by Barack Obama in February 2009. But each time there have been hot debates and discussions on the justifiability of the move. Even the Senators and Congressmen have been sharply divided over the issue. Many other countries too have resorted to bailout packages to restore health to their crisis-ridden financial systems. In fact there are clamours for stimulus packages in almost every country. Indian corporates are vociferous in their calls for financial help and other sops to boost liquidity, production, and demand. Some people find a sense of injustice and politics at work in such solutions, particularly in the Indian context: "The moment the interest of empowered lobbies is affected by such crises, there is a clamour for direct intervention, for support funds, for bailout packages. Yet these same insistent voices would preach the virtues of a purist, non-interfering capitalist system if large targeted schemes are implemented as bailout packages for the poor like, for instance, the loan waiver package for poor farmers or the National Rural Employment Guarantee Scheme (NREGS). At those moments, all the horrors of deficit financing loom large, at moments of global recession, such intervention becomes the imperative need of the hour."[10]

The sanctioning of bailout packages has also brought some key questions to the fore, such as: As the cries for Government bailouts increase and get the label of legitimacy, is capitalism dead? Does the use of taxpayers' money to prop up free markets herald the rise of socialism? Are we heading towards a new capitalism in which the workers' and investors' interest converge? And if so, does it signal a change in labour dynamics? Will public-private enterprise be a major instrument of state policy? And, finally, are these moves and deviations temporary to last only till the end of the present global downturn, to be discarded after that? "We need to find answers to these questions before venturing into mindless bailouts."[11]

It is believed in some circles, and rightly so, that capitalism is reinventing itself. They feel that capitalism is not dead. "Recessions are not aberrations of capitalism but an intrinsic part of it. Markets create boom and bust cycles, arising from human tendencies to swing from euphoria to fear and back. A bust is an occasion for cleaning out deadwood and failed experiments, and reinventing capitalism."[12]

The communist parties in India and elsewhere may have declared after every recession that capitalism is on its last legs, but the fact remains that capitalism has a knack of reinventing itself and "growing constantly stronger while the recession free communist system collapsed."[13] The world's economic history bears testimony that capitalism has risen like phoenix out of the ashes of every recession.

As discussed earlier, Karl Marx kept on waiting for the end of capitalism in the latter half of 19th century, but it never came and he gave up his theories of capitalism collapse. In *The Accumulation of Private Capital* (1913), Rosa Luxemburg wrote: "Though imperialism is the historical method prolonging the career of capitalism, it is also a sure means of bringing it to a swift conclusion." But this conclusion (end) has still not arrived though nearly a century has passed since then. Ferdinand Fried of German radical right expressed similar thoughts in his book *The End of Capitalism* (1930). In the US, Howard Scott's technology movement predicted the replacement of market prices by central planning. British sociologist Karl Mannheim went as far as saying, in his book *Man and Society in an Age of Reconstruction* (1940), that democracy could survive only by delinking from capitalism. Negative statements about capitalism continued even after Second World War. Historian A.J.P. Taylor declared in 1945:

> Nobody believes in the American way of life, i.e. private enterprise. Or rather those who believe in it are a defeated party, and a party which seems to have no more future than the Jacobites in England after 1688. Noted economist Joseph Schumpeter, a great supporter of entrepreneurship, suggested in *Capitalism, Socialism and Democracy* that capitalism could die through self-inflicted wounds.

After the Second World War, all capitalist nations became welfare states earmarking large sums for the sick, aged and the poor. Some people interpreted it as the fading away of capitalism. There was a stagnation of capitalist economies in the 1970s which brought a new hope amongst the Leftists in Europe. Francois Mitterand came to power in France on a platform breaking with capitalism. He took some unprecedented steps like nationalizing major French industries, raising taxes, shortening working hours and increasing holidays. He said that he "would not take the Thatcher-Reagan path to disaster" and would instead follow a path of welfare and relief. But soon, France found itself in a deeper recession than the US and England. Mitterand gave up his policies and re-privatised nationalised companies. Another economist, Jerry Muller, chronicled in 1989 the predictions of the demise of capitalism. These again proved inexpedient.

As things spanned out over the last one and a half century, all these intelligent and learned people have been proved wrong about capitalism because of the two main reasons. First, that capitalism has been construed as a system with no role for Governments at all, whereas it is not a *laissez-faire* system and allows state intervention in important matters and critical junctures. Modern capitalism is in fact a Government-business joint venture. Second, "these critics have been underestimating capitalism's ability to re-engineer itself and evolve into new forms that can get rid of the old defects."[14]

The current global economic crisis calls for capitalism to reinvent itself. The world is searching for a new financial order. There is a talk about the need to expand the role of International Monetary Fund (IMF) so that this multilateral body can alleviate the misery wreaked by the financial tsunami that is currently sweeping the globe. However, it is increasingly being felt that the IMF has rather been "inept in understanding the crisis and that the neo-liberal economic ideology it has blindly espoused has been responsible to a considerable extent for the present mess."[15] Donald Greenlees, a veteran Australian journalist, is of the opinion that Asia will play a big role in reshaping world's financial system. When international finance officials gathered at the annual meeting of the World Bank and IMF in October 2008, there were muffled admissions that the resolute mission of global free-market liberalization these institutions had set for themselves, termed as Washington Consensus, was dead. The entire East Asia believes that the IMF interventions and so-called plans in the financial meltdown of 1997-1998 that affected most parts of East Asia, actually exacerbated the crisis. Similarly, some experts have criticized IMF's policies which, they say, have contributed to the present economic slowdown:

> The doctrine of downsizing Government, trade and capital market liberalization, privatization and cutting Government regulation of markets was imposed...without regard for local conditions or national sovereignty. Moreover, the ideological faith in light-handed regulation was one of the proximate causes of Wall Streets excesses and the current crisis.[16]

IMF's insistence during the Asian Financial crisis that emergency financial aid would be offered only if stringently applied market reforms were undertaken, did not go very well with countries like Thailand, Indonesia and South Korea "which were given that medicine in return for IMF funds." South Koreans usually refer to the events of 1997 as the "IMF crisis." According to Yung Chul Park, a professor of finance at Seoul National University, "At least in East Asia, the IMF has not regained its credibility because it has so far refused to engage in frank and constructive dialogue with Asian stakeholders."

The global financial crisis has busted some myths about the power of the Wall Street, G8 and the Bretton Woods institutions. Now the world needs to look beyond the old Western powers which have been setting the global economic agenda since the end of Second World War. It is time to include countries like China, Japan, India and Brazil where the regulatory system prevented a complete meltdown. The USA is still the world's strongest economic power but the developing countries of Asia and parts of Latin America have emerged as new centres of capital accumulation and no longer form the periphery of global economy driven by Western Europe and North America. Global competitive capitalism is becoming increasingly multipolar. For Asia, notably for China, Japan and India, it is potentially a historic period as the presumption that their unprecedented economic success during the last two decades would translate into increased global leadership may become a reality. Their high annual GDP growth, business, industry and exports "not only gives them more flexibility to respond to tough economic times, but also puts them in a unique position to contribute in minimizing the distress of the worldwide crisis and create a "new economic and financial landscape in the year ahead."[17]

Obama Supports Free-market Economic System

US President Barack Obama has said that he supports the free market economic system as he sought backing for his efforts to revive the ailing economy. During a meeting with CEOs and other top leaders, Obama said he wants

Government "to right the ship and then let private enterprise do its magic." "At these moments, Government has stepped in not to supplant private enterprise, but to catalyze it, to create the conditions for thousands of entrepreneurs and new businesses to adapt and ultimately to thrive," said the President. He said his Government must move quickly and aggressively on the most immediate threats to the American economy and financial stability—jobs, housing and credit. "And that's why we've already passed a recovery plan that will save and create 3.5 million jobs over the next two years, more than 90 per cent of which will be located in the private sector," he explained. "That's why we've launched a housing plan that will help responsible families lower their monthly payments, a plan that's already helping responsible homeowners save money by refinancing their loans," he added.

Meanwhile, Obama vowed to enact tough, common-sense regulatory reforms, which he said will prevent a crisis like the current one from happening in future. "There are going to be a series of fairly complex issues around regulation in the financial markets which we believe is necessary," Obama told business leaders. "But we are also very mindful we've got to do those regulatory reforms in a way that doesn't strangle innovation and creativity and entrepreneurship but deals with the systemic risks that obviously we were unprepared to deal with when this latest crisis occurred," he said. However, he also stressed that his Government believes the financial market reforms should not lead to a new "super-regulator." "We think it is very important that there is coordination, not necessarily a super regulator," Obama said.

Indian Economy: 2009 Forecast

The year 2008 started out well enough with growth figures approaching 10 per cent. However, with the massive financial troubles which began towards the end of 2008, the year 2009 does not look quite as good. The Asian Development Bank (ADB) has projected growth of a mere 6.5 per cent. Previously, it had forecast 7 per cent, down from another earlier estimate of 7.4 per cent. ADB stated as under:

India, South Asia's most dynamic economy in recent years, is reeling from the direct effect of the global financial crisis on its banking systems and financial markets. The growth projection for India has been revised down to seven per cent in 2008 and 6.5 per cent in 2009, from 9 per cent in 2007.

In the first week of December 2008, the World Bank anticipated the Indian economy would grow by 6.3 per cent in 2008 and 5.8 per cent in 2009. It realized a 7.8 per cent expansion in the first half of 2008 against 9.3 per cent a year ago. The economy grew by 9 per cent in the year 2007.

Inflation was a threat in India, especially when it reached a peak of 12 per cent in early August, 2008. Much of what drove this inflation was the country's rapid growth and rising oil prices. Oil has fallen considerably since then, easing inflation. As a matter of fact we are staring at deflation with inflation figures reaching below half a per cent in March 2009.

Manufacturing is expected to be hit in 2009 due to a decreased demand as a result of the global downturn. India's growth is not totally dependent on the West, but the slumps in the US, Europe, and even the Far East will be felt in India's exports. The Indian Government will need to accelerate its reforms and push for more investment if it wants to maintain good growth rates in the face of the global slowdown. In a news conference with the World Economic Forum (WEF), CII Director General Chandrajit Banerjee said, "There is a pressure on bottom lines of companies. Production is down. We do see economic growth moderating between 7.4 and 7.8 per cent this fiscal." "Since inflation is down, we expect more fiscal and monetary measures to give a momentum to growth. The Government should increase expenditure in infrastructure sector and put ongoing projects on the fast track," he continued, but dismissed fears of large-scale corporate layoffs.

The worldwide credit crunch has led to foreign investors dumping shares amounting to more than $12.5 billion, and the rupee has fallen in excess of 20 per cent.

The WEF said that the global crisis "could also weaken the balance sheets of the financial institutions, cause a further fall in share and asset prices, and challenge the macroeconomic situation due to shrinking global growth."

India's Exports and Imports Decline

With external shipments contracting for six months in a row, the country's exports aggregated $168.7 billion in 2008-09, growing marginally by 3.4 per cent over 2007-08. Imports, which have been falling for last three months, recorded a growth of 14.3 per cent in 2008-09 to $287.7 billion as against $251.6 billion in 2007-08. Because of the sharp fall in imports, the trade deficit in March 2009 declined to $4.1 billion as against $6.3 billion. However, during 2008-09, trade deficit increased to $119 billion from $88.5 billion in the previous year. Imports fell mainly due to decline in the oil import bill with falling crude prices. Oil imports bill at $3.8 billion in March fell by 58 per cent. However, during 2008-09 oil imports increased by 17 per cent to $93.2 billion as against $79.7 billion in 2007-08. Because of the slowdown in the economic activities, non-oil imports also dropped by 19 per cent in March 2009. However, due to sharp increase in the first nine months, non-oil imports bill in 2008-09 went up by 13.2 per cent to $194.6 billion from $171.9 billion. Exporters and economists feel it would take a few more months before the contraction bottoms out. Federation of Indian Export Organisation President A Sakthivel said as inventories in Europe will be over by August 2009, they have started visiting India and international trade fairs for procurement. He said that India's exports will pick up from July 2009 onwards and may touch the $185-billion-mark in 2009-10 on the back of diversification to countries in Latin America, Africa and Asia.

However, ICRIER Director Rajiv Kumar said, India will be lucky if it can retain the 2008-09 level of exports. The slowdown in the non-oil imports also not augurs well for the economy. "The fall in non-oil imports during January-March, if concentrated in the areas of machinery, equipments and project goods, would entail slowdown in the industrial production," FICCI President Harsh Pati Singhania said.

Slower, But Still the World's Second-fastest

At 7 per cent growth, India would still rate among the fastest-growing economies in 2009-10, perhaps next only to China, despite being buffeted by an extraordinary global economic meltdown. "Current indications of the global situation are not encouraging," Pranab Mukherjee said in his Interim Budget speech for 2009-10. "Forecasts indicate that the world economy in 2009 may fare worse than in 2008." Latest national income figures show that India's GDP growth rate would fall sharply by nearly 2 percentage points from the sizzling growth of 9 per cent recorded in 2007. This is still higher than the US and many countries in European Union that have clocked negative growth in the last few months amid a global financial meltdown. With an inflation rate of around 4 per cent, India could well be the envy of the world economy. "The GDP in the nominal terms is a function both of estimated growth and inflation," economic affairs Secretary Ashok Chawla said at a post-budget press conference. "These are expectations. We expect growth to be at the order of 7-7.5 per cent during 2009 and inflation to be no more than 3-3.5 and maximum 4 per cent," he added

The Government has taken a slew of fiscal measures, including sharp cuts in excise duties and increased plan spending, to help the economy tide over the ripple effect of a recession in the world's developed countries. But those sops are set to push up the central Government's fiscal deficit to a worrisome 6 per cent of GDP. Add to that, off-budget expenses like oil and fertiliser subsidies, and Government finances could be left with a gaping hole of over 10 per cent.

Analysts sounded more bullish about the prospects of the Indian economy than many of its Asian peers. "India offers a unique combination of having a relatively less open economy and an open equity market," said Rajeev Malik of Macquire Securities. "While India's export dependence has increased in recent years, it is still significantly less than that of other Asian economies."

India will see signs of recovery from the economic recession in the second half of 2009 and a distinct improvement in growth will be witnessed in 2010-11, according to Rajya Sabha member and economist C. Rangarajan. Speaking at a symposium on 'Global Financial Crisis—Impact on Indian Economy', organised by the Department of Economics of University of Hyderabad, Rangarajan said that it was false to contend that the country escaped from a serious impact of the crisis due to economic reforms. The financial reforms were intended at improving efficiency and the global crisis would have a ripple effect on the structure of capitalism. "Acceptable capitalism would require more regulation," he said. He underscored the need for cut in excise duty and enhanced public spending, especially in infrastructure development. The revised estimates of total expenditure by the Union Government for 2008-09 were 20 per cent more than the budget estimates. As a result, the fiscal deficit was estimated at six per cent of the GDP, he observed.

Rangarajan said the capital inflow, which was put at $100 billion in 2008, would not be as much and exports would be impacted due to global slowdown. He said the huge current account deficit in the US and surplus in China and a few other countries needed to be balanced. The crisis had its roots in the subprime lending crisis which was a result of housing loans obtained beyond their capacity by borrowers. Rangarajan said that the rating agencies in the current crisis were irresponsible in creating a booming market in suspect derivative products. Regulatory failure was another cause for the global crisis. Former RBI Governor Y.V. Reddy said regulatory capture by the regulated, moral and intellectual failure contributed to the economic crisis. Only 15-20 institutions, which received maximum bailout packages, had a role in this as they did not do business with one another due to mutual distrust.

The Indian economy has shown signs of recovery in the financial year 2009-10. Powered by increased Government spending on infrastructure, the cement industry witnessed a dream run with a robust 12.75 per cent sales growth in March

2009 over February and a healthy 9 per cent growth in the last quarter of 2008-09. Not just cement, the steel industry, which has been reeling under the slowdown, saw consumption rise 3.8 per cent during the quarter. Cement and steel are considered bellwethers of economic activity. A rise in demand for steel and cement augurs well for the economy as it will lead to infrastructure development and consequent boost to manufacturing, transportation, distribution, and marketing of various types of goods. India's equity market has also shown an upswing on global cues, with Bombay Stock Exchange (BSE) index now sustaining above 10,000 mark. Foreign Institutional Investors (FIIs) are reported to be showing a renewed interest in the shares of select Indian companies, as things are improving, though slightly in America and Europe.

China Economy: 2009 Forecast

The Chinese economy grew a whopping 9.9 per cent in the first three quarters of 2008, and 11.9 per cent in 2007. Forecasts for 2009 are nowhere near as rosy. In 2008, the Chinese Government took significant action to encourage growth amid the worldwide financial slowdown. It unveiled a US$585 billion stimulus package which will extend into 2010, and slashed the interest rate three times. It also relaxed credit regulations.

Despite these aggressive measures, global uncertainty, a general bleak outlook, and lack of liquidity between financial institutions will drag China's growth figures, resulting in 'only' 8.6 per cent growth in 2009, according to China Galaxy Securities. Firms, excluding those in the petroleum, finance, power, and steel industries, should see the earnings grow by 7 per cent in 2009, according to Galaxy.

The World Bank has made more conservative forecasts. It once expected China to grow 9.2 per cent in 2009, but now has that revised down to 7.5 per cent. The World Bank projected China's GDP growth rate would be 7.5 per cent, significantly lower than the 9.4 per cent gained in 2008. It also expects China's export growth to shrink to 3.5 per cent as against a huge 11 per cent in 2008. David Dollar, the World Bank Country Director for China said:

In terms of the effect of China's slowdown on the world, there's good news and bad news. China's recently announced stimulus package is good news because it will keep China's growth rate up at a pretty healthy rate and so imports will continue to go into China at a fairly good rate. That's good news for countries like Mongolia and Australia that export commodities like copper and iron ore to China...it's also welcome news for countries selling primary products, machinery and parts to China. The bad news is there won't be as much stimulus to these exporting economies as China was giving in the past.

President Hu Jintao is making socially and environmentally -sustainable efforts which should help guide growth. This new policy will take effect in 2009, and is sure to appeal to Western investors and Governments, if done right. Nevertheless, Jintao is sending the right message.

The human rights issues will continue to loom as ethnic struggles in Tibet and Xinjiang remain unsolved. However, these are not expected to dampen economic forecasts or even political stability.

The Government budget is expected to report small surpluses in 2009-10 after an approximate surplus of 0.4 per cent of GDP in 2008. And while inflation has been a recent issue—much due to rising oil prices—it is expected to decline to about 3.8 per cent in 2009. Utility costs will remain high, but these will be compensated by low consumer goods and food costs. China is likely to maintain a current account surplus due to its massive amount of exports.

LATEST MEASURES—2009

London Summit Pledges $1.1 Trillion to Boost Global Economy

Leaders of the world's largest economies at the G20 summit in London pledged additional $1.1 trillion in resources for the International Monetary Fund and other multilateral institutions to boost global growth.

Addressing the media at the end of the summit, British Prime Minister Gordon Brown said this would be in addition to the fiscal stimulus packages that the individual countries had unveiled that would total $5 trillion by the end of next year. There was agreement on the biggest stimulus package in history, the biggest interest rate cut, the biggest infusion of resources into multilateral institutions and the biggest boost to trade finance in history, he said.

The leaders agreed to treble the resources available to the IMF to $750 billion and support the allocation of new Special Drawing Rights of $250 billion, support at least $100 billion in lending by multilateral development banks that will be available to all members and ensure $250 billion in trade finance while allowing the IMF to sell gold and provide concessional finance to the poorest countries.

Mr Brown said there was "substantial agreement" on the need to do whatever it took to restore growth. The outcome represented the "collective action of people working together at their best."

The summit for the first time agreed on a set of principles to reform the global banking system. The shadow banking system including hedge funds would be brought under the regulatory regime and new accounting standard would be formulated.

In a strong move against tax havens and banking secrecy, the leaders warned: "We stand ready to deploy sanctions to protect our public finances and financial system" and declared that "the era of banking secrecy is over". They noted that the Organisation of Economic Cooperation and Development (OECD) had published a list of countries assessed against the international standard for the exchange of information. They would, in addition, put in place new rules on pay and bonuses in the financial institution that do not reward failure.

Addressing the issue of rising protectionism in different countries, they reaffirmed the commitment made at the Washington summit in November 2008 to refrain from raising new barriers to investment or trade in goods and services, imposing new export restrictions or implementing measures to stimulate exports that are inconsistent with World Trade Organisation rules. They would also minimise any negative impact on trade and investment that may arise from their domestic fiscal policy actions and said they would not retreat into financial protectionism.

The leaders called upon the WTO and other international bodies to report publicly on the adherence of all countries to these commitments. They also called for "an ambitious and balanced conclusion" to the Doha Round of trade talks that could boost the global economy by at least $150 billion a year.

In addition, they pledged to assist the less developed countries to meet the Millennium Development Goals and "lay the foundation for a fair and sustainable world economy". The fiscal stimulus packages would also be directed to ensuring a green, low carbon recovery.

Slight Improvement

According to Federal Reserve's influential report called Beige Book there has been a moderation in the pace of decline in some districts in America while others were stabilising. President Barack Obama and Fed Chairman Ben Bernanke said that recession was easing. The report said that retail spending remained slow in the quarter ended 31 March 2009 but did comment that "some districts noted a slight improvement in sales as compared with the previous reporting period. Signs of interest from buyers in the property market were also visible: "Home prices and construction were still falling in most areas, but better-than-expected buyer traffic led to scattered pick-up in sales in a number of districts", the report said.

According to the report, although the industrial production fell by 1.5 per cent in March 2009, it was noted that the decline had slowed and that factory activity had stabilised. Michelle Meyer of Barclays Capital said, "Although conditions are weak right now, there are signs that there is stabilisation in certain sectors."

In his major address at Georgetown University, Obama proclaimed signs of economic progress but also warned American people by saying "by no means are we out of the woods." The excerpts from his speech, given below, are quite reassuring:

> There is no doubt that times are still tough. But from where we stand, for the very first time, we are beginning to see glimmers of hope. And beyond that, way off in the distance, we can see a vision of an America's future that is far different than our troubled economic past.

According to Obama, a complete recovery depends on two things: (i) building a new foundation for the US economy, and (ii) making changes in the political landscape. He said that the rules governing the financial system must be brought into the digital age and that the economy must be transformed from one less dependent on clean energy, to that with good education and healthcare costs brought under control. "We cannot rebuild this economy on the same pile of sand", he said, making a Biblical reference to Jesus Christ's Sermon on the Mount. "We must build our house upon a rock. We must lay a new foundation for growth and prosperity—a foundation that will move us from an era of borrow and spend to one where we save and invest, where we consume less at home and send more exports abroad."

Referring to cancelled Government-sector layoffs, new clean energy industry hires, a spate of refinancings, and signs of increased credit flows, Obama said, "Taken together, these actions are starting to generate signs of economic progress."

Obama, pointed to the US Government's housing plan as a factor in boosting the economy, as the number of people refinancing their loans increased. He added that support for the auto and student loan markets had also contributed to an easing of credit conditions along with progress at the London G20 meeting. But he warned that more work needed to be done and that "credit was not flowing nearly as easily as it should". He also said 2009 would be a hard year for the US economy, when there would be more job losses, more repossessions and "more pain before it ends".

Bernanke, who was talking to students at Moorehouse University in Atlanta, said, "A levelling out of economic activity is the first step towards recovery". But he added, "We will not have a sustainable recovery without a stabilisation of our financial system and credit markets." The central bank has reduced interest rates to near zero in a move to boost the economy and encourage spending. But problems in the credit markets have continued to make borrowing for individual and firms hard and expensive.

Housing Market Momentum

Interest from home-buyers is starting to gain "real momentum", although sales remain low, UK surveyors said. New inquiries in the housing market increased for the fifth consecutive month in March 2009, the Royal Institution of Chartered Surveyors (Rics) found. However, it said surveyors had still been selling, on average, fewer than 10 homes each over the past three months. There was increased optimism that sales would pick up during the year, but it remained tough for first-time buyers. "Buyer interest is starting to gain real momentum, but will remain frustrated while mortgage finance is scarce," said Rics spokesman Ian Perry. "The market is still in a fragile state, but with demand continuing to pick up, there may be more signs of stabilisation in the coming months," he added.

Surveyors have been among the most optimistic when predicting the turn in the market, and have been reporting interest in property from people who are failing to get much interest from other investments. Surveyor David Richardson, from Norfolk, said, "Those with cash in the bank on close to nil returns are considering and often actually moving back into the property market." Martin Pendered, of Northamptonshire, reported "significant numbers of viewings", but stated that it remained difficult to persuade buyers to commit to buying a home. The survey backs up the latest home loan figures from the Council of Mortgage Lenders (CML), which suggested that the number of mortgages handed out was rising. Both groups said it remained tough for first-time buyers, with the CML claiming they typically needed to provide a record deposit level of 25 per cent.

China Offers Funds to Boost ASEAN

China has unveiled plans to establish a $10 billion (£6.8 billion) investment fund for South-East Asian countries.

It has also offered credit of $15 billion to the Association of South-East Asian Nations (ASEAN). ASEAN was set up in 1967 in part to counter influence from communist China but has since become a vehicle for close ties. That deal is intended to create the world's largest free trade area, covering nearly two-billion people. China's Foreign Minister, Yang Jiechi, announced the new funding plans in Beijing to a gathering of envoys from the 10 members of ASEAN, viz. Indonesia, Singapore, Malaysia, Thailand, the Philippines, Brunei, Burma, Laos, Cambodia and Vietnam. According to Jiechi the $10 billion investment fund was designed for cooperation on infrastructure construction, energy and resources, information and communications.

China planned to offer $15 billion over the next three to five years in credit, including loans with preferential terms of $1.7 billion in aid for cooperation projects. China also planned to offer 270 million yuan ($39.7 million) in special aid to Cambodia, Laos and Myanmar to meet urgent needs, inject $5 million into the China-ASEAN Cooperation Fund, and donate $900,000 to the cooperation fund of ASEAN Plus-3, the side grouping of ASEAN plus China, Japan and the South Korea. China said it would provide 300,000 tons of rice for the emergency East Asia rice reserve, and more Government scholarships. "The overall thought for China-ASEAN cooperation is that the two sides should rise to difficulties in face of the grim global financial crisis, and make efforts to convert unprecedented challenge into opportunity for closer pragmatic cooperation and common development," Yang said.

G20 Communiqué—and a Guide to the Decisions

The G20 London Summit took place at a time when the world was confronting the worst economic crisis since the Second World War. The London Summit aims were to bring together leaders of the world's major economies and key international institutions to take the collective action necessary to stabilise the world economy and secure recovery and jobs. Leaders faced an unprecedented range of challenges including that of averting an even more severe downturn and restoring growth in the short term, while at the same time reshaping the financial system, preserving the world trading system, and laying the foundations for a sustainable recovery. The leaders agreed to take the following steps:

1. Restoring Confidence, Jobs, and Growth

A series of financial market events beginning in 2007 has culminated in the worst international banking crisis in generations. Despite unprecedented interventions by Governments to fix the financial system, this crisis has triggered a global recession. Before the G20 Leaders met, forecasts suggested that most of the advanced economies and many developing and emerging economies would remain in severe recession over 2009, with world growth in real terms resuming and rising to over 2 per cent by the end of 2010.

In response to these events, Governments of the G20 nations agreed to take action to accelerate the return to trend growth and support families and businesses through the recession. In the UK, for example, the Government increased spending to support homeowners and people at risk of losing their job and provided support to get the financial sector lending again. The Bank of England interest rates to their lowest level ever, making it cheaper for businesses and households to borrow. Other countries across the globe also took similar action.

At the London Summit, leaders of the G20 reaffirmed their commitment to work together to restore growth and jobs. They expressed their confidence that the new actions and commitments agreed at the Summit would accelerate the return to trend growth; and they committed to taking whatever action was necessary to secure that outcome. Recognising that further action may be needed, they called on the IMF to assess regularly the actions taken and the global actions required. Not only did leaders agree to take further action on fiscal policy and in other policy areas, but they also tied the need for such action to the achievement of quantified and time-bound objectives for growth; and put in place a clear monitoring mechanism for judging progress. This represent a significant step forward in international macroeconomic coordination to deal with the crisis.

2. Strengthening Financial Supervision and Regulation

Problems in the financial sector and weaknesses in supervision were one of the fundamental causes of the crisis. Increased lending and securitisation of assets reduced transparency and exposed the banking system to high levels of systemic risk. While market participants were unable to understand the nature of the risks they were exposed to, the regulatory system allowed them to increase leverage dramatically in the run-up to the crisis. The tendency of the financial sector to over-expand during upswings was exacerbated by a number of factors: over-reliance on Credit Ratings Agencies (CRAs) assessments of the credit risk and potential CRA conflicts of interest, inadequate accounting standards and capital requirements that served to reinforce rather than dampen financial market over-expansion, and remuneration policies that encouraged excessive leveraging and risk-taking.

At the Summit, G20 leaders agreed to a blueprint for reforming the regulatory framework of the financial sector. Key principles underlying the framework include the need to strengthen macroprudential supervision; for capital requirements to explicitly incorporate countercyclical elements —but that in present circumstances it would be inappropriate to raise them until recovery takes hold; for all systemically important institutions, including hedge funds, to be subject to regulation and supervision; for common principles for remuneration so as to discourage excessive risk taking; to ensure credit rating agencies do their job properly and without conflicts of interest; and to deal with tax havens and non-cooperative jurisdictions. Leaders also agreed that a central role in coordinating the agenda should be taken by the Financial Stability Forum, renamed as the Financial Stability Board and incorporating all G20 countries.

Agreement on specific measures across all of these areas and all of the G20 countries represented an unprecedented degree of international regulatory coordination, and will lead to major reforms of the global financial sector—reducing the risk of a recurrence of this crisis.

3. Funding and Reforming Our International Financial Institutions (IFIs) to Overcome this Crisis and Prevent Future Ones

The global financial crisis has resulted in the seizing up of international financial markets that are essential for keeping the world economy functioning. The effects of this have been particularly felt in developing and emerging economies. Governments as well as households and businesses in these countries have found it more difficult to borrow, adding to pressures on economic growth from reduced global demand and exports and increasing unemployment. International financial institutions like the International Monetary Fund (IMF) and the World Bank have an essential role in ensuring the stability and recovery of emerging markets and developing economies.

To ensure international financial institutions have the resources needed to provide responsive and effective support to developing economies—which have been key factors in world economic growth over the last ten years and are vital to ending the global recession—G20 Leaders have agreed to resources available through the IFIs by $850 billion. They agreed to treble IMF resources to $750 billion, initially funded through bilateral borrowing to be then incorporated into an expanded and enlarged New Arrangements to Borrow of up to $500 billion. Leaders also agreed to an SDR allocation of around $250 billion—to provide an additional $100 billion in liquidity to emerging and developing economies (including $19 billion for the poorest)—and urged ratification of the 4th Amendment for an additional $30 billion SDR allocation.

Leaders urged multilateral development banks (MDBs) to make available at least an additional $100 billion in resources over the next few years, and also committed to providing up to $50 billion of trade liquidity support as part of the global effort to ensure the availability of at least $250 billion of trade finance.

Leaders also agreed to ensure that the international financial institutions have the facilities they need to address the current crisis and meet the needs of emerging markets and developing countries: welcoming the IMF's new Flexible Credit Line (FCL) for eligible countries, urging the IMF to reform its surveillance and lending facilities to address the causes of countries' balance of payments needs, supporting the World Bank Vulnerability Framework through voluntary bilateral contributions, increasing individual country limits on World Bank lending to enable large countries to access required levels of finance, allowing low income IDA countries with sustainable debt positions and sound policies to gain temporary access to non-concessional IBRD lending, and a temporary lifting of caps on the proportion of concessional lending by the MDBs provided as budget support to low income countries.

Besides as increasing resources, it is important that each country has confidence in the institutions' relevance, effectiveness and legitimacy, to ensure credibility. At the London Summit, leaders recognised that action needs to be taken to improve the credibility of IFIs. The G20 therefore agreed as under:

- Reform of representation on IFIS—IMF quota reform to be brought forward to be completed by 2011; and similar reform of the World Bank to be completed by 2010;
- Selection and recruitment of heads of IMF and World Bank to be based on merit;
- Consideration of greater involvement of the Fund's Governors in providing strategic direction to the IMF and increasing its accountability.

4. Promoting Global Trade and Investment and Rejecting Protectionism, to Underpin Prosperity

Trade is vital for the health of the global economy. The more open to trade economies are, the greater the benefits. History demonstrates this: since 1945, average tariffs for developed countries, like the UK, Europe and the US, have fallen from nearly 40 per cent to less than 5 per cent; world exports have risen 27-fold; and world income has risen eightfold. However, world trade is forecast to fall by 9 per cent during 2009—the largest decline in 60 years—due to lower global demand and reduced exports. This decline is exacerbated by growing protectionist pressures, but also the drying up of trade credit—essentially the insurance exporters pay while their goods are in transit, which roughly 90 per cent of world trade relies on. The G20 leaders stated that reinvigorating world trade and investment is essential for restoring world growth and leaders agreed on action to stop the slowdown in world trade. Specifically, leaders resolved as under:

- They committed to ensure that countries do not resort to protectionism, by extending their pledge made in November 2008, not to raise trade barriers or impose any new trade restrictions to 2010, and rectifying any such measures promptly;
- They committed to minimise any negative impact of domestic policy action on world trade and investment including fiscal policy and action in support of the financial sector, and not retreat into financial protectionism;
- They committed to notify promptly the WTO of any such measures and called on the WTO, together with other international bodies, to monitor and report publicly on adherence to these undertakings on a quarterly basis;
- They decided to take measures to support trade, including a commitment to make available $250 billion in trade finance over the next two years, through both national agencies, and the Development Banks, as well as making better use of financing that is already there;
- They expressed their personal commitment to the Doha Round and agreed to prioritise the negotiations.

5. Ensuring a Fair and Sustainable Recovery for All

The global financial crisis affects all countries, rich and poor, and the response will also affect all—both rich and poor countries now, and also future generations. Leaders recognised the human dimension to the crisis and committed to support those affected by creating employment opportunities and through income support measures. And they stated their determination not only to restore growth but also to lay the foundation for a fair and sustainable world economy.

The effects of the current crisis on developing countries could result in an additional 90 million people a year living in extreme poverty, and threaten progress made towards achieving the Millennium Development Goals. A global recovery will not be sustainable unless it benefits the poorest and provides them with the opportunities they need to escape poverty. Recognizing this, the leaders decided as under:

- They reaffirmed their commitment to meeting the Millennium Development Goals and to achieving Official Development Assistance pledges, including commitments on Aid for Trade;
- They made $50 billion available to low income countries, including through the Rapid Social Response Fund, investing in food security and supporting the World Bank's Vulnerability Financing Framework;
- They agreed the IMF should double concessional lending access limits and capacity to increase its support to low income countries, and requested the IMF to bring forward proposals to use the proceeds of agreed gold sales to do so;
- They called on the UN to establish a mechanism to monitor the impact of the crisis on the poor. Understanding that a return to business-as-usual growth will leave them vulnerable to rising oil prices and the potentially catastrophic impacts of climate change, several have committed sizeable parts of their economic recovery packages to low carbon investments. Leaders agreed to pursue a path of economic growth that creates green business opportunities. The opportunities will not only provide jobs and contribute to the economic growth, they will also ensure that the recovery is sustainable in the longer term.

World Leaders Welcome Summit Outcome

The Communiqué of the London Summit was acclaimed by the G20 leaders—from developed, emerging and developing economies—as well as the regional organisations and international institutions that participated in the meeting. Welcoming the Communiqué, Gordon Brown said:

"This is the day that the world came together to fight recession not with words but with a plan for economic recovery and reform. In this new global age of interdependence global problems require global solutions."

The leader's remarks which throw light on the seriousness of the situation and show global commitment of take preventive measures are given below:

Barack Obama, President, United States:

"This will be a turning point in our pursuit of global economic recovery. By any measure the London Summit is historic. It is historic because of the size and scope of the challenge that we face and because of the timeliness of our response. We owe it to our citizens to act now. Today the world leaders have responded with unprecedented effort."

Luiz Inácio Lula da Silva, President, Brazil:

"It was good, not only for Brazil or any single country, but for the hopes and the future of humanity."

Nicolas Sarkozy, President, France:

[The results of the summit] "are beyond what we could have imagined.... We are all happy with the results."

Angela Merkel, Chancellor, Germany:

[It is] "a very, very good, almost historic compromise.... We have agreed to set up a clear financial market architecture.... We have taken an important step toward creating order in an area in the world where there was previously no order."

Kevin Rudd, Prime Minister, Australia:

"...agreement begins to crackdown on the cowboys in financial markets that have brought global markets undone with real impact on jobs everywhere."

José Luis Rodríguez Zapatero, Prime Minister, Spain:

"We have set in motion the greatest concerted plan of fiscal expansion in history. It is unprecedented. It reaches $5 trillion.... This amount will contribute in a decisive way to facilitate a recovery of the world economy and to preserve millions of jobs."

Dmitry Medvedev, President, Russia:

"This is a step forward, this is a step in the right direction. Of course we could not solve all the issues, but such a goal wasn't on the agenda."

Abhisit Vejjajiva, Thai Prime Minister—Representing ASEAN:

"The various reforms in terms of the global financial institutions and the new facilities again respond better to the needs of emerging and developing economies. We are not losing sight of medium and longer term goals in terms of development."

Dominique Strauss-Kahn, IMF Managing Director:

"The global crisis is hitting emerging market and poor countries hard. The G20 leaders have today sent a powerful signal that the international community is committed to support these countries, including by ensuring that the IMF has the tools to act."

José Manuel Barroso, European Commission President:

"It is an historic moment, a defining moment for our global response to the crisis.... We took the right decisions."

CONCLUSION

There is no question that the global financial crisis has crippled economic growth around the world. But there is a lesson in this crisis. The rumours about the demise of capitalism may be exaggerated but the warning signs are clear and scary. In the present age of globalisation, an unregulated market—which is susceptible to manipulation by a few rogue characters—can plummet and send out strong ripples. Capitalism may have an in-built self-correcting mechanism, but how painful such mechanism is, can be realized from the present global economic conditions which have jolted the entire world.

"The financial crisis roiling the world today is the result of serious shortcomings in domestic financial governance that have exposed gaps in the global governance of institutional finance and capital."[18] Its immediate roots lie in the excessive and not so transparent leverage of complex securities and derivatives that inflated the real economy to excessive proportions. The US regulatory regime governing its financial and banking worlds—which had far-reaching repercussions for the entire globe—can be euphemistically described as light, incomplete and fragmentary. Thus, the need for efficient, effective and transparent regulatory and surveillance instruments and institutions is quite obvious. The role of global governance institutions, now more than ever before, is to contain the contagion. Only a new regulatory regime will reassure the world at large that the balance has been restored between the risks and the benefits of integrating with an open world economy.

The comity of nations has joined hands to take short-term emergency measures to deal with the financial crisis. There is a growing recognition that the system to manage the modern world of banking, capital and finance has to be redesigned. The corporations, markets and financial flows are global, but regulatory and financial systems are national—or in a few cases like Europe—regional. The world at this juncture needs "some sort of visionary internationalism" like Bretton Woods Conference in 1944 that founded the IMF and the World Bank and restructured the international monetary system.

It is also being felt that the existing political or economic institutions like IMF and G7 have not proved equal to the task of coordinating an adequate response to global crisis. The way things are, it is hard to imagine that any major global challenge can be effectively addressed without involving all three Asian giants—China, India and Japan. But two of the them, viz. India and Japan are not permanent members of the UN Security Council, and two, viz. China and India are not part of the G7. These anomalies need to be removed to give these countries more say in international affairs. The decision to base the initial crisis summitry on the G20, at the Beijing Summit has been hailed as an evidence of changing global equation. The G20, which has effectively replaced G8 (G7 + Russia) brings China, India, Brazil, Mexico and Indonesia together with the major industrial powers and the EU. It is likely to become the architect of global governance and an effective tool of restoring and maintaining a durable economic world order.

The G20 meeting of 2 April 2009, held in London, can be termed as landmark in many ways. The member countries—which are virtually world's main financial powers—pledged more than $1 trillion for emergency loans to reverse the recession.

Emerging markets and developing countries, which have been the engine of recent world growth, are also now facing challenges which are adding to the current downturn in the global economy. It is imperative for global confidence and economic recovery that capital continues to flow to them. This will require a substantial strengthening of the international financial institutions, particularly the IMF. G20 members have therefore agreed to make available an additional $850 billion of resources through the global financial institutions to support growth in emerging markets and developing countries by helping to finance counter-cyclical spending, bank recapitalisation, infrastructure, trade finance, balance of payments support, debt rollover, and social support. They not only decided to reject protectionism but also to bring tighter financial regulation. Positive results can be expected sooner than later.

NOTES

1. James Joyner, "Protectionism Wave Crashing Over Global Economy"—http://www.acus.org/new_atlanticist/prot>
2. *Ibid.*

3. Sudipto Mundle, (Former Director Asian Development Bank), "Forget the Great Depression," *The Times of India.*
4. Alan S. Blinder, (2002), "Keynesian Economics" in *The Concise Encyclopedia of Economics.*
5. "Capitalism is dead. Long live Capitalism," *The Times of India.*
6. Paul Krugman, "Capitalism's Mysterious Triumph" quoted in *The Times of India.*
7. Pramit Pal Chaudhuri, "Adam Smith isn't dead," *Hindustan Times.*
8. Michael Heinrich, "The Current Financial Crisis and the Future of Global Capitalism," http://www.bulatlat.com
9. *Ibid.*
10. "Profit for All," *The Times of India.*
11. Gautam Chilkermane, "Dialectic Mysticism," *Hindustan Times,* 4 November, 2008.
12. S.S.A. Aiyar, "Capitalism is Reinventing Iself, "*The Times of India,* 15 February 2009.
13. *Ibid.*
14. *Ibid.*
15. *Hindustan Times*, 11 November 2008.
16. Donald Greenlees, "The Search for a New Financial Order," in *Global Asia* Vol. 3, No. 4.
17. *Ibid.*
18. "Rewrite the Rules", *The Times of India.*

Bibliography

Acknowledging the Positive Role of Taiwan in the Current Asian Financial Crisis and Affirming the Support of the American People for Peace and Stability...Session, on H. Con. Res. 270, May 21, 1998 (1998), United States, for sale by the U.S. G.P.O., Supt. of Docs., Congressional Sales Office.

Administration Struggling with 1999 Budget Proposal Because of Global Financial Crisis and Weak Oil Market: SourceMex Economic News and Analysis on Mexico.

Agénor, Pierre-Richard et al. (2006), *The Asian Financial Crisis: Causes, Contagion and Consequences (Global Economic Institutions),* Cambridge University Press.

Aghevli, Bijan B. (1999), "The Asian Crisis Causes and Remedies" (Financial Markets), *Finance & Development,* International Monetary Fund.

Akella, Anita Sundari (1999), *The East Asian Financial Crisis: Evolution and Environmental Implications for Indonesia,* World Wide Fund for Nature, Macroeconomics Program Office.

Altman, Daniel. *Connected: 24 Hours in the Global Economy,* New York: Macmillan.

Asia supera la crisis financiera: Talón de Aquiles: la política. (TT: Asia Overcomes Financial Crisis: Achilles's Heel: Politics), Siempre! (2005), Agustín Gutiérrez Canet, Edicional Siempre.

Asian Development Bank (2005), *Early Warning Systems for Financial Crisis: Applications to East Asia*, Palgrave Macmillan.

Baig, Taimur (1998), *Financial Market Contagion in the Asian Crisis* (IMF Working Paper), International Monetary Fund, Asia and Pacific Department.

Batra, Ravi. *Greenspan's Fraud*, New York: Macmillan.

——. *The New Golden Age*, New York: Macmillian.

Bedford, Richard (1998), *The Asian Financial Crisis and Migration: Perspectives from the Asian Region and New Zealand* (Discussion Papers), Population Studies Centre, University of Waikato.

Beeson, Mark (1999), *Politics and Markets in the Wake of the Asian Crisis* (Asian Capitalisms), Routledge.

Blustein, Paul (2001), *The Chastening: Inside the Crisis that Rocked the Global Financial System and Humbled the IMF*, Public Affairs.

——. (2003), *The Chastening: Inside the Crisis that Rocked the Global Financial System and Humbled the IMF*, PublicAffairs.

Bora, Bijit and Bot, Alexandra Nora (2003), *Tariffs and the East Asian Financial Crisis: Policy Issues in International Trade and Commodities Study, No. 13*, United Nations Publications.

Bowe, Michael (2000), *Did Foreign Investors Destabilize Equity Markets during the 1997 Asian Financial Crisis?: Evidence from Closed-end Country Funds*, Manchester School of Management.

Brownell, Charles and Brownel, Justine (2008), *Subprime Meltdown from U.S. Liquidity Crisis to Global Recession.*

Buckley, Richard (1998), *Asia's Financial Crisis (Understanding Global Issues)*, European Schoolbooks.

Burton, Theodore E., *Financial Crises and Periods of Industrial and Commercial Depression*, 1922 Edition-Reprint 2009, CreateSpace.

Carney, Richard (2008), *Lessons from the Asian Financial Crisis (Routledge Contemporary Asia)*, Routledge.

——. ed. (2009), *Lessons from the Asian Financial Crisis*, New York: Routledge.

Chang, Ha-Joon; Palma, Gabriel and Whittaker, D. Hugh (2001), *Financial Liberalization and the Asian Crisis*, Palgrave Macmillan.

Chang, Sea-Jin (2006), *Business Groups in East Asia: Financial Crisis, Restructuring, and New Growth*, USA: Oxford University Press.

Chan-Lau, Jorge A. (1998), *Financial Crisis and Credit Crunch as a Result of Inefficient Financial Intermediation: With Reference to the Asian Financial* Crisis (IMF Working Paper), International Monetary Fund, Research Department.

Choi, J. Jay (2000), *Asian Financial Crisis (International Finance Review)*, JAI Press.

Choudhry, T. (2005), "Time-varying Beta and the Asian Financial Crisis: Evidence from Malaysian and Taiwanese Firms", *Pacific-Basin Finance Journal*, Elsevier.

Chow, Peter C.Y. and Gill, Bates (2000), *Weathering the Storm: Taiwan, Its Neighbors, and the Asian Financial Crisis*, Brookings Institution Press.

Chu; Yun-Peng; Hill, Hal and Yun-Peng, Chu (2001), *The Social Impact of the Asian Financial Crisis* (Elgar Monographs), Edward Elgar Pub.

Chung, H. (2005), "The Contagious Effects of the Asian Financial Crisis: Some Evidence from ADR and Country Funds", *Journal of Multinational Financial Management*, Elsevier.

Claessens, Stijn (1999), *Resolution of Corporate Distress: Evidence from East Asia's Financial Crisis* (Policy Research Working Paper), World Bank, Financial Sector Practice Department, Financial Economics Unit.

Click, R.W. and Plummer, M.G. (2005), "Stock Market Integration in ASEAN After the Asian Financial Crisis", *Journal of Asian Economics*, Elsevier.

Consequences of the Asian Financial Crisis: Hearing before the Committee on Finance, United States Senate, One Hundred Fifth Congress, Second Session, February 4,

1998 (S. hrg) (1998), United States, for sale by the US G.P.O., Supt. of Docs., Congressional Sales Office.

Corsetti, Giancarlo (1998), *What Caused the Asian Currency and Financial Crisis?* (NBER Working Paper Series), National Bureau of Economic Research.

Coyle, William T. (1998), *The Asian Financial Crisis: Effects on U.S. Agriculture* (ERS Staff Paper), Economic Research Service, Market and Trade Economics Division.

Cronin, Richard P. (1998), *Asian Financial Crisis: An Analysis of U.S. Foreign Policy Interests and Options* (CRS Report for Congress), Congressional Research Service, Library of Congress.

Crotty, James and Epstein, Gerald (2005), "A Defense of Capital Controls in Light of the Asian Financial Crisis" (Papers from the 1999 AFEE Meeting), *Journal of Economic Issues*, Association for Evolutionary Economics.

Das, Dilip K. (2005), *Asian Economy and Finance: A Post-Crisis Perspective (Innovations in Financial Markets and Institutions)*, Springer.

Ding, D.K.; Chua, J.L. and Fetherston, T.A. (2005), "The Performance of Value and Growth Portfolios in East Asia before the Asian Financial Crisis", *Pacific-Basin Finance Journal*, Elsevier.

Discourses on Asianisation: The Asian Financial Crisis and Rediscovering Asianness (2008), Toru OGA, VDM Verlag Dr. Müller.

Donlon, J.P. (2005), "Is Asia on the Mend?" (Includes Related Articles on Singapore's Bright Economic Prospects) (*Asian Financial Crisis*) (Panel Discussion), Chief Executive (US), Chief Executive Publishing.

Endres, James (2001), *The Asian Financial Crisis and Its Impact on Korea-Australia Economic Relations* (Australia-Korea paper), Australian Centre for Korean Studies.

Financial Crisis in Asia: Hearing before the Subcommittee on Asia and the Pacific and International Economic Policy and Trade of the Committee on International...Congress,

Second Session (1998), United States, for sale by the US G.P.O., Supt. of Docs., Congressional Sales Office.

Francis, Bill (2000), *Operational Hedges and Coping with Foreign Exchange Exposure: The Case of U.S. MNCs during the Asian Financial Crisis of 1997* (Working Paper Series), New York University Salomon Center.

Frank, Thomas, *The Wrecking Crew*, New York: Macmillan.

Friedman, Milton and Schwartz, Anna J. (1963), *A Monetary History of the United States 1867-1960*, Princeton: Princeton University Press.

Friedman, Thomas L. (2008), *Hot, Flat, and Crowded*, New York: Macmillan.

Galbraith, James K., *Unbearable Cost, Bush, Greenspan and the Economics of Empire*, New York: Macmillan.

Gerlach, R.; Wilson, P. and Zurbruegg, R. (2006), "Structural Breaks and Diversification: The Impact of the 1997 Asian Financial Crisis on the Integration of Asia-Pacific Real Estate Markets", *Journal of International Money and Finance,* Elsevier.

Gersovitz, Mark and Stiglitz, Joseph E. (June 1986), "The Pure Theory of Country Risk", *European Economic Review*, 30, 481-513.

Ghysels, E. and Seon, J. (2005), "The Asian Financial Crisis: The Role of Derivative Securities Trading and Foreign Investors in Korea", *Journal of International Money and Finance*, Elsevier.

Goh, C. and Anthony, C. (1999), *IMF & the Asian Financial Crisis (World Scientific Asian Economic Profiles),* World Scientific Publishing Company.

Goldsmith, Barbara (2009), *Handbook for Surviving the Global Financial Crisis*.

Goldsmith, R.W. (1987), *Premodern Financial Systems: A Comparative Study*, Cambridge: Cambridge University Press.

Goldstein, Morris (1998), *The Asian Financial Crisis: Causes, Cures, and Systemic Implications (Policy Analyses in*

International Economics) [illustrated], Institute for International Economics; illustrated edition.

Gonzales, Juan (2005), "Asia Buffets, but Valley Holds Its Own" (The Impact of the Asian Financial Crisis on Tennessee Valley), *Business Perspectives*, University of Memphis.

Griffith-Jones, Stephany; Cailloux, Jaques and Pfaffenzeller, (1998), "The East Asian Financial Crisis" (IDS Discussion Paper), Institute of Development Studies.

Gul, Ferdinand A. and Tsui, Judy S.L. (2005), *The Governance of East Asian Corporations: Post Asian Financial Crisis*, Palgrave Macmillan.

Haggard, Stephan (2000), *The Political Economy of the Asian Financial Crisis*, Institute for International Economics.

Hellyer, Paul (1996), *Surviving the Global Financial Crisis: The Economics of Hope for Generation X*, Login Publishers Consortium.

Hill, Yun-Peng and Chu, Hal (2002), *The Social Impact of the Asian Financial Crisis*, Williston, Vermont, USA: Edward Elger Pub.

Hoa, Tran Van (2000), *The Social Impact of the Asian Financial Crisis*, Palgrave Macmillan.

Hoa, Tran Van and Harvie, Charles (2000), *The Causes and Impact of the Asian Financial Crisis*, Palgrave Macmillan.

Hoa, Tran Van, ed. (2000), *The Causes and Impact of the Asian Financial Crisis*, Palgrave Macmillan.

Hunter, William C.; Kaufman, George G. and Krueger, Thomas H. (1999), *The Asian Financial Crisis: Origins, Implications and Solutions*, Springer.

Jackson, Karl (1998), *Asian Contagion: The Causes and Consequences of a Financial Crisis*, Westview Press.

Jao, Y.C. (2001), *The Asian Financial Crisis and the Ordeal of Hong Kong*, Quorum Books.

Kane, Edward J. (2000), *Capital Movements, Banking Insolvency and Silent Runs in the Asian Financial Crisis*

(NBER Working Paper Series), National Bureau of Economic Research.

Kaufmann, Hugo (1985), *Germany's International Monetary Policy and the European Monetary System.* New York: Brooklyn College Press.

Kim, Yun-Hwan (2002), *Government Bond Market Development: A Post-Crisis Financial Agenda in Asia*, Asian Development Bank.

Kindleberger, Charles P. and Jean-Pierre Laffargue, eds. (1982), *Financial Crises: Theory, History and Policy*, New York: Cambridge University Press.

Knowles, James C.; Pernia, Ernesto M. and Racelis, Mary (1999), *Social Consequences of the Financial Crisis in Asia,* Diane Pub. Co.

Krause, Lawrence B. (1998), *The Economics and Politics of the Asian Financial Crisis of 1997-98*, Council on Foreign Relations.

Krugman, Paul and Norton, W.W., *The Return of Depression Economics and the Crisis of 2008.*

Kwack, Sung-yong (1999), *Capital Inflows and Monetary Policy in Asia before the Financial Crisis* (KIEP Working Paper), Korea Institute for International Economic Policy.

Lai, Joseph, *Global Financial Crisis—Cycle Analysis: Life Cycle-Business Cycle-Stock Cycle*, BookSurge Publishing.

Lai, Kon S. et al. (1998), "Asian Financial Crisis Shows Globalization can Promote Risks as well as Opportunities", *Business Forum*, Los Angeles: California State University.

Lane, Timothy (1999), "The Asian Financial Crisis: What Have We Learned?", *Finance & Development*, International Monetary Fund.

Lanyi, Anthony (1999), *Governance Aspects of the East Asian Financial Crisis* (Working Paper), Center for Institutional Reform and the Informal Sector, University of Maryland at College Park.

Lee, Chung H. (2002), *Financial Liberalization and the Economic Crisis in Asia (European Institute of Japanese Studies, East Asian Economics and Business)*, RoutledgeCurzon.

Lee, Eddy (1998), *The Asian Financial Crisis: The Challenge for Social Policy*, International Labour Office.

Lee, George (1998), *Crisis, Today Asia, Tomorrow the World: Causes, Problems and Cures of Asia's Economic/Financial Crisis*, Pioneer Publishing.

Leightner, Jonathan E. (2005), "Asia's Financial Crisis, Speculative Bubbles, and Under-Consumption Theory", *Journal of Economic Issues*, Association for Evolutionary Economics.

Lichauco, Alejandro (1998), *The Financial Crisis in Asia and Its Impact on the Global Economy: A Philippine Perspective*, Independent Review.

Lipper, A. Michael and Sease, Douglas R., *Money Wise, How to Create, Grow, and Preserve Your Wealth*, New York: Macmillan.

Liu, Pak Wai (1998), *The Asian Financial Crisis and After: Problems and Challenges for the Hong Kong Economy* (Hong Kong Institute of Asia-Pacific Studies Occasional Paper), Hong Kong Institute of Asia-Pacific Studies.

Mandel, Ruth and Humphrey, Caroline, *Markets and Moralities Ethnographies of Postsocialism*, New York: Macmillan.

Mclean, Roy (2001), "Globalization and the Asian Financial Crisis" (Anthology) (Brief Article), *Atlantic Economic Journal*, Atlantic Economic Society.

Mengkui, Wang (2008), *China in the Wake of Asia's Financial Crisis (Routledge Studies on the Chinese Economy)*, Routledge.

Mera, Koichi; Renaud, Bertrand and Sharpe, M.E. (2001), *Asia's Financial Crisis and the Role of Real Estate*.

Miller, John (1998), "Learning from the Southeast Asian Crisis" (Includes Related Article on the Impact of the

Asian Financial Crisis on the US economy), *Dollars & Sense*, Economic Affairs Bureau.

Miller, John (2005), "Ask Dr. Dollar" (Financial Crisis in Asia in 1997), *Dollars & Sense*, Economic Affairs Bureau.

Minskiy, Hyman P. (1977b), "A Theory of Systemic Fragility", *Financial Crises: Institutions and Markets in a Fragile Environment*, eds. Edward I. Altman and Arnold W. Sametz, New York: John Wiley & Sons, pp. 138-52.

Mohamed, Ariff and Khalid, Ahmed M. (1980), *Liberalization, Growth and the Asian Financial Crisis: Lessons for Developing and Transitional Economies in Asia*, Edward Elgar Pub. Co.

——. (2000), *Liberalization, Growth and the Asian Financial Crisis: Lessons for Developing and Transitional Economies in Asia* (Elgar Monographs), Edward Elgar Publishing.

Moreno, Ramon (1998), *Asia's Financial Crisis: Lessons and Policy Responses* (Pacific Basin Working Paper Series), Center for Pacific Basin Monetary and Economic Studies, Economic Research Deptt., Federal Reserve Bank of San Francisco.

Morrison, Charles Edward (1998), *The Asian Financial Crisis: Putting the Region—and the US—to the Test* (Update), East-West Center.

Nanto, Dick K. (1998), *The Asian Financial Crisis, the IMF, and Japan: Economic Issues* (CRS report for Congress), Congressional Research Service, The Library of Congress.

——. (1998), *The Asian Financial Crisis: Chronology, Press Releases, Exchange Rates, and Stock Market Indices* (CRS Report for Congress), Congressional Research Service, The Library of Congress.

——. (1998), *The 1997-98 Asian Financial Crisis* (CRS Report for Congress), Congressional Research Service, The Library of Congress.

Neftci, Salih N. (2000), "FX Short Positions, Balance Sheets and Financial Turbulence: An Interpretation of the Asian Financial Crisis", *The Financier*, Financier, Inc.

Noble, Gregory W. and Ravenhill, John, eds. (2000), *The Asian Financial Crisis and the Architecture of Global Finance (Cambridge Asia-Pacific Studies),* Cambridge University Press.

Nolan, Peter (2009), *China in the Asian Financial Crisis (Routledge Studies on the Chinese Economy)*, Routledge.

Okonjo-Iweala, Ngozi et al. (2005), "Impact of Asia's Financial Crisis on Cambodia and the Lao PDR" (Includes Related Article on Social Impact of East Asian Financial Crisis) (Lao People's Democratic...), *Finance & Development*, International Monetary Fund.

Park, Yung-cul (2001), *Reform of the International Financial System and Institutions in Light of the Asian Financial Crisis* (G-24 Discussion Paper Series), United Nations Conference on Trade and Development, Center for International Development Harvard University.

Phillips, Kevin. *Bad Money: Reckless Finance, Failed Politics, and the Global Crisis of American Capitalism*, Viking Adult.

Polzin, Paul E. (1998), "Global Strategies: What's Montana's Move?" (Includes Related Article on the Asian Financial Crisis), *Montana Business Quarterly*, University of Montana.

Quintos, Carmela E. (1980), *Structural Change in Tail Behavior and the Asian Financial Crisis* (Cowles Foundation Discussion Paper), Cowles Foundation for Research in Economics.

Radelet, Steven C. (1998), *The East Asian Financial Crisis: Diagnosis, Remedies, Prospects* (CAER II Discussion Paper), Harvard Institute for International Development.

——. (1998), *The Onset of the East Asian Financial Crisis (SuDoc HE 20.3852:2002014360)*, National Bureau of Economic Research.

Richards, Alan (1999), *The Global Financial Crisis and Economic Reform in the Middle East*, Middle East Policy.

Roth, William V., Jr. (1998), *Consequences of the Asian Financial Crisis: Hearing before the Committee on Finance, U.S. Senate*, Diane Pub. Co.

Satyanath, Shanker (2005), *Globalization, Politics and Financial Turmoil: Asia's Banking Crisis (Political Economy of Institutions and Decisions)*, Cambridge University Press.

Schutt, Ellen Noonan (1998), "Crash!...It's Never a Good Sound" (*Asian Financial Crisis*) (Editorial), Nonwovens Industry, Rodman Publications, Inc.

Sharma, Shalendra (2003), *The Asian Financial Crisis: New International Financial Architecture: Crisis, Reform and Recovery*, Manchester University Press.

Shaxson, Nicholas, *The Dirty Politics of African Oil*, New York: Macmillan.

Shiller, Robert J., *The Subprime Solution: How Today's Global Financial Crisis Happened and What to Do About It*, Princeton University Press.

Simpson, John (2000), *Labour Migration and the Recent Financial Crisis in Asia* (OECD Proceedings), Organization for Economic.

Snooks, Graeme Donald (2000), *The Global Crisis Makers: An End to Progress and Liberty*? Palgrave Macmillan.

Swedroe, Larry E., *What Wall Street Doesn't Want You to Know: How You Can Build Real Wealth Investing in Index Funds*, New York: Macmillan.

Talbott, John R., *Contagion: The Financial Epidemic that is Sweeping the Global Economy...and How to Protect Yourself from It*, Wiley.

Tan, Jose Antonio R. (1998), *Contagion Effects during the Asian Financial Crisis: Some Evidence from Stock Price Data* (Pacific Basin Working Paper Series), Center for Pacific Basin Monetary and Economic Studies, Economic Research Deptt., Federal Reserve Bank of San Francisco.

The Asian Financial Crisis (1999), W. Curt (EDT)/Kaufman, George G. (EDT)/Krueger, Thomas H. (EDT)/Federal Reserve Bank of Chicago (COR)/International Monetary Fund (COR) Hunter, Kluwer Academic Pub.

The Financial Crisis in Asia and Foreign Direct Investment: An Assessment (1998), United Nations Pubns.

The Human Resources Development Dimension of the Asian Financial Crisis: Towards the Definition of an APEC Response, A Report on the APEC HRD Task Force, held in Chinese Taipei in June 1998 (1998), APEC Asia-Pacific Economic Cooperation, Human Resource Development Working Group, Task Force on Human Resource and Social Impacts of the Financial Crisis in Asia.

Tsui, Ferdinand A. and Judy, S.L. (2005), *The Governance of East Asian Corporations: Post Asian Financial Crisis*, New York: Palgrave Macmillan.

Valdez, Stephen. *An Introduction to Global Financial Markets*, Fifth Edition, New York: Macmillan.

Veigel, Klaus (1999), *The Asian Financial Crisis: Facts and Explanations*, Diplomarbeiten Agentur diplom.de.

Vines, Stephen (2000), *The Years of Living Dangerously: Asia—From Financial Crisis to the New Millennium*, London: Texere.

Wallich, Henry C. et al. (1983), *World Money and National Policies*, New York: Group of Thirty.

Wang, Yunjong (2000), "The Asian Financial Crisis and Its Aftermath: Do We Need a Regional Financial Arrangement?", *Asean Economic Bulletin*, Institute of Southeast Asian Studies (ISEAS).

Wolfson, Martin H. (Spring 1990), "The Causes of Financial Instability," *Journal of Post Keynesian Economics*, 12, 333-55.

Woo, Wing Thye (2005) "The Asian Financial Crisis: Hindsight, Insight, Foresight", *ASEAN Economic Bulletin*, Institute of Southeast Asian Studies (ISEAS).

Woo, Wing Thye; Sachs, Jeffrey D. and Schwab, Klaus (2000), *The Asian Financial Crisis: Lessons for a Resilient Asia*, The MIT Press.

Woodward, David (1999), *Time to Change the Prescription: A Policy Response to the Asian Financial Crisis*, Catholic Institute for International Relations.

Yadav, S.N. and Khatri, Pooja (2009), *Global Financial Crisis: New Challenges for Corporate Goverance*, New Delhi: Jnanada Prakashan.

Yang, Tracy (2001), "The Asian Financial Crisis and the Architecture of Global Finance", (Review), *ASEAN Economic Bulletin*, Institute of Southeast Asian Studies (ISEAS).

Yean, Tham Siew and Gale, Thomson (2007), "Prosper-thy-Neighbour Policies: Malaysia's Contributions after the Asian Financial Crisis", *ASEAN Economic Bulletin*, Association of Southeast Asian Nations.

Zandi, Mark (2008), *Financial Shock: A 360° Look at the Subprime Mortgage Implosion, and How to Avoid the Next Financial Crisis*, FT Press.

Zandi, Mark M. (1998), "A Balanced Yet Booming Market" (Positive Effects of the Asian Financial Crisis on Consumer Demand and the Housing Market of US) (Cover Report: Market Research/Housing...Story), *Mortgage Banking*, Mortgage Bankers Association of America.

Zhang, Xiaoming Alan (1998), *Impact of the East Asian Financial Crisis on Trade of Industrial and Emerging Market Economies* (IIF Research Papers), Institute of International Finance, Inc.